Blood And Roses

Blood And Roses

Catherine Hokin

Available from www.yolkpublishing.co.uk
All major online retailers and available to order through all UK bookshops

Or contact:
Books
Yolk Publishing Limited
145-157 St John Street
London EC1V 4PW

books@yolkpublishing.co.uk
www.yolkpublishing.co.uk

Printed in the UK by Yolk Publishing Ltd
Yolk's policy is to use papers that are natural, renewable and recyclable products
and made from wood grown in sustainable forests wherever possible

With grateful thanks to:

James, Madelene and Carla at Yolk Publishing
for believing in the manuscript.
Vera Browne and Claire Green for being
my review guinea-pigs and making me realise
I genuinely could tell a story.
Jim Scott who started this whole obsession off,
read my first (terrible) attempt at historical fiction
and loathed Margaret but would have loved this.
Claire (again) and Daniel ('the Knight')
for all the love and encouragement.
And Robert Hokin, without whom
this book simply would not exist.

Chateau du Dampierre, France: 1481

The fog when it comes falls across the land like a shroud: thick and grey and cold. It settles on the skin like the fading breath of a dying dragon, a tainted folk-memory. It seeps through the chinks of the chateau walls, through her bones and taunts her with the promise of death coming too close until she paces and shakes with...with what? With fury? With fear? With an old woman's fancies?

Is that why I write? If I wield the pen like a sword, can I make the past hold the future at bay?

It's a question she asks herself often enough, too often aloud now-adays. The few servants she has left think she has become quite mad in her obsession; they think she has too much concern for herself, too much conceit. She knows that some of them, the few who can turn her scratchings into words, have picked up the scattered pages and mocked their self-importance. So now she locks her papers away each night to be found only after her death when others' amusement will be no concern of hers.

Silence.

She suffocates under it. Every day the fog falls around the castle and wipes away the world. What if all her words are silenced? What if her story dies with her? What if the name Margaret of Anjou has no more substance to it than the grey mist that veils the windows? There are days when only her pride saves her: she is not ready for silence, she is not ready to disappear. There are days when she refuses to believe the evidence of her own eyes.

The servants wonder what she does at the window, why she spends so much time staring into shadows. She hears them whisper but pays them little heed: the people in her mind are growing far more important than the fools that surround her; the ghosts of the past, the imagined

6

readers of the future, they are who matter. She holds that thought like a talisman: that the story she works at every day will be read. She has tried to picture herself as a footnote to history, she fears that will be her fate, but she cannot accept it so she clings to her scraps of paper and builds her story like Penelope weaving at her loom. She wants to leave her mark, to have some note of hers linger long after her tune is played out. She wants, well it is simple really, she wants to be remembered as more than the monster she feels sure history will paint her. A simple wish but it is out of her hands.

There are letters on her desk, well-thumbed letters that faithfully repeat every Yorkist slander that sticks like stagnant mud to her name. They are always softened, these words, by protestations of affection from the loyal supporters who are so insistent she sees every cruel jibe, but the kind words make far duller reading than the venomous ones and she knows which will hold.

So she writes. She writes what she remembers and what she has been told. She writes the truth and the lies as faithfully as each other, knowing better than most how such little words as those can cover so many meanings and so many twists of thought and deeds. A man could sit down tomorrow in any court in England, France or Burgundy and they would hear the same stories she carefully re cords, told in many different ways and yet few would match her own memories.

She knows so much but here is one thing hidden from her: whether this time, in this room, is the end of her story or simply a pause. She is not a fool: she is aware that, for so many, she is already little more than a memory, a forgotten woman condemned to the shadows of this silent, grey chateau, no longer consulted or considered, condemned to live on charity, no longer of any consequence. Perhaps that is true for more than she wants to believe; there are days, greyer than the rest, when it feels true even to her.

There are plots still against the Yorkist kings, there are always plots against kings, but she doubts very much that she will ever be in the centre of them again. No, she knows she will not be riding back to England to play the conqueror, that day has long passed. But it is not all lost: there are lighter days when they still come, they still write, her spies in the world.

The world is moving again.

The whispers reach her; those who stole what was hers may be no safer than she ever was. That is enough to warm old bones. She may be exiled; her husband, her son may be dead (God help her when she thinks on that) but still the Crown she once prized so highly (still does if truth be told) is not securely held; is it ever securely held by those who would lay claim to wear it? She hears the rumours: the dance continues around the throne but the dancers have grown lazy and now the Yorkist star trembles in its fragile heaven as much as the Lancaster's once did. It is strange to think she used to envy Richard Duke of York his three sons and thought they would secure his family's line forever when now she watches them turn one against the other as the dream of power destroys any promise of blood. There is a sweetness in that, a nourishment of sorts to be drunk from the news that ripples through the quiet castle in letters read again and again. The Duke of Clarence, ever the greedy drunken fool, is dead and whether of drink, stupidity or at his brothers' hands, no one knows but everyone whispers. Edward, the King, sees only his own golden glory, no matter that it is merely a memory now, and is too enamoured of his mistress to mind what stirs around him.

The most prized messages come from her little Anne, once her daughter-in-law but wedded now to the third brother Richard, Duke of Gloucester and High-Lord of ambition: they tell in barely coded words how the hawks circle now around their once beloved King, Anne's husband chief among them. She may be short of many things but she is rarely short of news and she knows that there are those in England and at Court who still hold her close so, if she cannot ever return, well she can watch and smile and lend a word to any who still comes asking. Meddling to the grave, perhaps, or keeping the grave away.

The cold, the silence of this place, it seeps into me, into my bones; my ghosts draw ever closer.

It is hard to live in exile, to live alone and she is not so old a woman; she is not yet ready to leave the fight, to leave the world, even if it is ready to leave her. And there it is, the truth of why she writes: her voice is not yet ready to be still. Her attendants tell her to take comfort from the peace of this place and there are times when she does: she has spent more of her life in plots and battles than in quiet and calm and loss, of which she has known so much, is a wearisome thing. But a little peace can stretch into an ocean. She chose her paths, she knows that; she never chose the easy paths, she knows that too. She has endured pain and loss that would have broken many but she still survives. She has enjoyed power and knows what a strange thing it is: she has learned how, once tasted, it is very hard to lose the love of it and, too often, the pursuit of it becomes more than the getting. She has had it and she has lost it; she has never learned not to want it.

Does she have regrets? That is a question no one left around her dares or cares enough to ask but it is the one she would most admire. She knows the answer: her regrets lie in what has been taken, and in what she failed to do, not in what she has done. What she has done: words enough to condemn her in so many eyes before the answer is even given but the answer, well that is what she has promised herself she will write. She knows she has done far worse than was ever thrown at her by songs, slander and rumour; she also knows that she would have done far more if it would have secured the throne. The Throne: it is at the root of every choice she made, every turn she took. Hers is not an easy tale, she knows that, it is not one for lovers of simple romances like the girl she long since ceased to be. There is more in it of defeat than of victory, there is little in it of love and there is no happy ending to warm the reader.

And yet I write and I know it will be read for it contains something far more enticing than conquests on the battlefield or in the bedchamber: it holds my secrets.

9

Anjou:
1430-1443

My childhood was shaped by women, women so strong they made the men around them fade to shadows.

'Where is Maman going?' Marguerite knelt on the cushions piled at the high window and looked down on a courtyard bustling with carts, horses and men-at-arms, her mother's blue gown a flash of colour in the cold, grey light of early morning.

'To Naples, child, to claim your father's birth right as the true King of Sicily; something he does not seem to be able to do alone.' Yolande of Aragon rarely smiled but the sight of her daughter-in-law Isabelle's whirling preparations had filled her with a softening rush of pride. 'Your mother is a remarkable woman, my child, truly remarkable.'

She was. Even at five years old Marguerite understood the truth of her grandmother's words. Her mother Isabelle was always laughing, a bright burst of energy, received with cheers and blown kisses wherever she went. So, knowing it was the best way to keep the smile on her grandmother's flinty face, the little girl smoothed her dress with a gesture copied from her mother and waved as graciously out of the window as any queen, oblivious to the fact that she was far too small to be seen by the milling courtiers.

'When I am older, I will be just as great a lady as Maman.'

If Yolande was amused by the imperious tone her grand-daughter adopted, she showed no sign of it.

'I do not doubt it. That is what I expected of your mother and it is what I expect of you. You will fulfil that, just as she did.'

'But I will be a proper queen with my own Kingdom; I won't have to pretend that my husband makes all the decisions like Maman does.'

The hand that pulled her back from the window closed on her arm like a trap; Marguerite would have cried out but the fury on her grandmother's face silenced her.

'Where did you hear such a ridiculous thing?' The tone was no softer than the grip.

'It's what everyone says.' Marguerite fought back the tears she knew would only infuriate Yolande. She struggled to get the words out. 'I heard the servants talking one night when I was in bed. They said it is the Anjou women who are strong, not the men, but everyone pretends different. They said mother was the real King, everyone just pretends that it is father. It was what they said, I heard them.'

The words the child had heard so many times tumbled out in a rush and Marguerite braced herself for the blow she expected to fall. Instead Yolande dropped her arm and sank into a chair.

'Dear Lord, out of the mouths of babes.' She shook herself and pulled the child closer. 'My sweet girl, you cannot say such things.'

Even if they are true.

Yolande knew what the servants said: that Rene was only good for painting and for being put in a cell when he couldn't pay the money he owed; that without Isabelle there would be no claim on Anjou or anywhere else. She knew what they said and she knew the truth of it; she could not, however, acknowledge it.

She saw the tears falling down the child's cheeks now and brushed them away with a far softer hand. There were lessons Marguerite had to learn and she had to deliver them.

'We are strong women in this family, it is true; we have had to be, but, you must understand that it is the men who hold the power, not us. No,' she had seen the protest rise to her granddaughter's lips and stopped it with a gentle finger. 'You will be a great lady one day and you need to know the world you will live in. Your father Rene is a noble man and a man of learning, everyone who knows him will tell you that but it is also true that he doesn't always act the way people want him to.'

She smiled suddenly at the intent look on Marguerite's face. 'People want kings to be soldiers, Marguerite, they want men of action not men who can lose themselves in books and paintings for days on end the way your father can. That is what the servants grumble about but that does not mean that you should listen.'

'Father likes things to be quiet, he likes to talk not argue.' The child knew little of her father, she barely saw him, but she knew that much and Yolande nodded her assent.

'He does indeed, so your mother helps him with the things he does not do so well.'

'Like what?'

'Like making laws and governing his subjects and trying to explain to people who might not agree why he should hold the power in the places where he has his titles, like Anjou and Naples.'

The things a king should do that he cannot.

'But I still don't understand. If Maman does the ruling better, why doesn't she do it instead and let the King paint all day? He would be happier.'

Yolande's laugh was such a rare sound even the attendants raised their heads. 'And wouldn't the world be a simpler place if we let children organise it!'

She shook her head and pulled the child onto her knee, a gesture so unexpected Marguerite barely heard the rest of her words. 'Because people believe that power rests with kings and with men and they believe that a woman's greatest strength lies in her virtue and her meekness. They like their queens to smile and obey their husbands like all women are expected to do. You may not like that, you may not find such a part an easy one to play but it is what the world expects and you have to learn it.'

You will struggle with it as we all struggle, that is the real truth you need to learn.

Yolande looked down at the child and knew she could not say anymore.

Please God you marry a strong man and not a weak fool like your mother and I were cursed with.

She and her daughter had both had to bear the burden of ruling from the shadows. Years of pretending that they knew less of the world than their husbands. Years of sweetening their mouths to hide their scorn, making every act as though a man had conjured it, even though the strategy that shaped each decision made was theirs. She roused herself, looking for a kinder message to give the girl but she need not have worried: the child, cocooned in the heavy satin skirts and soothed by the rhythm of a lesson far too complex for her to follow, was lost to sleep.

***

'Marguerite, child, let me look at you.'

The room was finally quiet, the waiting women dismissed to make their own preparations before the delegation arrived. It had been only a matter of hours since the Anjou entourage had come from Angers to Saumur and the Chateau de Tuce but Yolande had already firmly established herself as its chatelaine. She was not a woman to be ignored or denied and she had every servant and every lord in the Chateau equally as afraid and equally as desperate to do her bidding. The woman who would retell the stories of their fawning flattery with unrestrained glee and mimic their pretensions was expertly concealed from everyone but her grand-daughter; the bond between them, established so firmly since the early days of Marguerite's childhood, was unshakeable.

'You look very well, my dear, very well indeed.'

It was true: Marguerite was not a beauty and neither she nor her grandmother would pretend such a thing but the burnished silver of the mirror reflected back a face lovely in its pink and white smoothness and eyes that held the promise of laughter in their inky depths. Yolande had chosen the crimson material for the gown deliberately to accentuate the creaminess of Marguerite's skin and the gold crescent moon of the headdress deepened the auburn notes in the dark hair peeping below it. The mood of the face, however, contrasted far too sharply with the twinkling jewels on the gown.

'They will expect a smile, Marguerite, as will I.'

It was a gentle rebuke but no less serious for the quiet tone. Marguerite heard the warning but refused to acknowledge it.

'What difference will it make if I smile or if I don't? The ambassadors will come; they will look me up and down, fawn over me until they run out of words but all I am is a pretty ribbon. If they want a treaty, they will buy the package we offer them; if they don't, then I will dress up for the next one and the next one until someone is satisfied.'

There was silence as petulance met anger and both sides waited for the explosion. It did not come. Yolande's frown vanished as fast as it had appeared and, once more, she confounded her grand-daughter with an unexpected peal of laughter.

'I have taught you too well and you, I fear, are wiser than your years even if your tongue is younger.'

She tucked a stray curl back behind Marguerite's veil and tapped her lightly on the cheek. 'It is true, you are only a part of the offering but you are such a pretty part and this dressing of the treaty as you call it is more important than you allow. This is a good betrothal for you, remember, far better than the ones we made before and far better than your sister has achieved.'

Marguerite grinned, as her grandmother had intended: there was more of competition than love between the sisters and Yolande had always made her favourites clear.

'That is better.'

Marguerite's smile, sometimes too hard to win, lit her face far better than any jewel; something Yolande knew but the girl did not.

'This is a good match. Think about it, Marguerite: I had looked to make you a Duchess but this marriage to Frederick of Hapsburg would make you an Empress. It is a great honour my child, so charm his ambassadors and bring the prize home.'

And charm them she did but it was pointless. No matter how strong Yolande's diplomatic skills might be, her own rules, so long ago explained to her young charge, still held sway: without Rene, who had finally joined Isabelle to play at kingship in Naples, the discussions could come to no conclusion. The delegation left, laden with gifts and good words but leaving nothing more than promises.

Marguerite, bored by the whole affair, pouted and sulked and managed a few tears but it was mainly for show. She had not imagined any other outcome and it was her pride that suffered the only real injury. In less than two years she had been dangled in front of every eligible family in the marriage market; offered to Luxembourg as a sweet little maiden to strengthen their line, to Charolais as the pretty trimmings on a debt her father owed, to an Emperor in the hope of a fortune. She had been danced, in fact, past every possible prospect like a puppy on a golden chain. It could not last, there was simply no substance to it. The news came a few weeks later that Rene's ambitions had once again run too rich for him and Na ples was lost to the Spaniards, that her parents were penniless kings without a kingdom and she herself had lost any value. The sudden stillness in her fortunes would have been a relief had it not been for the dreadful impact the blow had on her grandmother.

The realisation that Rene really was no more than a foolish, deluded child who she could not rescue, who had reduced her to poverty and her grand-daughter's glittering future to ashes was too much even for Yolande. She took to her bed and would not leave it, finally giving into the old age she had refused to acknowledge for so long. Marguerite's grief as she held her dying grandmother's hand, willing the life back into her body as she refused to accept the last ragged breath, was all too real. Her mainstay was gone. The only voice she would ever truly listen to was gone. The only person who would see both the dark and the light in her and guide her to their balancing, was gone. If Marguerite had known then the true depth of her loss, the blow would have felled her.

England and Tours:
1444

I was such an innocent: to be suddenly a prize again in the marriage market seemed a blessing, not the curse it surely turned out to be.

'Marguerite of Anjou.'

William de la Pole, Duke of Suffolk pushed the portrait across the table towards Henry; the lack of any reaction was exactly as he had expected but that made it no easier for him to curb his irritation. 'Your Majesty, please, at least look at the painting. I have seen the girl, it is a good likeness.'

The boy's evident distaste (and how could he think of him as anything but a boy when every action was so meek and tremulous) at even touching the miniature was too much; Suffolk gulped his wine in an attempt to still his tongue and hide his annoyance, thrusting the goblet back again at an attendant far too slow for his liking. It was of little help: the King's lack of care for any earthly pleasures was all too evident in the roughness of the vinegar that filled his cup.

'Your Majesty, she is a good candidate for marriage. I know how important your books are to you but it would be the right thing, the Godly thing, to at least put them aside for a moment and look at the likeness.'

Cardinal Beaufort's gentler tones had a far more persuasive effect on Henry who at least now turned his attention as directed. Suffolk could admire Beaufort's tactics, it was quite beyond him to emulate them.

'I had intended to occupy myself with the study of the psalms today.' Henry's tone was petulant; it took all Suffolk's self-control and a far larger draught of wine not to betray his rising temper.

'And you will return to them,' Beaufort's words dripped like thick-churned cream. 'But the matter of marriage will not go away, we must address it.'

'I do not want to marry.'

There was a serenity, a certainty in Henry's voice that made Suffolk long to cuff him. How could he be so detached from what everyone else in the Kingdom so badly needed? But Beaufort was too quick for the Duke, knowing his temper too well; the Cardinal's warning look was enough to quiet him.

'I know how you feel, Your Majesty. I know that you see your life as God's and in so many ways it is but it also belongs to your people and they need an heir. You cannot escape that.'

Dear God, he is a virgin; we have a virgin monk for a king.

Suffolk had long suspected it but the reaction on Henry's face at the mention of an heir confirmed it: he looked positively ill.

'And peace, Sire, we need peace with France. Marriage to the Anjou girl would ensure that at least. Your Kingdom needs that too.' Suffolk spoke quickly and, for once, the look Henry turned on him was one of gratitude.

'Thank you.' Henry picked up his Bible and turned to leave the room. 'My Lord Suffolk, I know, has the country's interests at heart. We need peace; it is my duty to do everything I can to bring that about and I will. You may make the marriage arrangements and I shall seek to resolve...' he hesitated for a moment, his thin lips pulled into a tight line as he sought words he could bring himself to speak, 'the other matter through prayer. Cardinal Beaufort, you will give me spiritual guidance on this matter for I am determined to live my life as Christ lived his, without succumbing to temptation. I will not be persuaded to any other path.'

For a few moments after his departure neither men spoke, it fell to Suffolk to break the silence. 'He would live as a monk? He is the King of England, he is 23 years old and he would live as a monk?' Beaufort rubbed his hand across a face suddenly showing the strain of his 70 years, 'He is not like other men, any agreement to the marriage is more than I expected.'

'And what then?' Suffolk filled his goblet for the third time, no longer caring how rough the wine felt as it burned against his throat. 'We bring the French girl here and crown her and what then?'

The Cardinal shrugged, 'we pray she knows a whore's tricks or we pray for a miracle; take your pick.'

***

'I know it is an honour, Father, but I don't understand it. Why would the King of England think of me? What on earth could he want with a penniless bride?'

Rene smiled his empty smile but Marguerite stopped his flights of fancy with a look. 'Please don't tell me stories about my fabled beauty, be truthful: what is my value this time? Why would this ambassador, this Duke of Suffolk, even consider me as a queen?'

Her father hesitated: his refuge was always in pretty stories and flattery but his daughter had stopped indulging that when she was barely out of the nursery. He suspected his mother's hand in Marguerite's coldness but had never had the courage to challenge either of them. He had no option now but the truth.

'It is war, my dear, it is always about war, whether waging it or avoiding it.' He shrugged. 'The English no longer have the appetite to fight for their French claims or perhaps no longer the coffers to pay for it. They have begun to talk of peace.'

Of all the things Marguerite expected to hear, that was the least of them. She laughed, she could not help it.

'The English tired of war? That makes no sense; waging war is all they have ever done. When have English kings not claimed French lands as their own and fought to keep them? I thought the English still believed the spirit of Henry V and the great days of Agincourt flowed through them, their ambassadors certainly claim it until everyone at Court is bored witless by their rantings. So what now, they have become lovers of peace?'

She could see her father's frown deepen at her levity but it was hard to treat his words seriously. 'I am sorry but I don't understand and, even if what you say is true, what has any of it to do with me?'

'I am glad you know so much of the world that my scant knowledge amuses you.' His words were meant to admonish her but he could see she was indulging him just as his wife and mother had always done. If he thought it would have mattered, he would have let her see the hatred she so often made him feel. There was no point: it would have glanced off her like a raindrop.

'What you don't see, daughter, is that the English pretend that they are civilised but they are not: the English Court is pulled apart by its own lords like a pack of dogs tear at a deer.'

He had her attention at least. 'They call it a Court that forms around their King but it is really a battleground where every lord has an eye to power and not a thought of loyalty. King Henry is a man now but he was a child with a crown for too many years and his country has suffered for it. Power has had to be shared between powerful men; powerful men do not sit well with that.' He paused but she waved him on.

'This new ambassador, Suffolk, presents himself as a man of grace but he is as bad as the rest. He detests and distrusts his rival for power, the Duke of Gloucester. The Duke of Gloucester who was once Lord Protector would do anything to see Suffolk out of favour.'

He leant forward, enjoying his story now, knowing that a girl brought up on tales of Joan the Maid and her terrible fate would be fascinated by the scandals he had heard from England. 'I mean it, these men would do anything. You have heard the rumours: Gloucester's wife was charged with witchcraft with no motive except to destroy her husband and Suffolk's hand was in it. The Milanese Ambassador talked of little else when he was last here. The evidence against her was nothing but nonsense yet she is lucky she escaped a burning. Believe me Marguerite, the English court is full of factions, the war in France bleeds their treasury; they need an heir and they need peace. The Duke of Suffolk has come to France looking to settle English affairs here simply so they may be more easily settled at home.' He stopped and looked at her with an appraising stare, noting how still she had become.

'And as for your role in this? It is easy. You please Suffolk because he feels you will be his to command. You are not some princess brought up in expectation of a crown; you will be so grateful for his suit of you that his influence with the King, once you are Queen, will rise and eclipse the other lords. You please your Uncle Charles because he will use you to secure the return of Anjou and Maine from the English to the French crown and so secure his kingdom. You please me because the English ask no dowry except the gift of my lands in Spain which I get nothing from but grief. And, as if the offer wasn't tempting enough, they will meet the expenses of the wedding to please your uncle. Whether you please the King of England, well that, I think, is your affair. We have done well, daughter, do not find fault with it.'

There was no more to be said.

***

I shall be a Queen and not just Queen of some half-held province but Queen of England!

Even when the seamstresses arrived and the goldsmiths came and silks and satins and cloth of gold were stretched out in front of her, it seemed like a dream. She danced through the days, her head full of crowns and coronations and empty of warnings, indulged by her mother, petted and pampered and spoilt. Even the Duke of Suffolk, as quick to irritation as he was, could not fail to fall for Marguerite's delight in what was to come and, if he slept ill at night for knowing the truth of what faced her, for once he kept his counsel and left her to her dreams.

And such dreams they were as only a 14 year old girl promised to a king could have. She knew he would be the golden knight of story tellers and the more she weaved the fantasy, the more those around her helped her spin the web she had no idea she was caught in. Marguerite of Anjou, she held herself with such grace throughout every ceremony: curtseying to King Charles at the head of the greatest procession of royalty the people of Tours had ever seen; receiving the ring made specially from one of Henry's own; accepting the title of Queen of England with dignity and grace. Marguerite of Anjou, the public face of peace awaiting her place in History and smiling, always smiling, at Suffolk as he led her blindly into disaster.

France and England: 1445

It is strange to look back from such a distance and see the girl I once was, so buried now in the woman I have become. Strange and not of any comfort for I do not know her, I do not know her at all.

The girl who whirled round from the window as he entered was a flash of light, a beacon of fire against the grey stone of a chamber that barely seemed to contain her.

He will never catch her: she will blaze into England and he will fade in front of her. This cannot work.

'Suffolk, my dear Suffolk, I thought you had returned to England and forgotten all about me! Look at the preparations, people expect a wedding; are we to disappoint them? Have you found a wealthier princess to dangle in front of your King?'

'And are you going to play with me like the besotted fools I see you have enchanted all around you?' His scarred face broke into a grin. 'You have grown up, I think; where is the sweet girl I saw betrothed? I recognise the daisies but little else.'

Margaret, for that was how she tried to think of herself now, in the English manner, smoothed the gown of her white satin dress, admiring the gold and silver marguerites that encrusted it and made her smile match his. The effect was rather ruined by the edge she could not keep from her voice, an edge Suffolk heard all too clearly.

'I am not a girl, I am quite grown up. I am waiting to be a queen and I am tired of it. I have waited while my father subdued the rebels in Metz, I have waited while my sister married, I have waited for the Pope to pronounce my marriage valid. I have waited for you to come and see the matter done. I am sick with waiting! It is nearly a year since I was betrothed. I am impatient to see my husband;

I am impatient to be Queen.'

'You, Madame, are merely impatient; King Henry may find that far less endearing than I.'

He will hate it; he will hide from it.

It was his chance to warn her but he saw the glow in her face and could not do it; there was something in her that made him weak, that made him care about the impact of his words so much it stilled his tongue. And so he laughed to soften his words, words he knew she did not even heed, and smoothed her ruffled feathers with presents and stories of how much her betrothed longed to see her. Perhaps Beaufort was right and there would be a miracle, perhaps her very innocence would turn Henry's head. Of one thing he was quite certain: there would be no whore's tricks here.

I am too old to be cast like this, too tired of games.

Knowing he was powerless in the face of Margaret's excitement, Suffolk had thought to enlist his wife's help. Alice was now chief among Margaret's ladies and he had charged her with finding out just how innocent her new mistress really was. The response 'as a babe' had brought him no comfort and Alice's opinion that Henry himself was only 'shy and fearful and would become a husband when it was needed' had ended a conversation he had no appetite for.

As for Margaret, she had created Henry as a golden figure straight out of the pages of a chivalric romance: what had begun at the betrothal had only become more elaborate with waiting and Suffolk was powerless to stop it. Standing days later as proxy husband to her in the great Cathedral at Nancy he could see the girl was lost in a rosy haze. And all through the following week, when joust followed joust and pies the size of towers filled the banqueting halls and men staged battles on stately and exotic camels all to honour her, he could see she saw the spectacle but thought only of her dream-summoned husband.

Suffolk had schooled everyone well: Margaret knew Henry had been King for 20 years, since he was a baby; she knew he was thought of as a good and pious man but she knew no more and Suffolk made sure no one would speak to her about him in anything other than compliments. No one would answer her questions about what he was truly like with anything other than smiles. The Duke fooled himself it was for the girl's own protection; he persuaded himself that all she needed was to be in love with the thought of a king. If a voice pricked at his conscience that the reality might crush her spirit, might turn her sunny nature dark, he did not allow it to speak. Suffolk, with all the arrogance of his position and all the lack of understanding that brought, thought he could control the world around his little Queen and did not see the seeds of destruction that slipped away and took root all around him.

In return, Margaret, so caught up in her own enchantments, thought the world would fall smiling at her feet. How could she think otherwise when the evidence pointed to nothing else but triumph? A peace treaty had been signed declaring a two-year truce between two ancient enemies and her marriage was the seal on it. The English ambassadors laid out a carpet of flowers and Suffolk so skilfully hid the thorns: everyone in her train carefully picked so that she would not hear a dissenting voice; every face trained to smile at her. Every face except one but, when she finally met him, the one who would never smile with kindness at her from their first meeting to their last, she could not read the warning. Suffolk's job was too well done.

***

'Six hundred archers?' Suffolk looked out of the window at the escort massing in the courtyard below and grimaced. 'Is all this pageantry intended to glorify the new Queen or yourself? It is a little hard to tell.'

'I thought the answer to that was quite obvious.'

Richard, Duke of York smiled lazily at the older man. 'Add the can ons I have ordered to fire and the bells I have ordered to ring and even your little French girl should be able to see where the real power lies.'

Suffolk did not return the smile; it was all he could do not to throw his wine in York's smirking face and wash the self-satisfaction away but he had been charged with keeping the peace and he would keep it, no matter the provocation.

'Whether you like it or not, Margaret of Anjou is Queen of England. She knows your claim to the Throne and she will grant you every courtesy for that and for what is due to you as Lieutenant of France but you must repay her in kind. Do not treat her like a child.'

York's response was a roar of laughter that clenched Suffolk's teeth. 'Are you threatening me?'

He kicked the chair away and strode towards the window, his powerful frame suddenly making Suffolk all too aware of the 15 year age gap between them; at 34, York was still strong and handsome and all too aware of it.

'Look at them again and think about what they mean,' he gestured towards the bustling men below. 'Six hundred archers and all loyal to me; I could command double that number, ten times that number if I chose. So she knows about my claim to the English throne does she? Does she know that it is stronger than her husband's? Does she know my father lost his head pursuing it? Does she have any idea what that means to me?' The malice thickened with every question, he made no attempt to hide it.

Suffolk turned to face him, 'and why would you think she cares? You have a claim through the female line; it means nothing. You want revenge for your father; again, it means nothing. Margaret of Anjou is the Queen, she will be the mother of sons who will dispossess you completely so let me repeat my question: why would you think she cares?'

There was a moment's silence and then York's laugh rang out even louder, no more welcome this time than the last.

'Sons? My God, you really have fooled the girl! Does she think that pious little monk you have married her to will give her sons? I could almost feel sorry for her!' He shrugged. 'Unless of course you plan to do the job yourself?'

As Suffolk reached for his sword, York merely smiled, brushing the threat away with no more attention than he would have paid to a fly.

'Really, you would attack me here, moments before I am due to ride out and welcome your precious Queen?' He watched, his pleasure at the other man's impotence all too evident, as Suffolk clenched his sword hand into a fist but held it away from the weapon. 'I thought not, you aren't man enough.' York turned to the door with a mocking bow, 'and you aren't man enough to tumble the girl when the husband fails her. If her sons are the biggest threat she poses to me, my path to the Throne is all the straighter.'

I have failed her and there is nothing I can do. I have strengthened Margaret's greatest enemy against her and given her neither a warning to be wary of him nor weapons to ward him off when he chooses to strike.

Through the open casement came the canon roar and the thunder of bells just as York had ordered.

That is no welcome: that is the opening volley of a war.

***

As Suffolk knew it would, the pageantry turned Margaret breathless with delight. He watched her clap her hands with childish glee as York, with barely a bow, presented Henry's wedding gift: a white palfrey whose crimson velvet cloak was covered in roses, a vision of storybook prettiness. As she ran towards it, Suffolk tried to put out a restraining hand, to remind her to exercise a queen's de tached elegance but it was too late.

'It is the most beautiful thing I have ever seen and you, My Lord of York, are the kindest!' She had seized the bridle with its tinkling golden bells without noticing how cold his face was. 'I shall ride her to the ball tonight and you will lead me in!'

She looked properly at York then and her dazzling smile lost a little of its brightness as she saw the stony countenance turned towards her. Her confidence faltered a little but she pressed on, unused as she was to receiving anything but flattery and acquiescence to all her demands.

'If you think that would be proper, of course.'

'It will be both my duty and my pleasure, Your Majesty.'

The response was courteous, she could not fault him for that, but the voice and eyes were like ice. And still she continued trying to charm him, uncertain what else to do.

'And will we dance?'

'If that is your wish.'

He looked as though nothing could be further from his thoughts. Unsure of herself but not wanting to look foolish in front of Suffolk or her mother who were coming closer, Margaret cast around for some question that might warm his response to her.

'It is my wish tonight but really I long to talk to you about my husband.' She smiled at him again; still nothing. 'You are praised everywhere for being a truthful man and I would know more about the King. Tell me, is he a good man, a kind one? Will he find me pretty do you think?'

She knew the question sounded clumsy as she asked it but she was still not prepared for his reaction. He laughed and it was surely not the laugh of a courtier.

'Pretty? I doubt he will notice you unless he is instructed to.' There was a smile now on his face but she wished for stone again: it was like watching a snake warm itself in the sun.

'Your husband is indeed a good man, Your Majesty,' he paused and stared at her then for far too long, as though he knew her in a way far too intimate; Margaret's face grew warm but she could not look away. 'He will not see you as I think you want to be seen. It is a pity for you deserve to be looked at; you deserve to be brought properly to bed by someone who knows how to steady you.'

Her face was as crimson now as any of the roses around her but that only seemed to entertain him more and there was an ownership in his lazy smile that made Margaret's blush move more to anger than embarrassment.

He saw the change and he laughed. 'Well, perhaps you are full of surprises, perhaps he will be able to do his duty by you and get himself an heir.'

He moved closer and, for a moment, Margaret thought he might touch her, almost wanted him to do something so unacceptable she might be able to break the spell that seemed to hold them both separate from everyone around them. His breath was warm on her cheek, his mouth too close.

'He might, by some miracle, get an heir by you but the thought does not trouble me for I think he will prefer his prayer books to any diversion you think you can offer. And then what will you be? Ah yes, the French Queen who took our lands without an heir to heal us. I wish you joy of England, Madame; it does not wish it for you.'

Dear God, he hates me. It seeps from him.

He dropped a deep bow and moved back; letting other courtiers take his place before any response could find its way to her lips. It was a warning and she knew it and all the smiles around her suddenly seemed as false as a mummer's mask. A warning and a challenge: as young and cosseted as she was, she could see the glove laid down and could see an enemy even if she had little perception of the cause.

The rest of the day passed as though she was not in it. She did not attend the evening's welcoming banquet, feigning sickness and letting her mother take the lead. She dismissed her women with a sharp tongue they were not used to and lay alone on her bed, feeling not fear but fury rise. If Suffolk's smiles and seeming joy at her marriage where but a pretence, if York's words were a truer reflection of the reception that awaited her, she knew she would need to build her defences and keep her distance until she had the skills to fight the battles she now suspected would come. What she also knew was that she would fight back, she had no choice.

Suffolk saw the onset of a war and he was right but what he failed to see was the truth of the girl he had tried to defend: Margaret was not merely the pretty, biddable child he wanted her to be, she was Yolande's granddaughter.

***

The room was as dark as a cell and as poorly furnished. All the tapestries and trappings of the outer chambers were banished from Henry's most private space. There was an altar, a plain table, a single chair and books, piles of them, but nothing of comfort. Beaufort shivered.

It is his monk's room: we can make him play the King outside but this is who he really is, this is what we have to hide.

He shook himself and forced a smile, coughing gently so that Henry was forced to look up from the pages he pored over.

'She has landed, Your Majesty, there is a message from Suffolk.'

Henry's stare was as blank as ever. Beaufort resisted the urge to shake him, reminding himself that this pale-faced boy who showed little interest in anything beyond his books and his prayers was his King. It was not always easy.

'The Queen, your Majesty, she has arrived from France.'

'Then I must go to meet her.'

The Cardinal struggled to hold his composure.

Dear God, he sounds as if I would drag him to meet his executioner rather than his bride.

'In a few days, yes, you should. Preparations are underway to receive her at Southampton to allow her to recover from the crossing. Her journey was a difficult one according to Suffolk's letter; he describes a storm so bad they feared they all might die.'

Beaufort picked up the letter Henry had not even glanced at. 'It does not make easy reading. Suffolk describes a wind that whipped so fiercely the mast itself crashed to the deck, its standard ripped to shreds and the French women wailing so hard the sailors thought it was the end of the world. Apparently the storm didn't abate even when they finally brought the ship in; he says here the poor Queen's first taste of England was not cheering crowds but howling winds and a sea that seemed intent on eating up the land. She was made quite ill from it.'

Henry's attention was suddenly caught but not in any way Beaufort would have wished.

'Do you think it might be an omen, My Lord Cardinal, a portent? Perhaps God does not truly want this marriage, perhaps he is telling us it is not where my duty lies.'

Omens and portents; tricks to catch the ignorant.

Beaufort might have been a man of God but he had little time for the superstitions that daily surrounded him unless they were weapons to catch the unwary. To hear them repeated with all a peasant's simplicity by his King brought him no comfort; to have to counter them simply made him weary.

'I do not believe, Sire, God would have saved the Queen unless he meant for you both to have a happy and fruitful marriage together.'

Another pale smile and Henry detached himself as the Cardinal raised a silent prayer that the Queen might prove herself more practical than her increasingly unworldly husband.

**

'He is handsome, don't you think My Lady? As handsome as any king should be, as any husband should be?'

Lady Alice spoke the truth and Margaret's smile as her husband approached through the Great Hall shone with it. Her husband: despite the ceremonies and the pageantry, now that he was before her, she did not know what to do. She had pinched her cheeks unmercifully that morning, conscious of her pallor from the dreadful crossing, she had rubbed scented oils into her hair until its coppery lights gleamed and fretted over every gown she had and now there he was, walking slowly towards her, his face equally as pale as hers.

The crowded room had quieted: all the chatter Margaret had struggled to understand stilled as the courtiers struggled to catch a glimpse of the couple's first meeting.

Conscious of the whispers, the expectation, Margaret took a deep breath, willing the butterflies dancing in her stomach and the nervous giggle rising to her lips to be still and gone. Alice was right: Henry was handsome, with his gold hair and crown catching the light coming through the high windows, there was almost something ethereal about him. At 23, she could see that there was nothing of the soldier in his slight body, nothing of the heavy strength Richard of York paraded, but his features were very fine and his eyes and smile, when he eventually raised her from the deep curtsey she had swept into to hide her sudden trembling, promised a kindness.

'My Lady Wife, it is my humble honour and my spiritual joy to welcome you to England. God watches our union and can only be glad of it.'

His words are strange and his tone too dry and cool no matter how elegant his French.

She tried to push the thought away. The more watchful courtiers noticed that he dropped her hand as quick as he had taken it and barely met his new wife's eye; Margaret saw it too but chose to see the gesture as the dignified behaviour of a king greeting his wife in public. What else could she do? And if there was a moment's misgiving, it was only a moment. She was dazzled by the gold of his cloak, the sapphires in his crown and the sweeping bows of his attendants. She was dazzled by the pageantry of kingship, as Beaufort and Suffolk, carefully orchestrating every step, knew that she would be. No response was expected of her, her husband was swept away as quickly as he had come and Margaret was left to her ladies to learn the customs of her new country so that she would come to her real wedding a fit and proper bride for a king. The web continued to spin about her, the threads so fine she could not see the bindings.

***

I am going to be alone with him. He will come here and everyone will leave and then...what? What will I say to him, what will I do? He is so...distant.

'Alice, doesn't it strike you as odd that my proxy marriage was grander than the ceremony today?' Margaret tried to keep her voice light as Alice fastened the neck ribbons of her creamy bed-gown but there was a tremor in it she could not hide.

33

'Everything today was as the King wanted it.'

Alice smiled, pressing a goblet of wine into Margaret's hands and making her drink it, knowing without daring to say it that the girl might need courage for the night ahead. 'He told William that your wedding day was one for prayer, not pomp and spectacle.'

Margaret sipped the wine, grateful for anything that might calm her nerves. Alice's words had a certain logic given what she had seen of her new husband but still the day had not been what she dreamed.

'It was so very quiet. Was your wedding like this?'

Alice remembered the laughter and celebration of her marriage to Suffolk, the bawdy shouts and instructions as they were led to the bedchamber and turned to the fire to hide her blushes. 'It does not matter surely, My Lady. You are married now, your husband will be coming to you; it all begins now.'

To Alice's relief a knock on the door announced the King's arrival and her excuse to leave the bedchamber without further comment. She could not help notice the awkward silence that fell on the room as the attendants began to withdraw but that was no longer any of her business. Many a young couple began in such a state, they would have to find their own way through it.

Margaret stood in the centre of the bedchamber, feeling a chill despite the fire and the thick hangings.

What do I do? Do I go to him? Do I go to the bed?

It was Henry who spoke first, his voice oddly thin and empty of any expression a new wife might hope to hear.

'You are a good woman, Margaret. I can see it in you and I hope that soon your devotion to God will come to match mine in its joy and the comfort you take from it.'

Margaret looked at him uncertainly, suddenly even more unsure of herself.

These are not words of love, not even words of desire; surely they are words of prayer?

She continued to stand, increasingly unsure of herself, grateful that it was Henry who moved to close the space between them.

'Come with me now as my wife, it would give me such pleasure.'

He said it as softly as a lover and took her hand in his. Margaret felt the coolness of his fingers and breathed a sigh of relief: he clearly felt as shy as she did, all would be well. But he did not lead her to the bed. He led her instead to an altar tucked away in the corner of the room and gestured to her to kneel. As she did so, the candle-light suddenly caught the shadows of her body beneath the thin bed-gown; Henry gave a strangled gasp, looking about him he grabbed a heavy fur mantle, only calming when it was wrapped tightly about her shoulders.

'Pray with me.'

He fell to his knees on the hard stone beside her, clasped his hands, bowed his head and was lost to her.

What could she do? He spent the night in prayer, the whole night, on his knees before his God. Margaret left him there when she could no longer bear the cold and crawled into bed; he did not even notice. She slept fitfully, alone, too confused even for tears. Her mother had taught her what her duty was, her women had teased her enough for her to have some thought of what she should expect. It was not this.

And, after the strangeness of that night, he simply did not come to her. His new wife was left every evening with the chastest of brotherly kisses while he withdrew to his prayers and his books and his priests. By the time she entered London for her coronation, Marga ret was a shadow of the exuberant girl who had once spun such pretty dreams.

***

The sky was such a deep blue it was as though the painters had prepared it specially; the clouds so fluffy white she could almost belief the craftsmen had placed them there and tinged their tips with silver. Even the sun had the look of a golden disc better suited to dangling from a necklace. It was picture-perfect and she hated it.

'They must love you, they must really love you. It is breath-taking!'

Osanna Herman, the youngest and giddiest of the women who had accompanied Margaret from France clapped her hands in delight as she squirmed beside her mistress in the litter.

'Look, there are marguerites everywhere!'

She was right. The spectacle that greeted the young Queen's final arrival into London was breath-taking and clearly no expense had been spared, despite the lack of a dowry to fund it. Against the backdrop of the sky, builders had positioned delicate, flower-decked arches. The aldermen, all cloaked in crimson, and the guildsmen in bright blue had placed themselves around the bowers as though they were the most perfect of the blooms. There were cheering crowds and pageants on every corner whose great poems and prayers demanded careful attention and the right smiling responses, making Margaret very glad for the English she had finally mastered.

The progress had been slow and halting for there were so many tableaux to entertain the royal party, each demanding a stop and a smile and applause. It was exhausting and relentless and Margaret could no longer tell one set of symbols from another. At Southwark, she was shown the figures of Peace and Plenty, both declaiming how it would be Margaret alone who would set aside warring Mars and bring unity between France and England. At Leadenhall, Dame

Grace urged on her the virtues of Truth, Mercy, Peace and Justice. At Cornhill, images of the Virgin and now, at the Eleanor Cross, a chorus of angels serenading her beauty.

London has made my coronation a triumph; I do not trust a word of it.

'What are they saying?' Osanna was pointing at the heavenly choirs as they struggled to raise their voices over crowds made loud by fountains of wine. 'What are they saying? I cannot follow any of it, their accents are so rough.'

'It's not their accents, it's your English or rather your lack of it. You need to make some effort to learn!'

Margaret tried to sound stern but there was barely a year between them and Osanna rarely took anything she said seriously. The girl still hadn't made the switch from friend to subject and Margaret was loathe to put the barrier between them that would come soon enough.

'Listen to the music, it's a hymn.'

Osanna continued to look completely lost.

'They are saying that I will bring peace between France and England through this marriage; they are comparing the unity between our countries to the perfect unity of God's kingdom in Heaven. It is exactly the same sentiment we heard at Leadenhall and at Temple Bar. They certainly have very high hopes of me.'

'Then you should be honoured. It's such a wonderful welcome but you look as though they want to eat you! Madame, are you ill? Why don't you smile?'

Osanna frowned, her pretty open face wanting Margaret only to enjoy the day as she was doing.

How can I answer her? How can I tell her that the English I want her to learn has brought me more care than comfort today?

She simply could not spoil Osanna's day by telling the truth of what she heard on every corner. The prayers for her happiness were not shared by the crowds. She had heard too many shouts demanding to know who had paid for her golden necklace, the pearls threaded through her hair and strewn so richly over the heavy damask of her gown. Men who had clearly enjoyed the fountains of wine too much asked where their French lands had gone in voices thick with menace. And if she could not tell her closest friend that, she most certainly could not confide that her husband still had not so much as touched her, that he left Margaret's room each night almost as soon as Osanna did and her pretence of tiredness in the mornings was simply that; pretence.

But even that was not the reason for her silence, her struggle to smile: she did not have words enough in any language to confess that the loudest voice she heard, the voice behind every muttered insult that rose from the streets, was Richard of York's: mocking her ignorance and blighting her marriage. So many unspoken words; Margaret felt herself choking on them. But she was no longer the trusting girl who had sailed from France: she was beginning to learn the truth of the English Court. If there was to be a pretence, she had to show belief in it, even to her friends.

With a smile as bright as she could make it, she turned to her companion.

'Forgive me, dear Osanna. You are right, I am nervous and it is making me a misery. Hold my hand and we will wave and smile and everyone will see a bride who is glad to come among them, who wants only to be their beloved Queen.'

And so she did but she saw that day how well the people of London could act and she hardened her heart a little against them. She did as she was bid. She journeyed to the great palace at Westminster, this time alone in her gold-draped litter. She walked in stockinged-feet beneath their purple canopy to the Abbey, her hair flowing down her back like watered-silk. She received the holy oil and the silver sceptre topped with its dove of peace and, finally, she sat on her throne, the crown at last upon her head, crimson and ermine cloaked about her and watched them come. All the great lords, bowing their knees and swearing their oaths, Suffolk at their head. She did not trust a single one of them

.

***

The banquet that followed Margaret's coronation had been long, the Hall at Westminster crowded, the clamour from the watching tables loud. She had clapped dutifully as the lords entered on horseback, pretending to hold back the press of people like knights from the volume of romances she had been given as a wedding gift. She had pleased the cooks by exclaiming in delight at the jewelled-coloured jellies studded with golden lozenges, the subtleties shaped like castles and fountains and even a dragon. She had received the Lord Mayor's speech of thanks and golden cup of wine with gracious smiles. She had enjoyed playing the part of a queen but now, as she welcomed her husband finally into her room, she longed to be a wife.

'Henry, husband, stay with me.'

She tried to keep her voice steady: she had quickly learned that any note of censure and he would be gone.

Sensitive as she was to his crippling shyness, she had dismissed her women and seen to it that a fire was lit despite the warmth of the May night. Anything to bring some comfort to the chamber. Her nightgown was closed to the neck and her velvet-thick hair was caught back in a modest plait; the common tricks a wife might use to charm a husband had no place in this room.

And yet she had looked forward to seeing him: despite their physical distance, they had begun to form a tentative friendship. Having not seen him all day, for the coronation rituals were hers alone, she was ready to replay the experiences of the ceremony, enjoy them again in the retelling.

If Margaret was honest, she wanted more: she was heady with the adulation heaped upon a newly-crowned queen and she longed more than ever for her husband to look at her at least with the pretence of the adoration she had been surrounded by everywhere outside her bedchamber. Surely this night, when she was now his Queen as much as his wife, he would not leave her alone like a nun in her cell? But, even as she began to frame her hope in words far more delicate than the longing she felt, he had turned to go.

'It has been a long day, Margaret, you should sleep, gather your strength; there are three more days of banquets and tournaments to come. Everyone wants to see their Queen, to celebrate her, to enjoy her beauty.'

He was courteous as ever in his withdrawal; for courtesy, she could not reproach him but neither could she match him.

'Everyone wants to enjoy her except the one who should! How am I supposed to get a son for my beloved subjects when my husband runs from my room like an animal sprung from a trap? By praying?' She stopped, horrified by his sudden whiteness. 'Henry, husband, Your Majesty, forgive me. I shouldn't have spoken so.'

'Then why did you?'

His voice was so quiet, Margaret could barely hear him. Carefully she moved over to where he stood and reached for his hand but he flinched away. There was no going back, the words were said. Holding herself as steady as she could, she made her voice as quiet as his:

'Because it is the truth. There were as many voices in those crowds cheering for the hope of a son as for the hope of peace.' She took a breath, curbed her tone so no possible note of accusation could be heard, 'You need an heir, Henry, surely that is why you married me?'

He finally looked at her but it was a look of such blankness a shiver ran through her too strong to be controlled. When he spoke, there was not a trace of emotion in his words.

'I did not marry you, Margaret, you cannot think of our union like that. My councillors married you to secure peace and, yes' he paused slightly but his face, his voice showed nothing 'as you say, to get an heir. Neither the deed or the ambition was any of my doing.'

She watched him but she could not understand him and her anger, an emotion she had barely known growing up but one that was now an almost constant push, started to rise. Biting down hard on it, she tried to sound coaxing.

'Don't you want a child? Is it me who is at fault? Am I in some way displeasing?'

Still no smile, nothing of tenderness from him just the strangest sense of absence, as though she was an idea he had fretted over, a problem from a tract to be solved by thought and prayer, not a real woman whose feelings and emotions might have some place in his life.

'This is not about your person, Margaret; that is of no consequence to me. This married life is simply not what I would have chosen: my life is God's.'

He spoke slowly as though explaining a perfectly reasonable position to a troublesome child.

'My country may wish for an heir but that is not a wish I can fulfil. I explained this all to Beaufort and to Suffolk when they spoke of our marriage. Salisbury my Confessor, has helped me to know that any sin of desire I might feel for you is merely that, a sin. And, in time, that will leave me; I pray daily for it.'

They all knew, all of them: Suffolk, York, Beaufort, they all knew and still they had brought me here into this pretence of a marriage. And if there is no child...

They would blame her. She would be removed, by God knows

what means, but she would be removed. Fear and fury both at the vulnerability of her situation screamed through her; she knew he would recoil from the shrillness in my voice but she could not contain it.

'How can you say such things? You are a King, not a monk! You have a duty to your country: you cannot live the way you choose and nor can I! Dear God Henry, if you do not have an heir, your great advisors will fight around your crown again like a pack of rabid dogs, surely you must see that? You will never be safe.'

She was crying now, the tears tumbling down her face; whether they sprang from fear or anger, she did not care.

'And if I do not give you a child, what will be said of me? It is not hard to know: they will say that I am a worthless wife, a Queen to no purpose who has cost the country more than she ever brought it. I have heard the taunts already: London thinks that I am not worth the price England has paid. You could change all this and yet you refuse, you would throw me to them!'

The tears had become a flood and finally something in him stirred. Slowly, he broached the space between them and took his weeping wife in his arms; no matter those arms were stiff and awkward, she still clung to them.

'Forgive me, forgive me.'

It was all he said, over and over until finally the crying stopped.

'Margaret, forgive me. I do not want to hurt you; I did not want to put you through this but I am as lost as you. I am a good man, you must believe me, but you should not be here, we should not be married.'

'But we are, Henry, we are.'

Margaret looked at him, properly looked at the man who held her and saw the truth of his distress. He was deathly pale, his face as tear-streaked as her own, and so young-looking that his frailty caught at her and pushed her anger aside.

We are trapped, both of us. I need a protector or a saviour and he can be neither. There is no one to heal this but me.

The truth of her marriage, of her position threatened to engulf her but she could not let it. Quickly drying her eyes, she took his hand and led him gently to a chair, pressed a goblet of wine into his trembling hand. She made every movement small as though she had caught a delicate bird in a snare and did not dare to move too quick lest it was startled into flight.

They sat in silence for a time, watching the fire flicker, Margaret's hand barely a pressure on his arm so that he would sense it as a kindness not a restraint. When Henry eventually spoke, his voice was barely more than a whisper and had such tiredness in it, she could have cried again.

'I know what is expected of me, Margaret, out there as their King and in here as your husband but I can do none of it. No, don't try to placate me, let me talk.' For she had immediately moved as though to contradict him in her fear at his words. 'I can do none of it and you must know that. I do not want to be King; I do not want to be a husband. When I say my life is God's, it is not a choice, it is the truth. I am a monk who wears a crown and I wish you had no part of this charade they make me play. You are so lovely, Margaret, but you cannot be a diversion from my true purpose: I live to honour God, as a monk or as a priest would honour him.'

A diversion: Richard of York's words.

A fool would think it a curse but she knew it now for the truth that nobody else had dared tell her.

He cannot be a husband to me.

His words were plain enough and yet, fool perhaps as she might be to try, she could not admit their truth. She had to persuade him to a different course.

'Henry, husband, think for a moment. Wouldn't the birth of a son honour God? You are King by his divine will so surely there can be no wrong in anything you do?'

She could see as soon as she spoke the hopelessness of her attempt. Henry had a lifetime of pious prayer to support him and the soul of a saint; she had nothing to counter him with but the seductive abilities of a desperate virgin, a foolish virgin who thought she was wise. There was an answering smile to her words but it had more of despair than pleasure in it.

'And are you Satan, Margaret, that would tempt me from my path? Or are you so wise that you can know the will of God better than any confessor of mine?'

She could not stop herself: she jumped at the Devil's name, whitening as she remembered Gloucester's wife and the accusations made against her. He saw her distress and caught up her hand, raising it clumsily to his dry lips.

'Forgive me; that was unkind and undeserved. Margaret, I wish I could give you what you want but I cannot, I am not that man.'

She could not give up. 'But you could be, Henry, you could be.'

She forced her voice once more to cajole not plead. With great care she moved one hand to his cheek and laid the other on his knee, so thin beneath his nightgown.

'You could be and, then, once there is a child, well your duty is done and you can go back to your prayers and your devotions and everyone will know the future of the country is settled and they will love you for it.'

It was as cruel, she knew, as tempting a naughty child with a sweetmeat only to thrash it for its misdemeanours once the hand was caught. She could see the trust in his eyes and knew he had barely thought about what must happen if he believed in her words. Gently, she rose and began to move towards the bed, his hand loosely entwined in hers. If he looked more like a man going to his death than a young husband following a willing wife to bed, she chose not to think about it. Keeping her gaze firmly fixed on him, as though to break the contact would break the spell she had caught him in, she undid her gown at the throat, for he would neither look nor touch, and did the same to his.

'Margaret, no, I cannot...' but she quietened him with the softest of kisses and felt him begin to stir. With a delicacy of movement she did not know she had, she sank back into the pillows, pulling him with her and moving their garments aside. For a moment she had some hope of him: she could feel him begin to tremble, felt a pressure as his lips began to return her kiss. It was a moment only. She took every one of her mother's lessons and every bit of kitchen gossip she had ever heard and tried to make a lover of him but it was too hard a task. Her inexperience could not challenge his pious distaste.

As she guided him inexpertly between her shaking thighs, he groaned, but any hardness in him lasted barely a moment and his groan was one of such misery she could not carry on. There was an emptiness in him, a shrinking away that set a coldness in her heart no matter how much she tried to fight it. He pulled back and turned his face away and, when she tried to touch him again, he pushed her hand roughly from him, called her whore and witch and names she did not recognise but she smelled the scent of the fire and heard the fall of the axe in all of them. Finally he fell into an exhausted sleep, having failed and wept and prayed until he had no more strength in him, leaving Margaret alone in the dark, finally free to let her own tears fall. Richard of York was the only man who had spoken the truth: this was not a man who would give her sons to keep her safe. This was a man who would destroy her.

***

'Is it consummated?'

Suffolk saw Beaufort wince at the directness of the question but would not apologise for it; this was a concern too important to merit a care for sensibilities.

'Cardinal, you have the King's Confessor under your control and probably half the women of the bedchamber in your pay. It is a reasonable question.'

The older man sighed.

'You flatter my abilities. Salisbury has become very evasive of late and the women are far more loyal to her than I expected.'

'Then it has not.'

Suffolk shook his head as Beaufort began to speak. 'If you do not know, you suspect as much. He barely visits her rooms and you hear the talk as much as I. The whispers in the corridors of Westminster are thick with how the King prefers his books to her bed.'

'At least he does go to her now, she has made him stay in her rooms until morning at least one night in every week.' The Cardinal raised his eyebrows, 'she is clever, cleverer than I thought she might be given her age. She knows there must be a hope of a child at least but in truth I think it is only a hope. The King has told me how much he likes her company, how well read she is but he is not a man who has unlocked the pleasures of the bedchamber, that much is clear.'

'By Christ, how did we come to this?' Suffolk's grip on his goblet looked fit to shatter it. 'Where did Henry get the idea that piety was so closely entwined with chastity? He can hardly take the churchmen around him as an example of that.'

Beaufort heard the insult and chose to ignore it: his own daughter was a poorly kept secret but not one that troubled his conscience.

'The King is a deeply religious man; you may as well shout at the sun for disappearing at night as try to change the truth of that.'

'That is all well and good but there needs to be an heir; an empty cradle is no use to England. You have seen the Court. It is no better than a battle-ground, a bear pit.'

Suffolk made no attempt to hide his frustration, Beaufort knew him well enough not to expect it.

'We finally lose the Regency, get a king on the throne and yet we have achieved nothing: the Court is still split into factions, all these families, all used to fighting for position, all crowding now round the King, looking for preferment, for the best route to power. The Percys, the Nevilles, the Beauchamps, the Cliffords, the Stanleys, so many of them and all with their own private armies, their men filling the city, parading their liveries and brawling without fear of consequence. And above them all the Dukes of Gloucester, York and Somerset...'

And Suffolk,' the Cardinal could have said but he chose to keep his counsel while the Duke blustered on.

All intent on their own personal gain, fomenting division, plotting and planning as the King dreams and prays and founds colleges to make more men like himself in a country that has no need of them. He may as well still be a child for all the good he does us.

Beaufort waited for the storm to abate as he knew it would.

'And what would you do to remedy things? Have the Queen take a lover and fill the cradle that way?'

Suffolk's expression of horror was so pronounced, Beaufort took it as proof that the rumours he had heard about the Duke's interest in the Queen was merely mischief-making.

'Let us pray she is as clever as you think and doesn't do something

47

so foolish. The nobles crowd around her as thick as flies as it is waiting for some favour from her; can you imagine the feeding frenzy if she was to place any of them above the other?' Suffolk shook his head. 'She is young; she probably still has hope that she can win her husband away from his priests. If she loses that hope, you had best pray her women suddenly find the appeal of your purse far stronger than any bonds of loyalty. If her belly swells, she could cuckold us as much as Henry.'

The South:
1446-7

I wonder if I would have been source of pride or disappointment to my Grandmother? It is a foolish thought and matters little but I think she would have judged the lessons she taught me badly learnt and that saddens me still.

'You are, my dear Beaufort, the best of teachers. Had my grand-mother only lived to know you, you and she would have made a team nobody could outwit.'

'You flatter me, Your Majesty, but too few beautiful women do that these days and, I confess, it is very pleasant.'

The Cardinal smiled warmly. Suffolk might have charged him with spying on the Queen but spending time with her had proved no hardship. Under the guise of acting as her guide through the political factions that were her daily life, they had become firm friends: Margaret listened to his opinions and made him feel far younger than his 70 years, his wisdom made her feel far older than her twenty. It was a good match. If Suffolk knew how deep the friendship ran, he would have trusted the Cardinal less but Beaufort had little care for that.

'If I am to be a good teacher, you need to be a pupil who will listen. You favour Suffolk too much.' He shook his head as Margaret opened her mouth to argue. 'Credit me with some sense before you start protesting. I no more believe the rumours that you and he are lovers than I believe Gloucester's wife is really a witch but rumours there are and your behaviour does little to counter them. Suffolk is a very entertaining man but you are seen too much in his company; you would be as well to have Gloucester a little more on your arm and thinking himself a little more in your ear.'

He saw the mew of distaste and made no effort to hide his irrita tion; Queen or no Queen she could still behave too much like a petulant child.

'Whether you like it or not, Humphrey, Duke of Gloucester, is the last living brother of Henry V, he is heir presumptive and, I have no doubt, a thorn in your side. But you cannot be so obvious in your preferences: you make it far too clear that you are already heartily sick of the mention even of his name.'

Margaret frowned and balled her fists against her anger in a gesture he was becoming all too familiar with. 'You are right, I know that you are right but, by God, Gloucester is a difficult man to like and he cares little for me.' She looked at him as though expecting a contradiction; he did not respond.

'I swear he hates me because he still thinks of himself as a soldier. He wants nothing more than to fight so what am I but the constant reminder of the peace treaty he hates so much? Every time he looks at me he sees his glorious brother's betrayed legacy. And God help me if I was to get with child and deprive him of the crown he so lusts after. Maybe the imprisoning of his wife has made him bitter but I don't care to be in his company.'

Beaufort shrugged; he had heard her complaints too often.

'They are all soldiers and so your presence insults them all. As for his wife, you could benefit from a little more compassion: he loves her and the loss of her is sharp. You know that she is to be moved again, Kenilworth Castle is too close and he tries too hard to see her. He has taken that hard but, whatever your feelings towards him, the truth of what I said remains: you do not play your enemies well.'

He saw the fists tighten until the knuckles were white and shook his head.

'Margaret that temper of yours will not help you. You push your enemies too far away when a little flattery would keep them closer and easier to sweeten and you push too hard for those who please you. Just consider: the letters you have sent to your uncle King Charles, against all my advice, promoting the continuance of the peace treaty sound to everyone like Suffolk's words in the Queen's mouth.' He leant forward so the words would be heard by them alone, 'which means that they sound like Suffolk's words in the King's mouth for Henry only signs what you clearly write. You need to have a care.'

He watched the conflicting emotions play across her face: she knew he was right but she was still too uncertain of her place and authority to allow him too much mastery. He sighed inwardly as he watched Queen win over pupil and knew his words were only half-regarded.

'I have done no more than my role demands.'

Her tone was haughty, a girl playing at power; he let it pass.

'The King wishes for peace with France to continue, Gloucester's war-mongers still fight against the promised cessation of Anjou and Maine without which the peace will collapse. I am sorry Cardinal but the process drags on too long. King Charles needs to know that the English are serious in their intentions to return what he sees as his lands or he really will call for a war that we can ill-afford. I merely acted as mediator with my uncle; my letters to him were intended to smooth the way and quicken the discussions. I am sorry if that offends you but I thought it was what a queen should do.'

'Margaret, you are not sorry but you are a delight!'

Beaufort's laugh was loud enough to make the maids in the corner look up from their embroidery. Here was the cornerstone of their friendship: neither could stay angry with the other for long and both delighted in each other's characters, flaws and all.

'A delight! Yes, my dear, a queen should be a patient, gentle medi-ator, acting only to advance the ambitions of her husband. You are quite right so let me play pupil to your teacher. You have read your

Cessolis, I think that you have, and what does he say? Ah yes, that a queen should be well-mannered and timid.'

She was starting to laugh now and he knew his advice had a stronger chance of being heeded if she was amused by him.

'And de Charny , I have seen his book in your chamber, and he too is very clear on how it is a queen's duty to handle no great matters without the permission of her husband, the husband who she should at all times revere.' He wagged his finger at her and was rewarded by a peal of laughter.

'Perhaps I should be the teacher after all. I know that you have read the books but you have paid them very little regard; the gentle supplicant indeed! Tell me how exactly your letters to your Uncle Charles, in which you made so much of the importance of maintaining the peace and the importance of the promises the English made to him, fulfil this humble mediator's role? You, my dear, have written to the French King directly, put words in your husband's mouth and made Suffolk's pledges at your wedding, that all at Court thought we in England would simply ignore, into a reality.'

His tone became serious now. 'Maine and Anjou, in name at least, are French once more and the English are furious. You have put French needs above English needs and there will be more bloodshed despite your oh so innocent attempts at conciliation, already our captains at Le Mans refuse to comply. Don't you see: your attempts to prolong the peace will merely extend the war.'

'Because the English are fools!'

He had misjudged the mood; her laughter had vanished.

'I do not put French needs first, how dare you charge me with that, I think only of England. We cannot afford to drain the resources of the Crown any further with wars that cannot be won. You want me to listen to Gloucester? Gloucester is too in love with past glories to accept that war is a fool's errand and my husband is too weak to control him. Someone had to act. And it is not just Suffolk whose voice is in this, York also supports me: he favours the marriage I proposed between his son and Charles' daughter so I have done what you wanted and pulled some of my enemies closer. Never mind Gloucester, isn't York a prize worth having?'

She was angry now, genuinely angry and Beaufort could do nothing to mollify her. He had seen this quick temper of hers flare too often lately, suspecting the cause was of little use in trying to calm it.

'You talk about de Cessolis and de Charny with their treatises on how the perfect queen should conduct herself as though they are the only works that matter. Perhaps, my Dear Cardinal, you should read Christine de Pizan: the women in her City of Ladies are skilled in the art of rhetoric and the practice of government and encouraged to speak their thoughts boldly, not timidly. They were the works my mother and grandmother put their faith in but perhaps they are a little too rich for the English Court.'

With practice borne of long service, Beaufort acted as though her outburst had not happened.

'While there may be truth in what you say, York acts purely out of his own self-regard. He does not thank you for your efforts, he sees you merely as meddlesome as does the rest of the Court. And he sees Suffolk's hand behind it: York knows Suffolk does not want to run the risk of any loss of face over the promises he made so eloquently at your marriage. As, again, does the rest of the Court.'

Beaufort sighed and passed a hand across his brow, his age suddenly all too apparent.

'You will do as you will, I have no doubt of that and, perhaps, your strategy is the right one but the English won't forgive you for it. You do not understand: they are no lovers of warrior queens except in stories told to children. And no, they have not read the books you set such store by and would not care for them if they did. You are fooling yourself if you think you can push your husband to one side: whatever else he may be or may not be, he is still the King and you would do well to remember it.'

Whatever else he may or may not be; he knows.

There was silence: it was Margaret's moment to confide in the Cardinal, it was his moment to help her but the chance was lost. Whatever the King's failings, however close their friendship, some subjects could not be aired. Margaret swept from the room, her pride hurt, and refused to see the Cardinal while she licked her wounds. By the time she was ready to admit that the fault was as much hers as his, it was too late. Beaufort was too ill and too frail to give her real counsel or comfort and her sorrow at his dying when it came was made far worse by the knowledge of how easily she had thrown away one of the few honest men who had truly befriended her.

***

It was wet. It had been wet for days and the Court was weary with itself and fractious. Books had been discarded, the musicians went unlistened to, everyone needed a diversion; Margaret, unable to calm her restless nature in the hunting fields, was more than happy to provide it.

'Good Duke Humphrey. It is an interesting title. Do you deserve it?'

She made no attempt to hide the mockery in her voice but she could not push him to a public reaction. The hatred in Gloucester's eyes could have forged a weapon strong enough to defeat an army but he was too clever a courtier to openly rise to the insult and his answering tone was as smooth as buttermilk.

'I cannot answer that, Your Majesty, what modest man could? It is a title I have heard, I admit, but you must ask the men who use it not the man who wears it for its truth.'

Margaret inclined her head in a show of admiration neither of them believed. 'Shall I rename you then 'Clever Duke Humphrey' for that was certainly well-said.'

She moved closer but kept her voice loud enough for the surrounding room to hear.

'Well, my clever Lord, perhaps you can give me some guidance on matters other than names. We are not a happy group, you must agree. Factions still plague us and never let the Court settle despite how much your King hates his subjects to be divided. If you are good or clever, however we shall style it, perhaps you can find some way of binding their loyalty a little closer.'

She tapped him lightly on the arm as though in play, 'and, if that doesn't work, well perhaps your wife can weave a healing spell and enchant us all to friendship.'

There was an audible gasp from the groups scattered around the Hall which did nothing to mask Gloucester's sharp intake of breath. Beaufort looked up from his conversation and began to rise but Margaret was enjoying baiting her quarry far too much to pay any attention.

'Do you think your wife is as good and clever as you, my dear Lord Gloucester? Remind me what she was accused of: oh yes, obtaining potions from a witch, wasn't that it? And what was your Lady's defence? Wait, I remember but let me get it right, that's it, "she wasn't learning the arts of witchcraft, she was merely seeking help to conceive".

Gloucester was livid now, his face a purple mask, but there was nothing he could do in the face of such an attack and, with another little tap as though she offered nothing more than comforting advice, Margaret pressed on.

'You see, my dear Duke, I think your wife was not so much clever as foolish. And lucky of course, yes, she was very lucky to avoid the executions her accomplices couldn't escape, but she was also very foolish. Wouldn't you agree?'

There was complete silence. Beaufort's limping progress across the flagged floor had stopped: he could see that Margaret had abandoned any thought of consequences and her anger would run its course no matter what he might say or do. He was far too old and far too tired to become the next target.

There was no pretence between Queen and courtier now, neither was smiling and it was clear from his stance that, could Gloucester have struck her and survived it, the Queen would have been on the floor. And yet she still would not stop goading him.

'Perhaps she is not the only one who is foolish. Isn't it only foolish men who marry their mistresses and then let them play at sorcery? So not clever or good then; I shall call you "Misguided Lord Gloucester" and let us see how that sits.'

It was a declaration of war and he took it as one, storming from the chamber without permission and without any attempt to hide his fury.

***

'You have made yourself an enemy and now what will you do with him?'

Beaufort was exhausted; it was etched in the deep lines of his face, the tremors of his hands. The bones were too close to the surface now.

'You cannot humiliate a man like that and expect him not to strike back; you have thrown him a challenge with your foolish spitefulness and God knows where it leaves us all.'

'I don't care.'

Beaufort grimaced at the petulance in the Queen's voice; the aftermath of fury always made her childlike but he had cautioned her about it too many times to care to revisit it now.

'Gloucester is an irritant, his judgements are poor, his war-mongering is a nuisance; I want him away from me and away from Court.'

'So badly that you would have him killed?' Finally she took some notice of him.

'I have heard the rumours, they are ridiculous.'

'Perhaps. But they are everywhere, Margaret, and they are believed.

'What is believed?' Again she was on the attack and he no longer had the resources to soften her. 'That he will be murdered and they will find my hand...where? On the poison cup? What do people see me as? Some Locusta or Agrippina from Ancient Rome, prowling the gardens of Westminster in search of poisonous herbs?'

She looked at him and gave a laugh that had nothing of mirth in it. 'My God, they probably do. Can't they see the truth? That this is all Richard of York's doing? He has his little spies spreading word that I have brought the poisoner's arts with me from France; that I learnt them from the Milanese ambassadors I met at my uncle's court. It is such a pack of lies I cannot understand how anyone would choose to believe them.'

'Because they want to.'

Beaufort's words were blunt but he had to make her see the danger she faced while he still had the strength to do so. 'You are a French Queen without an heir; the people will believe anything that pulls you down until you give them what you were brought here to do. I know what you are doing: you treat the Court as though it is a chessboard, selecting the pieces you think you can manipulate best as though you were the one in control. You call Gloucester foolish; you would be better to keep that name for yourself.'

'Old-age makes you very brave Beaufort.' But his words had struck home and the bluster had gone. 'I know they hate me, I know it but do they really think me capable of murder? Do you?'

She looked suddenly so young, so vulnerable. He shook his head.

'Of course not but I understand how you could be accused and ill-judged. Margaret, you must learn how to control your tongue. If Gloucester was to die, you might indeed be blameless but I doubt you will be believed.'

'Unless I had a son in my belly. Then I could kill who I liked and I doubt anyone would care, that is the real truth isn't it?'

There was such bitterness in her voice, he wanted to turn away but he would give her honesty above all else, it was all he had left to him now.

'Yes. You need a son and then they will forgive you anything.' He paused, conscious of the difference in their ages, of his Cardinal's robes. 'There is no hope yet that...'

'There is no hope yet? There is no hope!'

The fury was back full-force, all her frustration spilling out. 'You have taught my husband far too much about God for him to be any use as a husband. You made him a monk but you knew that, you knew that and still you pulled me into this mockery of a marriage where I can do nothing but fail.' She waved away his protest. 'Don't insult me, do not. And don't tell me how much I need an heir, I know it every day.'

She laughed, that hollow, mirthless sound that made him wince each time he heard it. 'Well if I am to have a son, I will need to find a father for it; perhaps I should take Gloucester to my bed; that would certainly bring him closer.'

He could not bear it. Shaking with age but more with misery at what they had done to the laughing girl she had been, Beaufort rose to his feet and took her hands, pulled her into an embrace as though she was his own daughter needing comfort and calming.

'Stop, stop. You hurt yourself with such words and you would suffer even more if anyone but me heard them.'

She was in tears now but they were despairing not angry, he could see the shift in her.

'It will be alright Margaret. Gloucester will undo himself in time. The Duke is ambitious and full of pride; he does not need you to destroy him, he will do it himself. And your husband will accept his duty and give you your son; you are both young, there is time. Be patient.'

She might heed him, she might not but his last days were approaching, he could feel it; there was little else he could do.

***

The swish of her skirts, the way she tossed her hair and waited for every head to turn and watch her was enough to announce that Osanna was in possession of something that made her feel special. Margaret knew that claws were already sharpening with jealousy but she was too much in need of diversion to soften the audience.

'I have quite a story for you.'

Osanna looked not so much like the cat who had swallowed the cream but rather as one that had been given the run of the dairy. Margaret watched with amusement, she could not help it, as Katherine and Barbelina's reactions to their friend's announcement set the younger girl bridling. Her closest ladies-in-waiting had earned themselves the nickname 'the three French-hens' with their constant clucking, much to Margaret's entertainment and their irritation.

'You look far too pleased with yourself so I imagine it is just another tale of a poor courtier whose heart you have broken.' Katherine arched an eyebrow, a favourite mannerism that she employed far too often. 'It is quite astounding how your English has improved since half the men at Court who are meant to serve the King have started swearing loyalty to you.'

'It is nothing of the sort and, if my command of English has improved, then it is only so that I can be of better service to the Queen.' Osanna was torn between annoyance at the dismissal of her story and delight at the acknowledgement of the effect she knew she had on any man she chose to flatter.

'And we thought it was because you had used up all the nobles with their pretty French compliments and had moved on to rougher meat.'

Barbelina was well-named and Margaret could see an intervention would be needed if tears were to be avoided.

'Enough, both of you. I swear this wet weather is turning you all into hawks with too many talons. Osanna, tell us your news and I promise we will give you a serious audience.'

With feathers a little more mollified, Osanna settled herself as her audience chose to ignore her smug expression and the time she now took selecting a sweetmeat.

'I have just been told, by one of my closest confidantes, that there is going to be a Council hearing, that perhaps there will even be a treason trial.'

She had everyone's attention now.

'Why a treason trial? Has someone threatened the King?' It was Katherine who asked.

Osanna hesitated slightly, clearly fearful that her story might lose its weight. 'Well not exactly, no. But it is close enough: an apprentice has accused his master of treason because the master keeps proclaiming York as the rightful King.'

'Again? Oh Osanna, we hear these rumours all the time.' Katherine turned away, as did the others, and picked up her embroidery; she did not notice that Margaret still had her attention firmly on Osanna. 'Every apprentice with the slightest grievance or too much ale in him shouts the same charge and they are all meaningless. Why would you bring us such a silly trifle?'

'Because this one is different!'

The women jumped at Osanna's tone but she raced on. 'I promise this is different. The master who is accused is John Daveys, York's own armourer and the apprentice, Will Catour, well everyone says he is an honest man, not in anybody's pay at all.'

Osanna turned to the Queen who still had not reacted. 'The Council are taking it seriously, Madame, I promise you: they are afraid that the Duke of York is raising an army and that is why his armourer is confident enough to speak out. Who else would know the truth if not the man who makes the swords?'

He shows his true colours at last; if he comes out of the shadows, I can catch him.

This time it was different; they could feel it in Osanna's words and Margaret's steady smile. This time the response was left to the Queen.

'We should all apologise for doubting you, my dear. It is an interesting rumour and, as to whether it is the truth or not, or whether York is really involved or not, that is of no matter; it is a rumour we should feed.'

Suffolk, Gloucester, York. They all had their spies and their webs and their ways of making the Court dance to their particular tunes. They did not know how well-matched they were by the Queen and her flock of women willing to whisper and chatter and hide clever questions under blushes and compliments. It took little talent to spin Daveys' words into a whisper of a threat and the women, so skilled in collecting rumour, were just as talented in its spreading. Within days the Court was whipped to a frenzy and York himself was forced to utter denials on a matter he would rather have ignored, knowing as he also did that it mattered little where the truth lay: the words alone were enough to wound.

***

The monk's cell: she had called it that from the start and never felt comfortable there. Henry's withdrawing chamber had no comfort in it and no place for her but it had the luxury of privacy and there were times when that made it more desirable than any other chamber in the Palace.

'We must leave London, Henry; it is not safe for us here.'

Twice she had said it and still Henry looked at her as though he did not understand the words. Until, Suffolk had rather awkwardly announced her, Margaret had almost believed her husband had not even known who she was.

'Why?'

Suffolk winced at the childlike response but reined in his tongue; he had learnt that impatience would only result in further blankness. 'Why would we leave? Who are we in danger from? Hasn't York sworn his loyalty since that unpleasant matter with his armourer was dealt with?'

'That unpleasant matter? You can call it that if you choose; the rest of the Court calls it a challenge to the King's authority.' The reality of the King's withdrawal in the face of impatience was, unfortunately, a lesson Margaret still would not accept.

Henry looked down and began to knot his hands. Suffolk knew too well that any mention of a claim to the throne stronger than his own would turn Henry into a timid shadow. Margaret knew it too but any care she might once have had over her husband's sensitivities was long worn away.

'You are right, Your Majesty, it was an unpleasant matter.'

He heard Margaret's sigh of frustration but deliberately ignored it. 'But you dealt with it as a king should. A public rebuttal was needed, one whose words would make it clear that York and, by implication, any Duke who challenged his King, was acting against God's chosen agent on earth and you provided that.'

Henry smiled like a boy trying to please a favourite teacher.

'I did, didn't I? And the dual between Daveys and that apprentice boy was a clever idea: I knew the boy would win and he did. The people saw York's man proved to be a traitor and now York himself catches the taint. It was very well done.'

'Very well done, given that the dual you made them fight was so obviously fair what with Daveys being so much older and heavier and the fact that he had clearly taken the edge from his nerves with too many flagons of wine.' Margaret saw the fury on Suffolk's face and subsided but did not apologise.

'The point is, Your Majesty, that the people went to Smithfield and saw justice done. That was what was needed and you made sure it happened.'

'So if York is loyal, why must we leave? He made such an elegant speech, how could anyone doubt him?'

The child again; this time Margaret took notice of Suffolk's warning glance and bit her frustration down. She, Suffolk, everyone at Court knew that York's words were as hollow as an empty barrel but either Henry would not or could not accept the truth. York had sworn his loyalty because he knew the twists of diplomacy better than any of them; he knew his King might feel plots all about him but would be mollified by pretty words rather than call his enemies into the open. York also knew, as did everyone at Court, that he had protected himself well: if there was to be a sacrifice this time it would not be him but Gloucester who, unlike York, had never taken the time to learn the art of politics. With Gloucester so nearly in her grasp, Margaret too could afford to wait on the bigger prize and to take the gentler tone with Henry Suffolk so clearly wanted.

'York says he is loyal and so we must believe him, for now at least. But the City is still unsettled, Henry, and we cannot trust that. There are still rumours of plots to replace you and, if York is not behind them, then Gloucester surely is.'

Henry did not react so she carefully continued.

'Gloucester is popular with the people and I don't think we should pretend he still has any real love for you, or for anyone other than himself. He has a restless nature, Henry, you know it and we should, perhaps, think to curb it.'

I have frightened him; even the gentlest approach is still too harsh for him to hear but how can I soften what we have to do any further?

'You surely don't want me to accuse Gloucester of being a traitor?' Henry's voice was beginning to rise. 'How can I? There are no grounds. Besides, I could not do such a thing: there would be no proof and he would never forgive me for such an unjust attack. Margaret, you ask too much. I will pray on it, pray on it all and ask God to find a path for us.'

Henry's face twisted with nerves and he began to mutter the prayers they had seen him use to comfort himself like a child will twist at a rag until he calmed and quietened, still praying.

'Does he even see us?' Suffolk's face was pale as he watched the King retreat from them.

Margaret shook her head. 'I don't know. I've seen him do this before; it is as though he is lost in some private conversation with his

God. He won't hear anything else we say.'

Suffolk moved as though to touch Henry's arm but then dropped his hand, worry and distaste clouding his face. 'What ails him? Something is wrong and none of us speak of it. Every day we see him become more withdrawn from the world and we all pretend it isn't happening.'

Margaret sat down heavily; the relief of hearing Suffolk speak her own fears had drained the fight away from her.

'There are days, I swear, when he has the aspect more of a shadow than a man.'

She picked up Suffolk's wine goblet and drank without registering the taste.

'I talk to him about Gloucester and York and my fears for the Crown's stability but he will not listen beyond a moment: he will not hear the detail or discuss what we might do. He cannot make decisions, we all know it but still we bring them to him because he is the King. We make the decisions and pretend it his him and then we wonder why none of us can trust the other. Look at him,' she gestured to where Henry sat, still mumbling his prayers, oblivious to them both. 'Every day he becomes stranger. I would call in the physicians but what could I say? "The King seems a little nervous, a little more inclined to prayer than governing?"

She took another deep drink. 'The Court is riddled with mistrust as it is; what would happen if York or Gloucester saw him like this? In all honesty, Suffolk, how do I know I can even trust you once they start squabbling round the Crown?'

He opened his mouth to protest but knew she needed more than empty words.

'You are right. Whether he will believe us or not, the King must leave London. If you will trust me, and you can, let me make ar rangements to move the Court to Bury St Edmunds and hold parliament there. They are my lands, the nobles will be easier to control there and the King easier to hide from public view.'

She looked at him then for the first time since Henry had last spoken; there was a light in her eyes that once he would have found charming but now he saw nothing but danger in it.

'Arrange it and summon Gloucester. This time I will be rid of him.'

***

The Hall was deliberately empty: this was an audience that would take place in front of as few witnesses as possible and in front of only those she could trust. It was not Gloucester's words she cared about, he could speak any slander he dared, her concern ran only to Henry: if this went badly and he became afraid, she could not let anyone but the closest circle see the fool their King could easily become.

'Repeat those lies again and they will be the last words you speak.'

Gloucester's speech was brave enough, his hand on his sword foolhardy enough but even he, for all his bravado, knew how empty a threat it was.

'You would really draw your sword in the presence of your King?' Suffolk's tone stayed even but his smile was unmistakably insolent. 'Perhaps you did not clearly hear the charges brought against you.'

'I heard them.' Gloucester had withdrawn his hand from his sword hilt but the disgust in his voice was tangible. 'I heard them but I will not accept them. Plotting against the King? It is a lie. You think very well of yourself, Suffolk, if you think I would accept such an insult from you. If there are charges, and God help you to find them, let me hear them from the King, not from his wife's puppet.'

This time Suffolk's answering smile was a study in malice.

'You, My Lord, would do well to remember where you are and in whose presence you speak. Do you want to add slander against the Queen to the crimes I have listed here?'

He glanced towards the throne where Margaret sat, the very model of the obedient spouse.

'I speak at the King's command and with his authority; you are charged with plotting against the King's person, endangering the safety of the realm and showing nothing but contempt for the laws of your country. Will you answer the charges against you?'

'I will not answer lies and I will not answer you.' For the first time, Gloucester turned to the dais and addressed Henry directly.

'Your Majesty, you surely cannot believe these accusations? I have always been your loyal servant; I have done everything in my power to protect your interests since you were a child, why would I change now? You must see this for the deception it is: Suffolk looks to his own advancement at the expense of mine and does not care what damage is caused along the way. You are a good man, Sire, do not stoop to this.'

But Henry remained impassive as Suffolk and Margaret had gambled he would: they knew this was not a situation his increasingly fragile nerves could stand; the success of their plan depended on any direct appeal remaining unheard as the King closed his mind to things he would not comprehend.

The silence thickened and Gloucester, his words unanswered, took refuge once more in bluster.

'I will not stay here. I will gather my men and leave at once' but Suffolk's words stopped him as he turned to go.

'Your men are already gathered My Lord: your squires; your knights; your son. All gathered and all to be charged, as you will be, with treason.'

Before Gloucester could open his mouth, Margaret's steward Somerset, who had been waiting quietly at her side for the whispered word, had crossed the floor, his sword half-drawn. Gloucester was a prisoner before he knew what was happening.

'In the King's name, My Lord, I arrest you.' Such simple words but no one who heard them could mistake their fearful threat.

For a brief moment it seemed as though Gloucester would draw and fight and simplify his end but he was not quite such a fool and pride was all that he had left. There would be no trial, he knew that, there would be days in locked and guarded rooms waiting for poison or a sword or a smothering, but he would not give Suffolk or Margaret the pleasure of watching him plead. In the end it was a seizure that took him within a matter of weeks and, if he waited too long for the physicians and healing herbs that might have helped him, there was no one to complain to and no one to blame.

For all he did not think she had heard him, Margaret had taken Beaufort's counsel and seen the value of patience. Gloucester's men languished in their cells until July, until all had forgotten them and then five, including his bastard son, were executed for plots no one needed to detail and the rest were pardoned, with a great show of mercy and forgiveness from their loving sovereign. And with Gloucester gone, Margaret could turn her attention to York, moving against him not with weapons but with preferment: the Duke of York added the title of Lord Lieutenant of Ireland to his impressive array. It was not an exile, she knew York would not go to Ireland quickly if at all, but it was a clipping of his wings at least. The King's power was demonstrated, rebellion was averted and not a poison cup to be seen. And if Suffolk looked at Margaret with more fear than admiration in the weeks that followed, she was perfectly content with that.

London and the North: 1450

There are moments when it is as though we can feel the world turning, shifting on its axis so that nothing ever feels the same again. So many things cause it: chance encounters, a defeat where there should have been a victory or vice versa and loss, the act that leaves the deepest mark.

'Is every man in England who can bear arms poised to draw his sword? I swear every day feels like a rebellion is about to come!'

Margaret heard the shrill edge in her voice and saw the ripple it caused through the groups of courtiers gathered in the Hall but she could not contain herself. Rebellion was coming; she knew it but was powerless to act. With York's return to Court, posturing and preening like a conquering prince, her nerves were constantly stretched and her women were far too afraid of her tongue to try and soothe her.

'And if it does, then the King will deal with it as he will deal with war with France, if those rumours are also to be believed.' Jacquetta Woodville, wife to Lord Rivers, was a newcomer to Margaret's closest circle and usually a diverting one, but not today.

Margaret rounded on her, her eyes blazing. 'And that would be the same King would it who has just scuttled from the room like a crab about to be pecked by a gull because his wife dared to speak her mind?'

'And that would be the same wife who is about to stamp her foot like the smallest of my brood?'

Margaret stared at Jacquetta in shock at her presumption, as did most of the Court, but the older woman merely smiled at her.

She is like Beaufort, she says what she likes to me and I cannot stay angry.

As the thought struck Margaret she found herself suddenly smiling back. In so many ways Jacquetta, already blessed with a great brood of children and now pregnant again, was a reminder of everything Margaret was not and yet there was something captivating about her for she was a great spinner of tales and took such delight in her family and her marriage, even Margaret could not begrudge her such good fortune. Jolted out of her self-absorption, Margaret looked properly at Jacquetta and realised how breathless the woman was; her own anger was gone in an instant.

'Jacquetta, what is the matter? Sit down or you will have that child born before its time. Osanna, give her your chair; Katherine, find her some wine.'

The little flock was reluctant to move from their perches so close to the fire but Jacquetta's manner was so excitable and Margaret's so determined, they could make no protest.

'Thank you.' As Jacquetta sipped the spiced and warming drink, her breathing began to calm itself. 'I forget how hard it is for me to move so quickly.'

'Well why would you need to? What gossip can possibly need such ungainly haste?'

Barbelina's tone was cool but Jacquetta simply ignored her.

'It is not gossip, but grave news; I have just heard it from my husband and could scarcely believe it.' She paused, as always adoring the attention and clearly hoping for some reaction but, when none came her way, plunged on, 'Moleyns has been murdered, Madame, murdered and with such savagery; a mob took him in broad daylight if you can credit such a thing. None of us are safe, none of us.' She settled herself back against the cushions, clearly delighted with the gasps of shock that had greeted her words.

It was only Margaret who still looked at her blankly.

That makes no sense. Adam Moleyns, the Bishop of Chichester, the Keeper of the Privy Seal? Why would a mob murder him? And what mob?

Her silence gave Jacquetta just the excuse she needed to continue to command the room.

'It was soldiers, Madame, soldiers in Portsmouth.' She had settled into her tale now and was playing to her audience. 'Don't for a moment think I am justifying what they did, I am just repeating what I have been told. Apparently they were angry because they had not been paid, not for a long time and rumours that war with France is close again were all over the town. Well it seems that the soldiers thought they would be asked to fight even though there would probably still be no money to pay them.'

She waited for a moment, her tone growing ever more self-important when she resumed.

'There are many reports about what happened next and they do differ in the detail of exactly what was done but they all agree that the men were dangerous and could not be controlled. They had been rioting and looting so Moleyns went to calm them. Of course they would not listen to him or anyone and they set on him.'

She paused and then looked squarely at the Queen.

'My Lord husband says Moleyns was killed because he was Suffolk's man and the soldiers blame Suffolk for our losses in France. They say he did not send Somerset help quickly enough. And they say he stole the money that was meant to pay their wages.'

And so it begins: they will turn on me all of them and I have nothing in my hand to play.

'And do they blame me?'

Margaret's voice was quiet but Jacquetta heard the cold fury in it and she flinched away.

'Is that the real truth? Do they blame the barren Queen who has lost them France and has given them nothing in return?'

'They blame Suffolk, Madame; there is no mention of you.'

'I don't believe you. Look at me, Jacquetta, and answer me honestly: do they blame me?'

She was brave, even in her fury Margaret could see that, and she did not shy away a second time. 'There are proclamations, Madame, around the city, in the taverns and on the walls. They accuse Suffolk of treason it is true but, yes, they blame you. Every proclamation repeats the words that Cooper spoke against you at Canterbury.'

That slander again: 'Our Queen is no Queen of England because she bears no child.' Spoken by a common prisoner in Canterbury gaol and repeated by every man with a grudge against the Crown. Against me.

Margaret felt the old fear dragging at her and tightened her face into a mask.

'Where is Suffolk? Does he know about this?'

'He is with the King, Madame, trying to persuade him to act before the violence spreads.'

Trying to save his own skin would be closer to the truth.

Underneath the folds of her skirt, Margaret's fists were clenched so tight the rings dug into her flesh.

I should have foreseen this.

The treaty signed with such pomp at her wedding had not held: the losses in France were too much for the English to bear; all her attempts to reconcile these growling men had come to nothing. She had known it would happen, no matter how much her words of warning were ignored. Charles, his patience worn too thin, had grown tired of the English and their inability to keep the peace and, angered by the sack of Fougeres (Somerset, unable to restrain himself or his men must surely take blame for that insanity) had swept through the disputed French territories like an avenging angel. City after city, Lisieux, Gournay, Louviers, Evreux, fell like thistledown before him and Somerset, his bravery all forgotten, capitulated at Honfleur faster than anyone could get help to him. Help Suffolk was adamant he offered but that Somerset would not take. Whatever the truth of it, she knew it for a disaster and one that she had to separate herself from quickly.

'Osanna, Katherine, pack my dresses.' She waved their questions away, 'I am going to speak with the King: we need to leave London before this situation worsens.'

Jacquetta stared at me in dismay. 'But, Madame, Parliament was to be called, my husband...'

'Parliament will still be called.' If she had no time for Osanna and Barbelina's questions, she had less for Jacquetta's whose objections might carry far more sense. 'But it will be called in Leicester not here; there are signs that plague has returned to London, I want the King away from the city.'

And safe in my dower lands where no one can see the truth of him but me.

'But Suffolk will not go; he will not want people to think him a coward, running away at the first...'

She was no fool Jacquetta; Margaret's look was enough to silence her.

Ignoring the courtiers now openly listening, she swept from the room. Returning to London had been a mistake but Henry had been stubborn and Suffolk felt the danger over; it was not, it never was and now she had no choice but to put distance between herself and the man too closely identified with her name. If Suffolk was about to fall, that fall would be his alone.

It made sense, it was my only course of action and yet what was it if not a betrayal?

In the weeks that followed, Margaret told herself she had done everything she could to save her old friend. When Parliament impeached Suffolk as a traitor, as she knew it would, she spoke for him. She persuaded Henry that banishment was a fairer punishment than the execution the mob was baying for. She arranged his escort guessing, quite rightly, that attacks would be made on him as he left the Tower to take ship for the five year exile she knew he dreaded.

I may have wished death for Gloucester, I may have prayed for it for York; I did not want it for Suffolk. I do not want him dead.

All through those nervous days she whispered the same thought to herself as though it was a charm that would keep him safe. It did not work, how could it, and there were no words left to bring her comfort when they brought the news of his terrible death: butchered on board ship with a sword so rusty it took six strokes to take him, his headless body thrown onto the beach at Dover like refuse for dogs. There was no comfort to be had either when she heard how Alice took to her bed for days and woke her women screaming every night, begging for a sword to take her to.

There is no hiding from it: I betrayed my friend to save myself. I could keep the horror of that from the outside world but the knowledge is lodged in me like a poison.

***

The Great Hall at Greenwich was quieter than normal: the last rays of a warm summer sun had tempted people back out into the still heavy scents of the rose gardens and away from the strained atmosphere that had accompanied supper. Although Margaret had pretended to be at ease eating on the raised dais with an equally reluctant Duke of York, their play at friendship had fooled no one. As the last dishes were cleared away, she was unable to sustain it any longer.

'This is all your doing! Jack Cade is your puppet. He could never lead a rebellion like this alone, you are behind it, I know it.'

It was all Margaret could do not to fling her wine at York along with her accusations: the effect would have been as wasted as her words. 'You have such a vivid imagination, my dear Lady; I don't know where you get such ideas.'

He stretched his long legs in front of him as though they were merely discussing the latest flight of fancy from the pastry cooks.

'How could I have anything to do with a rebellion in Kent when I have been, as you well know because you sent me, so far away in Ireland?'

'The rebellion began the minute you returned; you had a hand in it.'

He shook his head and smiled as though she were a troublesome child worrying at him for a sweetmeat.

'The country has been fragile for months, you know it as well as I do. Did you really think Suffolk's death was the end of your problems? The timing of my return has nothing to do with this. Jack Cade is a hot-head, a clever fighter well-enough but a hot-head who would boil over at any provocation and London lets him in because London is London.'

He smiled and popped the last of the gingered almonds into his mouth as the servant reached to remove the platter. 'The City has never warmed to you, Madame, and you have never tried to woo it.'

He is too comfortable, too at ease: he acts as though the Palace is his and I am the inconvenient guest.

With an effort that gave York far too much amusement, she ignored the insult, desperate to see him falter before Henry (who was already beginning to shake at the turn the conversation had taken) forced her back into silence.

'If you and your family are so innocent, why does Cade also use the alias Mortimer? It is a bit of a coincidence surely? Half the citizens of London claim to believe that Cade is Edward Mortimer, your uncle and a claimant to the Crown. Why would he use the title unless your hand was in it?'

It was a foolish charge to throw at him and this time he did not even try to pretend to hide his laughter.

'Why on earth would I involve myself with a man who would make such a ridiculous claim? My uncle is long-dead, any man in his right mind knows it. Cade plays with the name because the people like it but all it proves to me, to anyone with any sense, is that he is a fool. I am loyal to the King; if you want to prove otherwise then try but you won't win any listeners with this nonsense.'

He is right and I hate him for it. I can lash out all I want but without real grounds, real proof, everyone will dismiss me as an hysteric and know I am afraid.

She turned to Henry but it was pointless. As York grinned and insulted her, Henry did nothing; he was too feeble with fear to make any move against York or anyone else. But she was right about York's involvement she knew it, no matter how much he twisted the truth. If Cade's army had not been so drunk on power, had not looted so mercilessly and murdered so many who resisted them that the citizens of London came to loathe and fear them, York would have openly joined his forces with theirs and seized his chance to make a play for the Crown he increasingly openly craved.

'He is no use to you, I warned you but you would not listen. Look at him, he is no use to you now against me and he never will be.'

That tone again, so low and mocking, meant for her ears alone; a twisted take on a lover's murmuring that made her stomach clench. And still he went on, dripping poison in tones of honey.

'Look at your husband, Margaret, really look at him. Kemp and Waynflete, your trusted bishops, Shrewsbury, all those men so loyal to you, they can pretend they don't see the truth of the man who rules them but you can't and I won't. They might make believe that the King is still the King but we know better, don't we? We know that the crown is set on the head of a ghost, that there is an absence where there should be a man. We know that you are pretending strength in the face of his frailty.'

The venom dripped and yet she could not move away, could not hush his tainted words.

'What can you really do? You cannot hide him away and you cannot put him in the field to face Cade. What can you do?'

There was not a sound in the Hall: the few courtiers who remained had stopped pretending and were now openly watching them, sat like two people entwined by the closest secret. Her control snapped: she flung the wine and stormed away from him as his laugh echoed across the emptying space and the Court began to gossip of a lover's spat. She raged through her bedchamber until every pot she could throw was in splinters and screamed at her women until they all fled in tears for he was right: what could she do but carry on the pretence?

All through the days that followed, she could not bear to think how York must have gloated in her discomfort as she played out what he knew was nothing but a charade. Setting the banners high and marching Henry to London where the rebels had made camp at Blackheath as though he would meet with them, then sending the bishops not the King to make the great pretence of listening to their grievances. It was a fool's game.

A king in control, quelling the rebellion? It was all make-believe.

Knowing she could do nothing else, she hustled Henry swiftly to Greenwich where he was happy dispensing pardons as though they were Easter coins with no idea of what he did or why. She knew the truth her husband would never have grasped even if she had tried to explain it: if the men who had found themselves caught up in it had not wanted the rebellion to end, if the people of London had not hated their butchery so much, if it had come to an actual battle, Henry's crown would have been lost right there. But she schemed and planned and then marched Henry back to Kenilworth as fast as she could, before his distracted air became too much the thing of gossip and the rebels really did find cause to replace a king.

And York was right in that to: she did not know what ailed her husband or what to do. It was no longer simple piety that kept him apart from his subjects, from the task of ruling them. The man was like a phantom: anything ill or unpleasant and he turned his mind away. Again she thought to call the physicians, again she dismissed the idea. What would she say? My husband will not speak of anything but religion? My husband quakes with fear at the slightest shadow? My husband seems to be out of his wits? York would have been on him in a moment.

Like a miser hunches over his gold, Margaret watched over Henry. The court began to comment on the couple's new devotion and the gossip made her weep: it was just another show. Margaret was Henry's protector; she was his gaoler by any other name. With a strength born of desperation, she kept up the pretence of a powerful but pious king whose prayers for guidance kept him silent and withdrawn from the world around him and it was believed if not admired. It could not last, York knew it and so did she.

But at night, in the dark when the mask was removed and she had to face her real fears, the thoughts that kept her awake and painted dark shadows under her eyes were not about rebels and pardons or executions. Cade's death, an execution she had ordered as a warning to the restless mobs, did not disturb her. York's plots and schemes were not the cause of her tired ill-temper. Even Suffolk's death and her fearful guilt began to fade. What haunted the little sleep she snatched and had her waking with a start night after night was the realisation of what she had really lost: not only did she not have the child she needed to heal the rifts around her, she had finally lost any hope of it. She was utterly alone and utterly desperate.

London: 1452

Betrayal: it becomes easier. Once one life has been destroyed to save your own, the senses dull so that the next slip of the knife comes at a lesser cost. It seems that need really is enough to make monsters of us all. I could pretend otherwise; it would be a lie.

Who could I take?

Her reflection in the burnished metal did not look like the face of a seductress: too many sleepless nights had left her pale and dark crescent moons swept below eyes whose brightness was too feverish.

Who would I want?

No, that is not the question; who could I trust?

She slipped off herrings as though to make each the symbol of a man and moved them across the table.

The ruby was the gaudiest: that would be Somerset then.

Not him, it cannot be him, the man is a disaster.

She turned the stone, watching it sparkle: Edmund Beaufort, the second Duke of Somerset; he had a reputation with queens since his long-ago love affair at 19with Catherine de Valois. He was, in his favour, a handsome man still, even at 45. He could charm any one of her little birds with his French manners and her too if she was in the mood for his nonsense, and he loathed York which was all to his credit. But, no matter, he was a disaster: hot-tempered, impulsive and reckless in decision-making. The mob had blamed Suffolk for the failures in France but they would have been better to blame Somerset. The loss of Rouen was his and the loss of Caen. The whole Court knew that, if York had not been the threat he was, Somerset would never have been made Constable of England on his return from France; such a promotion for such a disastrous showing, but the two men had to balance each other, cancel each other so that their claims to the throne could be controlled. No, not Somerset. She pushed the ruby away.

An emerald left, so York then? She shivered at the thought: he would not come meekly to her bed.

He acts already like a king, a king in all but name.

He wanted her; she could see that every time he looked at her.

But only to destroy me once he was finished.

No, that way madness surely lay.

All that remained was her diamond: clear and open, nothing hidden. In sudden disgust at her foolishness, she swept the rings to the floor. She was the Queen, she could not take a lover; she was lost.

***

She was exhausted. She had grown pale and thin. Her dresses hung from her frame and she no longer cared. Her rings slipped off fingers that were becoming bony and she left them where they lay. And yet still they came: messages and reports and accounts of York's movements on a daily basis, all demanding action and none of them giving her the weapons she needed to bring him down. It was little wonder she barely slept.

'He finally shows his hand.'

Something about Shrewsbury's voice, a suppressed excitement she had not heard before, caught her attention through the fog that seemed to fill her mind too often.

Margaret had barely glanced at the letter Shrewsbury had brought but now she took it back, studied it more carefully. Even in her distracted state, its contents were too clear to mistake: York had

stepped out of the shadows and openly accused Somerset of treason. The manuscript she held had been widely copied and distrib-
uted around the country and York's message was plain: if Somerset
was allowed to influence the King, the country would be destroyed;
Somerset must therefore go and only York was man enough to force
a charge of treason and to make it hold. It was carefully done.
There was no direct challenge to Henry and the demand for Somerset's removal was couched in the words of protection but it carried an implication of a weak king and a stronger duke, the balance
all wrong. The threat, the promise, of what would happen if York's demand was ignored was plainly there for those who wished to see it.

'Has he overplayed it?'

'It is certainly a bold move.'

Shrewsbury stopped but Margaret knew better than to press him for
he was a man who liked to consider all options before advancing
an opinion and she valued his judgement.

'It is bold but as to overplaying? No, not quite, I think it is merely
the start but it finally gives us some idea of where he is heading.
York is waiting to gauge support: if the people support him, if they
loathe Somerset enough, then I think he may declare himself.'

'As heir? You think he would make his claim so public?'

She hated to frame the question so bluntly with all it implied but
she had no choice.

The implication was not lost on Shrewsbury; it was clear that his
response pained him but he gave it nonetheless.

'Yes My Lady, as heir presumptive and the one who should be at the
centre of governing, where he most clearly is not. It has been a long
while waiting, Your Majesty; I think he feels safe enough to do it.'

She did not question him; what could she say? A long while waiting for an heir. Seven years a wife; seven years of stares and whispers as she showed not the slightest trace of a pregnancy. Dear God, the truth of it came so suddenly to her, she almost blurted the thought aloud.

If they knew I was still a virgin, the people would flock to York faster than bees swarm to a flower meadow.

She took refuge in questions she did not wish to ask with answers all too obvious.

'What does the King know of this? And Somerset?'

'Somerset blusters and shouts and demands redress. As for the King,' Shrewsbury shrugged, 'what does he truly know of anything that he does not wish to see? The merest thought of his nobles fighting between themselves and he is plunged into fear of civil war. It is not that he does not know of it, it is rather that he will not know of it.'

'And will not act.'

She waved away Shrewsbury's words before he could attempt excuses for a king his honour forced him to respect. 'Where is York now?'

'At Blackheath. He has gathered with him, well we would call it an army, he would claim it is a retinue. Whatever we choose to call it, he demands to meet with the King and have redress against Somerset. We cannot ignore him, that, at least, is clear. The King needs to meet York and Somerset needs to be restrained. Whether that course of action is real or a ruse, only you can say.'

And so she marched Henry out again and let York bluster and shout but stop short of battle as he watched Somerset arrested and taken away to the Tower as though York's accusations were both true and given a genuine hearing. It was a ruse, of course it was: Somerset was released almost as soon as he was detained. It was an appearance of conciliation but the time for that had passed and Margaret knew it: simple tricks alone could not keep her safe, York was only just beginning.

***

The diamond ring glittered on her finger as she twisted it to catch the light. It was the only one she wore, the ruby and the emerald were safe in her jewel chest; the diamond was the only one she needed.

'Leave us, all of you but Jacquetta. I want to speak with her alone.'

Her women looked up surprised: if she was ever to single one out from the other and request quieter company, it was usually Osanna she chose. But they gathered their needlework and their silks and bundled out of the chamber without complaint.

Jacquetta smiled complacently, comfortable in her new role as confidante. She had, as Margaret lately so often allowed her to do, commanded the conversation that evening, regaling the others with tales of her progress through England when she came twenty years ago as the bride of Lord Bedford, how the crowds had cheered her as though she was a queen herself. She barely saw her audience, she was so taken with the memory of her own splendour. At this extra sign of favour, she swelled and beamed, her tone dripping with concern the moment the two women were left alone.

'Are you unwell, My Lady? Is there something you require of me, some herb or potion perhaps to heal you? Some charm to bring you cause to smile?'

Margaret rarely laughed these days but it took all her self-possession to remain composed now. Jacquetta could be such a simpleton with her pretence of wise-woman's lore and her eagerness to flaunt it. Margaret knew she would soon be weaving some fanciful tale about her family, rambling legends of goddesses and healers whose power she knew herself heir to. Jacquetta had so little sense of how dangerous such nonsense was and her husband simply smiled indulgently at her whenever she began. Margaret smiled and smoothed the heavy satin of her skirt, watching the diamond reflect the deep reds of the embroidery as though it caught fire on her hand.

Such easy seeds to harvest.

'Do you really believe in such things Jacquetta? In herbs and potions and charms; that they can grant wishes, change fortunes, bring the things that would make me happy?'

Jacquetta puffed up like a wood pigeon at the Queen's interest and could barely contain herself. 'And more, Madame, if you know what you are about. The women of my family have long known such things and passed the lore from mother to daughter.'

She leaned in closer.

'I know what it is you most want, My Lady, and have often hoped you would ask me for my help.' She waited but Margaret did not speak, merely waited all innocence for the fool to accuse herself, so she continued unaware. 'A child, My Lady, a babe. I know how much you desire it and I can help you; there are so many ways I can help you if you would but let me. Old ways, perhaps, but proven.'

'Charms to bring a baby? You would get your Queen a child with witchcraft?'

Margaret watched as Jacquetta suddenly moved back, a new wariness in her eyes.

'Is that what you suggest, Jacquetta? That you know some secret spell that will end my barrenness, for that is surely how it sounds.'

It was as if she had been the one to cast a spell: Jacquetta could barely find her voice.

'Madame, I did not mean...I was not serious...it is nothing but a game, story-telling to entertain...'

Margaret smiled but there was no warmth in it and Jacquetta shrank back even further.

'But is it? You tell these tales, as you call them now, all the time, Jacquetta, and certainly make it sound as though you put a great deal of store by them. What If I was to ask you for your help, to believe in your words, what would you say then?'

Jacquetta gulped like a stranded fish, clearly aware that there was a trap but unable to see where it might fall.

'I do not understand your meaning, Madame. Have I offended you in some way? If my tales are upsetting to you then I am sorry for I meant nothing by them.'

'But I think you did. I think you like to be thought of as having, shall we say, a deeper knowledge than the rest of us, a secret power. It is a dangerous game to play but you never seem to worry about that. Don't you remember Eleanor Cobham? Margery Jourdemayne, the woman she went to for help conceiving?'

Margaret watched the play of light deepen in the jewel on her finger.

'The people do not like witches, Jacquetta; they fear them.'

At the word witch, every drop of colour had drained from the woman's plump little face and she was caught. All Margaret had to do was snap the trap shut.

'But you are right in one thing: I do crave a child and you do have something that could help me.'

Jacquetta was as still and silent as stone.

If Jacquetta could only use the tricks she claims she possesses to will herself invisible, I would be speaking to myself.

'The King needs an heir, Jacquetta, or the country will slip into civil war, so it is true: I need a child.' Margaret paused; Jacquetta was clearly afraid but she still had no inkling of where she was being taken. 'I need a child but I do not have the husband to get it. You, however, do.'

Margaret sat quietly back and watched Jacquetta's growing horror as the meaning of the words began to take shape. When the older woman spoke, her voice was a whisper.

'Madame, I cannot think what you suggest. I must be mistaken.'

'You are not mistaken, you heard me perfectly well. It is a simple matter: I need a child; your husband is good at getting them, mine is not. Look at you, what is Martha, your ninth? She is barely toddling and already you are letting out your bodices and laying out the cradle again, while I...' She shook her head. 'I need your husband and I will have him; that is an end of it.'

Jacquetta was on her feet now, outrage finally loosening her tongue.

'You cannot do it! Do you think I would let you? Do you think he would do such a thing? Besides, the King would know, the whole Court would know. It is impossible, it is treason; it is evil. Why would we consent to such a thing?' Her voice was rising, becoming hysterical; Margaret was afraid the women outside the door would hear her and intervene before the trap was fully locked.

'Sit down and remember who you speak to. I will do this and so will you and so will your husband.' Jacquetta was about to speak, to shout out her horror again, but Margaret had thought too hard about this to let her twist away now.

'If you do not agree to my plan, if you do not persuade your husband to agree, I will have you tried as a witch and destroy you both. Witchcraft would be such an easy charge: when a waiting woman is heard to talk too much of spells and charms, it is easy for a barren queen to claim she is cursed. You have already laid the foundation stones.'

Jacquetta was crying now but Margaret could not show her any mercy.

'And the King will not know because we will keep this plan secret, completely secret. If we do not, then we will all pay; if we do, you will be handsomely rewarded.'

She could have shown some mercy and left it there but it was far more satisfying to twist the knife. 'It is not an act of treason but an act of great loyalty, Jacquetta; you should be proud to be chosen.'

The hatred in Jacquetta's eyes was murderous; she knew how well she was caught but she still struggled.

'If there is a witch here it is you. Even if you can control me, you can't believe the King will fall for this. Henry is many things but he is not a fool; everyone knows he doesn't share your bed, so how will you persuade him that the child is his? What will you claim: some divinely ordained miracle, another virgin birth?'

Margaret shrugged: she could permit a show of anger now but it would be Jacquetta's last.

'And why not? You forget: it is Henry we have to trick. Who is more likely to believe in a miracle than my so very pious husband? He prays often enough for such a thing with little thought of how it may be resolved; well we shall give him the divine intervention he craves.'

'Dear God, you are quite mad.' But the fight had gone from her. 'Richard will never agree to it, no matter what you say.'

'He will because you will make him, not I.'

Margaret leant forward to deliver the blow she knew would break any resistance that was left.

'He loves you, Jacquetta; he loves you and your family but he loves his position more. He saw what happened to Gloucester: he will do anything to keep you safe from the spectre of banishment or burning and himself safe from the disgrace of it. He will do it Jacquetta, maybe he will even do it willingly.'

The beaten woman was weeping steadily now and went quietly when Margaret called Katherine back to tend her, fussing at the way her poor companion had suddenly fallen ill. Jacquetta would play her part, of that Margaret was certain: she knew the stakes they all played for and how much would be lost if York took the Crown. Jacquetta's family was too closely entwined with Lancaster to bring them any favour with York or to secure the marriages their growing brood would need; Margaret's plan may have been born out of desperation but she had chosen her target well and they both knew it.

***

I am alone.

She sat in a Court bustling with people and knew the truth of it.

I am alone.

If anyone of them knew what I plan to do, what I will make Jacquetta and Rivers party to, they would drive me from this throne and there would be no one to defend me.

I am alone but I am winning.

The thought brought a smile to her lips and everyone watching her wondered what brought such a sparkle to her eyes and a softening to her face the Court rarely saw these days.

I am winning because they hate me less than they despise York for his ambitions and pretensions.

Her smile deepened as she remembered the reluctance with which York had been forced to swear his allegiance to Henry just days before when the support he presumed would follow his second attack on Somerset had simply melted away. It was a smile so full of warmth, the courtiers began to look around them for the object of her delight.

She was no fool; she could sense the power in the country shifting. There were risings from Derbyshire to Devon, local grievances in the main but with the potential to become far more dangerous. It was already becoming treacherously unstable in the North where the Nevilles and the Percys had rekindled past hatreds and looked set to plunge the whole region into chaos. And she knew well enough how close York was to his nephew Richard Neville, Earl of Warwick, knew that he would watch the North like a hawk ready to swoop and make any rebellion his.

But, for now, she was winning and York was gone from Court and, if the real danger was not in the plan but in the execution, she was ready to face that. So she smiled and her women whispered and she hugged her secret close.

***

There was a chill on the room so thick it was as if the walls had dissolved and let the snow creep in. Creep in and settle so the tapestries, the furniture, everything was sculpted out of ice and coldest of all was the man in front of her.

'Say something.' This silence after so many words had run on so long. Jacquetta wondered if she had robbed him of speech, had caused a palsy to settle on his tongue.

'Please, say something.' She would have moved to sit by him but something in his stillness frightened her.

'You stupid bitch; you stupid, stupid bitch.' Now she would have prayed for a palsy to silence the bitter words she had unleashed.

'Did you never once think how foolish your stories were? How dangerous?'

His eyes were granite chips; she could not see her husband there.

'All your nonsense about charms and potions and river goddesses.'

'It is not nonsense.' Jacquetta saw the fury rising in his face but could not stop. 'It is not. The women in my family have the sight: we can weave spells, make things happen, it is our birth right.' She shook her head, 'call me what you want but it is true.'

The glass had shattered against the wall before she saw it leave his hand. The hand that was now twisting her arm behind her back so she could not pull away from his rage.

'The sight? You expect me to believe that? Where was your sight this time Madame? Why didn't you see the trap that was waiting for you? For a woman with the sight you have led us pretty blindly into danger.' She shook her head, 'that woman is stronger than me. She blocked me, I could not see —'

'By Christ, you never stop!'

He pushed her away hard so she stumbled against the table, the sudden pain taking her breath away.

'You never stop. Are you telling me now that the Queen is a witch, a better witch than you?'

And then the fight left him as quickly as it had come. His body sagged; she could have sworn there were tears in his eyes.

'You will get us killed, you know that don't you?'

'You can save us.' She put out a hand but he pushed it away.

'This time perhaps but at what cost? If she doesn't fall with child, if we are caught, what then?' He raised a hand to wipe away her words. 'No more, I will do what you ask, what choice is there? And then we will be the same as every other married pair.'

She frowned, 'what do you mean?'

He smiled at her then and she saw the man she had loved for so long caught somewhere still in its warmth.

'I loved you, Jacquetta. How many men can say that about their wives?' The smile faded. 'All these marriages for money and power and land but we had something different didn't we?'

She was crying now but he did not move towards her as once he would have done at any sign of her distress, he simply shook his head.

'I loved you.'

She never heard him say those words again.

***

'He is here.'

Three simple words but what they cost her. Jacquetta's face was cast from cold marble but her eyes were murderous black wells that promised nothing but poison.

Margaret knew how much Jacquetta loved Rivers, how enthralled she was by him. Her first husband had been an old man when she married him and Rivers had introduced her to all manner of delights in the bedchamber; once she had needed little encouragement to prattle about his prowess, now Margaret knew Jacquetta replayed every silly confidence and hated her Queen even more for what she had shared, for what she was about to share. It was of no consequence.

'Then let him in.'

There would be no respite, no last minute reprieve. Jacquetta stepped aside, she had no choice and she knew it. It was a freezing November night and the corridor outside the bedchamber was deserted but that could not last and this was no time for delicacy. Rivers came in and the door closed firmly on his wife.

'Thank you.'

It was clumsy and awkward but what else could she say? He had neither spoken nor looked at her and she suddenly felt her innocence and her ignorance like leaden weights. In all the planning Margaret had not given any thought to this: her only concern had been to force Jacquetta to deliver her demands, she had not wasted a moment's care on what must happen next.

Stupidly, as though her limbs had sunk into the floor, she moved towards the raised bed and, as he remained in silence, lay down, her back rigid, her eyes firmly on the gilded canopy above.

'Dear God, you have the manner of a corpse. I had thought I would at least get some pleasure from the night, some French trickery if nothing else.' The contempt in his voice was so thick it polluted the air.

'I did not ask you here for pleasure's sake.'

She did not move; she would not give him the satisfaction of seeing her shock at his words.

'Well, that is clear enough. Will you instruct me exactly how you want this done given how carefully you have arranged everything else? Perhaps I should bring my wife back in, at least she would warm things up a little.'

'How dare you!'

She was off the bed, flying at him with all the rage against Henry she had contained for far too long. 'How dare you speak to me like that, I am your Queen!'

She would have raked her nails across his face but he raised a warning hand and stayed her.

'My Queen? You are a whore who demands what does not belong to you and cuckolds her husband. Don't give yourself any more airs than that.'

'How can I cuckold a husband who has never laid a finger on me? How can I be a whore if I have never so much as kissed a man?' The words were out of her mouth before she had time to think.

'What do you mean?'

The contempt was gone, replaced with pure astonishment. 'What do you mean: not even kissed?' He stared at her, 'are you telling me that you are a virgin? How can that be? Henry has been your husband for years and if not him then...'

'Then Suffolk or Somerset or the kitchen boy? Or perhaps it's worse, perhaps it's York I sleep with?' Rivers had the grace to redden at that but Margaret was too sick of pretending to stop.

'That's what they say, isn't it, my enemies? That I try to tame my enemies by opening my legs? Dear God, can you really be so foolish? If I had a host of men pushing aside my skirts, why would I need to drag you to my bed to get a child?'

And then, to both their surprise, she burst into tears.

'Sit down.' Rivers took her hand as though she was a child and sat her down gently on the edge of the thickly covered bed. 'I did not know; I did not know any of this.'

'Did Jacquetta tell you nothing?'

Margaret rubbed at her wet cheeks with a corner of her nightgown, suddenly so weary all she wanted was sleep. Although she did not know it, it was a gesture of such simple innocence, all his anger vanished.

'Surely she must have given you some reason for this madness, at least explained how things stood with Henry?'

He sat down next to her, still keeping a distance between them but far less wary now.

'In truth we have done nothing but fight since she told me what you demanded.' He stared down at his hands. 'At first I refused to take her seriously and then, when I realised what her foolishness had led us all to, well I was angrier than she or I are used to.'

He turned to look at Margaret properly; she saw the sudden kindness in his eyes and could have wept again. 'She is not a bad woman, my wife, you need to believe that. She is foolish and too full of stories but she is not a bad woman.'

'I know, I know and I am sorry.' She tried to smile back at him, 'I know but I was desperate and she was easy to frighten, that is the real truth of it. I need a son; I have to have a son. If I don't then York will take the throne and it is not his to take. And Henry, my husband, I have tried but he can't —' But the tears were again too swift for her.

'Hush.'

It was the sweetest little word. She had been so starved of love; she had not known how starved until he said that simple little word. It fell like a caress on her skin.

'Hush, Margaret. Look at me. I am here and I will help you.'

And then he laughed and it was as though the sound rippled like a wave through her body. 'You are beautiful, Margaret, so very beautiful and you barely seem to know it.'

He raised her fingers to his lips and smiled and suddenly she knew everything would be well. 'Come here.' There was nothing more needed to be said.

He was kind and gentle that night and kind and gentle on every night as the strange courtship progressed, increasingly gentle so that she knew the act had become one of love as much as it had been forced out of loyalty.

For Margaret, the hours spent in the bedchamber became briefly more real than the hours spent anywhere else. There were times, when she lay in his arms or shivered under his touch, when she pretended that he was wedded to her not Jacquetta. She did not voice it, she saw shadows in his eyes and knew he would be haunted someday by what they did, but she felt it and it was enough. They all played their parts and, if she and Jacquetta were never quite so much in each other's company any more, no one remarked on it: fortunes were too easily won and lost at Court for anyone to enquire too closely into another's fall from favour.

They all played their parts so well there was never a breath of rumour and, if the Court did not notice, how would Henry? The more Margaret watched her husband continue a life spent deeper in conversation with his God than her, the less she concerned herself with how his virgin wife's pregnancy might appear to him and the more she began to believe he might declare it a miracle himself. He had to: their lives depended on it.

London and the South:
1453

My mother, my grandmother: they were both women of action, quick to make decisions, swift to carry out their plans. I saw how they acted and admired and copied them. Yet what I never fully understood was that they were also women without imagination: they could only ever see the outcome they intended, other possibilities were lost to them; unfortunately that trait became mine to.

Still so flat; how could she still be so flat when she was filled with such a secret?

Turning her back to the room as if it was the weather that captivated her, she ran her fingers over the wide belt of her gown. Nothing: her waist was as slim as ever, the lines of her gown were undisturbed. Biting down on the sudden burst of laughter she could feel bubbling to her lips, she returned to her chair and settled herself in its cushions.

'I think we shall make a journey.'

Her waiting women, too long confined in doors by weather that had been, until lately, more redolent of December than late March, looked up from their embroidery and smiled encouragingly; the Queen's words were as welcome as they were unexpected. Only Jacquetta kept her glance downcast as Margaret continued.

'The sky is finally clear and I am sure the days are warming.' She smiled back at her little throng. 'Spring is here and I long to be outside. This has been a hard winter in too many ways.'

That much, at least, was no pretence: Isabelle had died late in the previous year and Margaret, already so unsettled by the silent conspiracy playing out around her, had had little heart for the Christmas festivities. It had been a long time since she had seen her mother but the loss had hit her hard.

'Where shall we go, Madame; shall we give orders to have Kenilworth made ready?'

Osanna's assumption was a reasonable one: everyone knew that Kenilworth, after Greenwich, was the Queen's favourite residence and, had this been a simple move from palace to palace, the most likely destination. But Margaret was planning a far more public show. 'Not Kenilworth, no. I have a fancy to go to Walsingham. I would make a pilgrimage and soon; as soon as April arrives we will journey there and make an offering. It would do me good.'

Her women looked at her in surprise and, in doing so, missed Jacquetta visibly pale, missed her sharp intake of breath. A pilgrimage for one who had so recently lost her mother was understandable but the destination was not one so easily explained by a sudden need for mourning and not one anyone expected Margaret to suggest. Every woman in the country knew what Walsingham meant: the shrine to our Lady built by Richeldis de Faverches, where the vial of the Virgin's milk was kept, where women in need of a child went to dip their hand in the well and leave their gifts before the statue of the Mother and Child. Not merely one holy house, in fact, but a whole series of shrines to motherhood along the road the pilgrims called "The Milky Way".

In all the long barren years of her marriage, Margaret had never shown a moment's interest in such a journey: her women looked at her now with such pity in their eyes, she knew the first part of her plan was complete. They thought she was desperate; none of them could possibly guess the truth. None except Jacquetta.

She clapped her hands. 'We shall do it! Quickly now, go and start to prepare!'

Her women had already begun scuttling to their feet, the prospect of a change of scene already making them giggle and cluck. 'We will be gone from Court for quite a while and I need clothes that will show my piety as much as my position, you need to choose them with care.'

Jacquetta had risen to leave with the others but Margaret was too quick, 'Jacquetta, stay a moment and help me plan my offering.' The two women faced each other in silence as the room emptied; it was left to Margaret to speak first. 'I am with child. Our plan has worked.'

It was clear from Jacquetta's face she neither needed nor wanted the words

'Then I must congratulate you.' Her tone was stiff; her body held rigid. 'But I am a little surprised that you would choose to travel: your pregnancy cannot be long advanced; you would surely be better resting.' She would not bend, Margaret could almost admire her. 'And why Walsingham? You know that everyone will see it as a sign of your desperation for a child. You have never acknowledged such a need before; you have never paid any mind to pilgrimages or offerings or any of it. Why remind the people so openly of your failure when you no longer need to?'

'Because the people think of me as exactly that: a failure.' Margaret smiled at a word that had once so frightened her. 'I have never publicly acknowledged their fears that there will never be an heir, it's true, but that doesn't make them any less real or me any less aware of them. Well now I need to plant a new seed.'

As she spoke, Margaret had clasped her hands protectively around her stomach; Jacquetta shuddered, she could not help herself.

'Think about it Jacquetta, the people no longer speak of me and a baby in the same breath; I want to remind them that I am still young, that it is still possible. And I can only risk doing that now, when the hope is about to be met.'

'You want to ready them for a lie.'

Jacquetta made no effort now to speak with any of the deference due to a queen but her words carried too little importance for Margaret to react.

'You would have them see how pious you are so not a breath of rumour reaches this child. You would have us all believing in miracles.'

'And where is the fault in that?' Margaret smiled with all the confidence of a plan carried out. 'This has been a long time coming, Jacquetta, and I am no fool: I know I am not well-liked, I know that the people look at York and his growing brood and begin to see a safer bet than me and my empty cradle.'

Her voice suddenly hardened enough for Jacquetta to step back.

'Do I really need to explain it to you of all people? Everyone must believe that this babe is the heir who will secure Henry's throne, the heir who will push York and all the other lords who snap around us back into the shadows. Of course no rumour must touch my child but there will be plenty who will kindle them. I have to stop any suspicion before it starts and what better way to do it than a pilgrimage? When they see their Queen act the humble penitent, well who would doubt my virtue then?'

'And your husband? Will a pretty ride to Walsingham fool him too? You can play the people any way you choose but Henry? He is surely not such a simpleton as that?'

That was too far and Jacquetta knew it. There was no apology but she subsided. It was a simple truth: Margaret was pregnant; she was defeated.

And so the party went to Walsingham in the first sunshine of what became a very gentle April. They rode along paths made silken by light summer showers, through trees newly come into blossom, into a world that smiled its way into spring freshness. Margaret could not have asked for a sweeter backdrop and she knew it. She played her part all along the way with the greatest care: the penitent Queen, still young and beautiful but with a pleasing humility and a kindly smile. She made such a show of devotion along the route and at the Holy House itself, nobody could find fault with her.

Her fellow pilgrims were as simple a group as she had expected and as delighted to have a queen in their midst as she knew they would be. There were no dissenting voices anywhere and she played her audience well: bestowing alms with a generous hand and making a very public offering of a golden pax so heavy with jewels the angel it depicted seemed to blaze with fire. There were no protests here at her extravagances, many, to her delight, called out blessings, hoping that a child would be her due reward. She was careful, she gave her women no cause to suspect: there was little visible sign yet of her condition except tiredness and that was easy to disguise as fatigue from the journey.

And I want this.

The thought was always in her mind and always a surprise.

I want this, this child. Not just for England or for Henry but for me.

So, when the little group returned to the normal proximities of everyday life and the secret became one far less easily contained, she began to long to tell the truth of it, it became torture to hide it. As her bodices began to strain and her face began to develop a new plumpness, her women began to make amused comment about the skills of the pastry cooks. As May advanced and the weather warmed so that she could no longer take refuge in heavy cloaks, the whispering began to start. When she could no longer use the excuse of poor weather to disguise her refusal to ride, the whispering reached fever-pitch. She heard it all and longed to share her joy, because it was joy now, but one puzzle remained unsolved: how to deal with Henry?

The rumours had not reached him, she was sure of it: Henry paid no heed to the whisperings of the Court and there was no one who would have dared voice them to him direct. He still visited her at night but that meant nothing: he had never really looked at her, had never taken note of anything beyond the barest details and what would he know of the signs of pregnancy? More than that, Margaret knew he would not look for such a thing: for all her husband might be far distanced from the world around him, he was not a simpleton. They had done nothing that could lead to a child: she knew it and Henry knew it, no matter how she would pretend otherwise to the world. And so she could not share her joy because she had no plan. All she knew was that she could not tell the news, as might any normal wife, in private; the risk that he would refuse to accept it was far too great and that would be a secret not even she could keep. Neither a plan then nor a choice: Henry had to receive the news in public. His sense of Kingship would not, she prayed, fail her there.

'How long has he been gone?' The dark panelled room felt too close, as confined as a cage and Margaret could settle to nothing. 'How long and no word? Surely we should have had some word by now?'

'Madame, you must calm yourself, this agitation cannot be good for the child. You are fretting without reason. How could you doubt how happy the King will be, how happy the whole Court will be? We have all prayed for this for so long; today is a day for celebration not tears.'

Barbelina's voice betrayed her confusion at her mistress's restless state, at the fits of weeping and temper they had all been subjected to but Margaret could do nothing to reassure them.

'Why didn't you go to the King yourself?'

There was a coldness in Katherine's voice that Margaret would have challenged had she been more in control of herself. She knew how close Jacquetta and Katherine had grown lately and it unnerved her. Jacquetta had retired from Court, claiming exhaustion from her own advancing pregnancy; Margaret wished she could banish thoughts of her as easily.

'There is no danger to the child now surely and the King must long for it as much as you and yet you act as though the news is terrible. Why did you send his squire rather than go yourself?'

'Because that is how the news of an heir is delivered to a king.'

Sometimes Osanna's self-importance was a blessing; in her eagerness to show how well-versed in court-etiquette she was, she had turned Katherine's prying into an everyday argument.

'The Queen has to send Richard Tunstall if the news is to be delivered to the King in public, which is also the right place for him to hear it; she couldn't do it herself, I thought you would know that.'

'You are such a prig...' but the retort was lost to the sound of heavy knocking.

They have come for me. I will be charged with adultery. Dear God, they will execute me.

She thought she had spoken the words aloud but, from the confusion on Tunstall's face as he repeated his message, it was clear she had said nothing, had not even acknowledged him.

'His Majesty sends his kindest wishes, Madame, and has retired with his Confessor. He will attend you when he has finished at prayer.'

'That is all?'

It was all Margaret could do to stop herself clutching at him. 'You were gone some time, quite some time. Too long I think; why were you so long?'

Her voice was rising; they could all hear the hysteria in it.

'Madame, you must sit, listen to him properly. You have made yourself unwell.' Katherine pushed her into a chair, giving Tunstall time to collect himself.

'I am sorry, Madame but It was some time before...before he could make out the true meaning of my words.'

The squire shuffled a little, his face reddening as he tried to find some way to explain Henry's reaction without sounding disloyal to his King.

'It was as if he did not understand what was meant by a child or how such things come about. His Confessor had to remind him that this is how things are, between a husband and wife, I mean.' Tunstall was scarlet with embarrassment now; he looked at Margaret as though hoping she would let him go but she was struggling to concentrate on his words.

They think Henry is an innocent not a cuckold.

She could have laughed: it was even better than she could have hoped.

He does not react and no one expects him to; his strangeness seals my success.

She must have laughed then without realising; Tunstall stared at her and then continued, clearly not knowing what else to do.

'The King received the news first with confusion and then became very quiet. My Lord Somerset explained to everyone that the King was under great strain, that he is too much preoccupied with how our armies fare in Gascony to be able to switch his mind so suddenly to such joyous news. That it can, in truth, be difficult sometimes to rouse his Majesty to attend matters that are unexpected. And so that is why the news took a while in the telling.'

He tailed off, waiting for some sign from Margaret who was grinning at him so foolishly, he was convinced she had become ill. It was a relief when she finally spoke.

'My Lord Somerset is always very solicitous of the King's comfort, as I think you also have been.' Tunstall reddened again but this time it was from the pleasure at flattery rather than the fear of giving offence. Now he was all eagerness to please so she continued, quite calmly now the danger had so clearly passed.

'Just tell me one thing: did the King voice his thanks for the news that he will have an heir? Did he voice his thanks before the Court?' This was easier and Tunstall smiled delightedly, at last the bearer of better tidings. 'Oh yes, Madame. He gave thanks to God and asked that everyone say prayers for you and your child. Then he said he would retire to pray on the matter and withdrew. It was joyfully received by the whole Court; it is a very great day, Madame, a very great day.'

The relief of it made her giddy. She dismissed Tunstall with the promise of a generous reward for his services and made ready to receive the stream of well-wishers who were already gathering outside her chambers. The news that Rivers had left that morning, claiming a need to be nearer his wife as her time approached, was as well-received as any of the protestations of joy she listened to that day.

I came so close to disaster and yet all is well because my husband is a child himself; that is the miracle I hoped for.

Henry's reaction might have looked muted, questionable in any other husband; his words might not have stood close scrutiny if spoken by any other king receiving word that he finally had hope of an heir after such barren years, but this was Henry not some lusty, worldly man.

He did not come to her that night, despite his promise: he withdrew and he prayed as he said he would. No one who knew him would have expected anything else and Margaret was careful to make no show of any surprise or disquiet. He did not come to her for a week; he remained withdrawn from public view, seeing no one but his Confessor and his priests. And still no one thought it odd because it was Henry: they saw only a deeply pious man who saw no need to visit the bed of an already pregnant wife when he could spend his time praying for her safe delivery. He was praised for his devoutness by all, Margaret included. She would have gladly had him withdraw to his chapel until after the child was born and have no sight of her until she presented him with a son. Henry was not a fool, she knew that no matter how much she might want to believe differently, She could not trust that he would remain so easily played if he was to see her close, see the reality of the child she was carrying so visibly now. The web was too fragile to bear too much weight: one word of doubt from him and all would unravel even faster than she had spun it.

***

He had finally come to her, dismissing their attendants with a wave of his hand, refusing any refreshment with a curt nod. He had ignored her offer of a seat and, after that first appraising stare across her body, had kept his gaze pointedly fixed on her face.

'It is true then. You will have a child.'

Not questions but statements, delivered in a flat voice by an old man, a shell of a man with no more substance than a shade.

Dear God, I had not guessed how badly things ran with him.

'Our men are dying in Gascony, did you know?'

Margaret nodded, not wanting to speak, not sure how to deal with this husband suddenly hard about the face and so lost about the eyes.

'They are dying. We have not had any news from Castillon except that the French hold the town under siege. We don't know if Talbot's army will save them. But they are dying, I know it and yet here we have a miracle to ease our battered hearts. God truly does move in mysterious ways does he not?'

She gasped with the shock of hearing him speak so bluntly and with the sudden fear that perhaps controlling him would not prove quite so easy.

'Henry, I...'

But he waved a hand to stop her mouth and the hurt in his eyes was dreadful to look at.

'Please don't find excuses or invent lies Margaret; I don't want them and neither do you. I am to blame and my confessors are to blame and every advisor who forced a marriage onto me that I did not want is to blame but not you.'

He smiled then, a smile of such desperate sadness she would have withstood every torture not to see it.

'How could I blame you? You see what is needed and you take it. I envy you sometimes, Margaret, for your strength and your passion; I envy you but then I know it will never bring you what you want.'

'I don't understand.'

'And that is your tragedy as this marriage, this Kingship is mine.'

He laid a hand on her shoulder, a rare gesture from him but it had more in it of the benevolent priest than the caring husband and this time it was Margaret who flinched at the touch.

'They will never let you have the power you want. You will have your child, a son I do not doubt, but he won't be safe and neither will you. I have my God, Margaret, and I will turn to him when the demands around me become too great. I will find solace. You will have nothing.'

It was not a curse, it was not a threat; he said the words as though they were a simple truth and then he left her, bruised and shaking as though from a blow.

I have not fooled him then but I have surely destroyed some part of him.

Throughout the months of plotting and waiting, she had thought only of how to bend him to the way she had cast events; she had thought only of his strangeness and how she could use it, she had given not a moment's pause to his goodness. All along she had feared him denouncing her as an adulteress but he had taken the betrayal totally upon himself, there was never a trace of vengeance in him.

I have hurt him so much without ever knowing I could do such a thing; he is broken and at my hands.

It was a thought that would come back to haunt her through the long months ahead.

Windsor & Westminster: 1453

Sometimes, no matter how foolish I find such talk, I find myself falling prey to the nonsense so many speak of omens and premonitions, to the idea that somehow we know when a momentous event is about to happen; that a shiver, a coldness, a sign passes across the day that brings a calamity with it. And then I look at the days of my life which brought true horrors with them and I know there was no warning: they were days like any other when they began and days like no other when they ended. The 10th of August 1453 was such a day and no day after it ever felt certain again.

'My Lady, you need to come with me. Quickly Madame, please.'

The interruption was so unexpected, Margaret struggled to react to the obvious urgency in Somerset's voice. The perfume from the flowers in the rose bower hung heavy in the warm afternoon sunshine and more than one of the seated women had fallen gently asleep over her forgotten book. The Court had moved to Windsor in late July, the days were quiet and Margaret was glad of it: the baby was increasingly lively and she was tired, content to dream and await the birth. She was in no mood for the outside world to be pulled into their idyll.

'What can be so bad that it would spoil such a pretty day?'

She patted the grassy mound next to her invitingly and gestured to the wafers piled on a platter on the cloth but he barely glanced at anything.

'Madame, you must come, I insist. It is the King.'

His voice was shaking; she had not noticed it before and his face was the colour of milk on the turn. Somerset was clearly in no mood to be argued with and his unexpected terseness unnerved her.

'You will need to help me, I am not so light on my feet as I was.'

She tried to sound playful but there was no answering gallantry just a rough hand pulling her up. Margaret felt the baby kick against the sudden movement and snatched her hand from his grip.

'Somerset, stop, you're frightening me. What has happened, what is wrong with the King?'

He had turned and begun to stride away.

'Tell me what is happening or I will stay here. I mean it; I will not come unless you answer me.'

He turned and then suddenly sagged, holding a wall for support; that was enough to make Margaret run towards him then as quick as her ungainly body would let her. When she looked into his face, she saw she was not the only one who was afraid.

'I don't know what is wrong with him, I don't know.' He wiped a hand across his tired face. 'We had bad news from France, the worst news: Talbot is dead, thousands of his men killed with him and Gascony is lost. Lost after 300 years in our keeping.'

'Dear God, not Talbot, he was the bravest of our commanders.'

He was and his loss, Gascony's loss was not something Margaret wanted to hear no matter her enemies might still call her French. 'Has the King taken the news badly? Is that what it is?'

'I don't know how he has taken it, none of us do. He received it in silence and withdrew to pray, as he does when receives any ill-tidings and then, when he returned from chapel, he said he would go to his chamber, that he was weary and needed to sleep.'

Somerset stopped, clearly casting for words. 'It is as though the news has caught him a physical blow,' he shook his head. 'You must see him and judge for yourself, My Lady, for I can make no sense of it.'

But, when Margaret saw him, neither could she.

'Henry, husband, talk to me, how can I help you?'

There was no answer; he was hunched in a chair like a man twice his years, grey in the face and seemingly sightless although his eyes were open.

'He has not spoken, your Majesty, not a word since he said how weary he was and asked to retire to his bedchamber.' The physician would not look at her, 'we have tried to get some response from him but it as if he does not hear us.'

It is his old habit of blankness but far worse, like a waking sleep has wrapped itself around him.

'If it is sleep he needs, then allow him to sleep. I will wake him myself in a few hours and you will see your King restored to health.' She forced a confidence she did not feel into her voice and watched as Henry was led meekly away by his gentleman. Sleep came, it came easily to him but it was too heavy. She could not wake him. For a day and a night she could not wake him and when she did, that was when the nightmare began.

***

The chamber stank. From the bowl of blood that sat uncovered from his most recent bleeding; from the mixtures of garlic and lily root and henbane they had smeared him with; from the liquorice and wormwood concoctions they had boiled up as purges. Even the sweet herbs, the rosemary and lavender scattered around the room, had become cloying and sickly in the airless room.

'His mind has gone. His mind has gone, look at him.'

111

Osanna reached for Margaret's hand but could find no words of comfort for the truth was all too evident. Henry's eyes open but sightless, his head too heavy for his neck, his drooling mouth, his limbs as useless as a newborn's. He knew no one, recognised nothing.

'Perhaps we should try to move him. If he was out of bed, perhaps he would rouse a little.'

Desperate to do something, Margaret motioned the servants forward. It was useless. They sat him in a chair but he slipped to the floor. He could not stand without a man on either side. And so silent, not even a whimper as he was moved, cleaned, covered in ointments, cleaned again; treated with such roughness in the end as they tried to shock him back to some semblance of life.

'What do we do?'

Margaret had asked the gathered physicians the same question for three days running and still they had no answer.

'There must be something beyond bleeding; there must be some other potion you can try?'

But they only shook their heads and moved away from him, terrified that they would have the death of the King laid at their door as their bleeding and pricking and burning came to nothing.

'Try to stand him up again.'

She turned to Tunstall but he shrank away. 'What is wrong with you? I told you to help him stand again.'

'I can't, I'm sorry but I can't.' She could see the fear, the repulsion in his face. 'It is like a bewitchment, I can't touch him.'

'Dear God, are you really so ignorant you would blame this on witches? Your King is ill, he needs your help!'

But her words were worthless when weighed against Henry's broken state; Tunstall shook his head and moved further from the bed, the other squires copying him.

'Leave him alone; your anger will only make things worse.'

It was Somerset at her side, a hand on her elbow to draw her into the corner of the room.

'What do you expect them to think? He looks like a man enchanted out of the world.' His grip on her arm was tight but she was too stunned to shake him off. 'And isn't it better that they say that? What is the alternative, that he is mad like his grandfather?'

'Do not dare to say that!'

She saw the heads turn and lowered her voice.

'Henry is nothing like Charles VI; he is ill, that is all. We just have to find the cause. How can this be anything like his grandfather's delusions: Henry is in some kind of waking sleep, Charles thought he was made of glass, they are not the same!'

'Then you had better pray he doesn't wake up and start being able to see through his own hand or York will have your child tainted with the same curse and the throne away from Lancaster far faster than you can field an army.'

The fight went out of her: Somerset felt her sag against him and led her quickly to a seat.

'What do we do?'

'I don't know; none of us do.'

He stared at the figure lying on the bed and shuddered. 'It is like looking at a living corpse. Has he ever been like this before?'

Margaret's hands were drawn into fists in the folds of her skirt.

'Not like this. He withdraws from the world when things challenge him, you know he does, but not like this. You have to help me: we have to plan what we will do if he doesn't recover.'

Somerset could hear the fear in her voice, it matched his own but he had no comfort to offer her.

'If he doesn't recover? If he stays like this, like a simpleton? God help us then Madame, we will be finished, all of us.'

The rage of tears that followed his words shocked him: he had never seen her cry, never seen her lose control, even her temper was cold, not this heat of fury that made little sense.

'How could this happen now? Finally I make us secure and he does this? I get the child, I make the Crown safe and he collapses, it is too cruel! York cannot know, no one must know, we have to keep the Court away. I have not done all this to lose now, not now.'

Suddenly she clutched at his arm, her hand scrabbling at the ribbons on his sleeve.

'We have to keep him hidden until they find a cure. They will find a cure, surely? My child cannot come into this!'

He wanted to shake her off, her eyes were too wild, but she would not stop.

'Nothing will harm my child, nothing will take the throne from him, I swear it.'

She suddenly let him go and wrapped her arms around her stomach as though to hold the baby safe; he took the moment to step back a little, desperate to get out of the room and the nightmare it contained but she hadn't finished with him.

'They will make me go away soon, I will have to go into seclusion until the child is born; this,' she gestured at the bed 'this will be your secret to keep, Somerset. If there is to be any pretence of normality, then you have to shape it and make it real. I will not deliver my child to see its future destroyed, do you understand me?'

He was suddenly too afraid of her to do anything but agree.

***

Margaret was exhausted: the child inside her was never still and she barely slept. Every day she dragged herself to Henry's chamber, praying that she would find the nightmare ended and her husband awake but every day was the same: they could not rouse him. She did not know what to do or where to turn.

'You cannot delay any longer, Madame, it is becoming unseemly.'

Alice's mouth was pursed in unspoken censure. 'The child is due in a matter of weeks now, there will be a scandal if you don't go immediately to Westminster; there is already more talk than is good.'

Because none of us can risk any closer attention turning on our little Court, on the King.

The words were unsaid but her meaning was as clear as glass.

'I know, Alice, I know. What can I do? I am afraid to leave the King. Who will protect him if I am not here?'

Alice's face softened a little but she could not allow any more indulgence.

'You hardly protect him by staying, My Lady. There is nothing you can do. The Lying-in Chamber is ready and you need to take your place in it.'

She placed a gentle hand on Margaret's arm and spoke with the confidence of old friendship, 'Margaret, you have to think about the child. Henry is safest here, the household is small and Somerset will keep him hidden, will keep his condition hidden. Think for a moment: no one will notice that he is absent, the Court will be quiet; it will be holding its breath and hoping for a son, there will be no interest in the father.'

Margaret shook her head. 'You are right, I know you are but the thought of being closeted inside, with no word from the world frightens me. I can do nothing in there to help him.'

'You can have a son; that will help him. Perhaps that will bring him back to us.' She stopped; there was little comfort to be had in empty words.

Still Margaret resisted her. 'And what if I have a girl? Or a son who dies? How fast will the Court flock to York then?'

Alice shrugged, 'faster than you can control but that does not change anything today. You must go to Westminster and trust to God that you give birth to a living boy. There is nothing else that you can do but pray.'

***

I will go mad with fear. I will go mad.

'What should we do? Nothing soothes her; she will lose the child if she carries on like this.'

Katherine and Alice watched as Margaret paced backwards and forwards through the sweet herbs scattered on the floor of the birthing chamber like a tigress trapped in a cage.

Katherine continued, tears welling in her eyes. 'I feel so helpless. What else can I do to make her comfortable?'

She gestured at the room with its walls hung with deep blue arras patterned in gold fleur-de-lys and the great bed covered in scarlet velvets and satins and pillows thick with down.

'She doesn't see any of it. She complains the herbs smell foul, she won't drink the tisanes we brew, she refuses to even look at the Virgin's girdle we thought would bring her such comfort. What will calm her?'

Alice put an arm round the younger woman's shoulders, 'there is nothing you can do; none of this is your fault. She is whipped into a mass of nerves because of everything outside the room not because of anything in it.'

'Have you had any word from Somerset?' Katherine was not permitted to leave the birthing chamber but she knew Alice had slipped out.

'There is no change.'

Alice lowered her voice, not sure how much attention Margaret was paying. 'I had a note which could say little but I think word is starting to spread. York is suspicious at Henry's absence and more suspicious at Somerset's. I don't know how long the secret can hold...'

A scream from Margaret brought them to their feet and Alice to her mistress' side.

'Katherine, fetch the midwives, quickly. Madame, Madame, it is starting. You have to think about the baby now, nothing else.'

For hours there was no talk of anything else, no thought of anything else: everyone knew there could only be one outcome that would let Margaret leave the room with any hope of a future. When the child was finally born, it was not just the mother who cried genuine tears of joy.

'He is perfect! Look at him, he is perfect!'

It was so long since her women had seen Margaret look so young, so carefree.

'He is beautiful, quite beautiful.' Alice looked down at the pinkly plump child cradled against Margaret's dark hair and grinned. 'He is so strong! You have a soldier in your arms!'

'And now everything will be well, you will see; you have given us all back our hope.'

Osanna's words were heartfelt and no one, least of all Margaret, still lost in wonder at the sight of her son, could bear that day to deny them.

***

The casement was flung so wide open, Margaret was in danger of falling out but she did not care: to feel the sun on her face, to be able to smell fresh air after the stifling confines of the birthing chamber was intoxicating.

'I swear I had forgotten the sight of daylight!'

Archbishop Waynflete, who had just carried out the churching ceremony that had finally released Margaret from her confinement, attempted a frown but with little success.

'And you have forgotten how to behave in Chapel; you smiled so much I fear you did not take the ceremony seriously.'

'Can you blame me? Eight weeks, eight weeks of closed rooms and no conversation beyond colic and wet-nursing.'

She laughed at his sudden flush, 'I swear even your sermon was music to my ears after such an imprisonment!'

'I must congratulate you, Madame: your confinement seems to have left you more full of life than ever. Or perhaps it is the birth of a son that makes you so merry; on that too, of course, I also congratulate you.'

She whirled round to see York framed in the doorway with Somerset behind him and Alice in his wake, her pretty face a mess of confusion and apology.

'Is that how you enter a queen's chamber, with no announcing and no manners?'

Margaret had hoped to sound in control but her words sounded waspish and his response simply became more mannered and more contemptuous.

'Your Majesty, I apologise, I thought you knew that I had requested an audience. Would you prefer me to withdraw until you feel more ready to receive me?'

She was about to retort when she saw Somerset shake his head behind York's back so instead she sat slowly down, suddenly aware of the rising tension in the room. And still she did not guess why he had come.

'You may stay, of course.'

She kept her tone neutral and waved both men to sit; Alice had already muttered something about refreshments and fled. 'Thank you for your kind words; I am sure that you will understand how great my happiness is: my husband now has the heir we have both so longed for.'

The heir: the words hung between them like a blade yet York inclined his head and looked at her almost tenderly; it was unnerving and he knew it. 'And the little Prince, he is well?'

What does he really want to hear? That my child is sickly?

'He is well, healthy and strong. He seems to grow daily.'

'It is strange.'

York smiled but gave her no chance to respond to his odd statement. 'It is strange, I think, that most mothers in the early days of a baby's life hope more than anything that the child will sleep and give everyone their rest and yet for you Madame, that must be the greatest fear of all.'

Somerset would not meet her eyes.

Dear God, he knows. He knows and he will destroy me with it.

'The King must have dreamt of such an event for all the years of your marriage and now he can do nothing but dream. You must agree, Madame, it is strange.'

'How does he know?'

Realising there was no point in arguing with York, she turned the full force of her anger on Somerset. 'I charged you with Henry's keeping; I told you that not a word must escape and yet he knows. Is this how you carry out your duties?'

'Madame' it was York who spoke again, Somerset had his head in his hands and still would not look at her. 'Madame please, do not blame poor Somerset, what could he have done? You know what Court is like: gossip flows around it faster than water from a leaky pail.'

He shrugged as though he was discussing a rather irritating patch of bad weather, 'I heard rumours that the King had been taken ill but the symptoms hinted at were so peculiar that I had no choice but to go to Windsor and see the truth for myself.'

'And you admitted him?' Somerset flinched but it was York again who had the answers.

'What could he do to stop me? I have a right to know if my King is, well, how shall I put this: incapable. And, my dear Queen, surely I have a right to offer you my help? That is all I am doing, I assure you: offering you my help.' He spread his hands as though in apology, 'unless, of course, this state I found Henry in is simply a temporary thing and he has already acknowledged his son.'

It was like being caught in a hunter's snare: she could twist and pull but she could not get away. York's threat was plain: if the King was insensible, if he had not, could not recognise his son, what value was there in the Prince?

She watched him quietly, calmly observing her, waiting for her reaction and she knew: York was drawing battle lines. He would not openly challenge Edwards's position, he was not such a fool as that, but his stirring of gossip could do far worse. Almost as soon as she had left the birthing chamber, she had heard the murmurings about her son and his miraculous appearance, murmurings that would become a damning flood with every passing year unless they were staunched. York's voice was in every repeated rumour. And she also knew, for she had forced the truth from Alice and Katherine who had been released into the Court sooner, that the gossip was always the same: it was always Somerset who was named as the father and every favour granted him was held up as proof. Somerset, who now sat cowering in front of her like a dog waiting for a blow; it could have been amusing had it not been so desperate.

'My husband knows his son.' She kept her voice and her gaze steady but it was hard-won.

'And you can prove that?' He was pure hatred now; it was in his eyes and in his voice but Margaret could not let herself fall before it. Her nails under her sleeves dug deep into the soft flesh of her palms but all he would see was a mask.

'Prove it? What do I need to prove My Lord? I am your Queen and you ask me to prove that your King knows his son; what would you accuse me of?'

She thought for a moment that he would speak some words of

121

condemnation but it was too soon and he knew it.

'My apologies for any offence I may have caused.' There was not a quiver in his voice: this was simply a breathing space before the next attack, as he bowed and left the room, they both knew it.

'You fool!' She whirled on Somerset, all her pent-up rage lashing out.

'How could you let him see Henry like that?' There was no response. 'Dear God, how can everyone really think that you are Edward's father? Do they think I would really go from one idiot's bed to another's?'

'By Christ, Madame, you have few enough friends; you should treat those of us who stay with you with more care.' She had stung him but it did nothing to soften her contempt.

'Perhaps I should cultivate better friends.'

He began to rise but she waved him back. 'You are safe enough: if I drive you away now, the gossips will put it down to guilt. No, you will stay close and hopefully learn more sense.'

She laughed suddenly and all the soft notes they had heard in the weeks after Edward's birth were gone. 'I will make you Edward's godfather; that will infuriate York. Nothing will stop him now so I might as well anger him, appeasing him is pointless.'

'Is that really wise?' Somerset frowned at her. 'You do know that he is in league with Richard Neville, Earl of Warwick, that they have joined forces in the North? While you were cloistered, the two were inseparable. Waynflete wants you to name York as godfather; he wants you to try to build alliances.'

'No.'

'But Madame, this is an unholy alliance. With the Nevilles behind him and the Percys quashed, York clearly feels invincible and he is bent on revenging old hurts. Hurts that he blames you for.' Somerset sighed. 'Rather than fight him, could you not try to charm him?'

'Charm him?'

That laugh again.

'I tried to charm him when I was fifteen and I was the fool that time. It would be easier to charm a mad dog. No, I will keep him at bay until Henry recovers.'

She shook her head as Somerset tried to speak. 'He will recover and we will beat York. You have to trust me and you have to do as I say.'

He had no choice but he had great cause to regret her hold on him. Within weeks York struck: dragging Somerset to the Tower, branding him a traitor, waving away Margaret's horrified protests as though she were of no more interest than a meddlesome child. It was cleverly done: an act of revenge couched in fine words as a pledge of York's devotion to Henry and his promise to protect the King from false friends. It was a declaration of war.

London: 1454-5

I have lived my entire adult life, perhaps my entire life, against the backdrop of war: the fear of it, the reality of it. It has been an ever-present shadow. It is hard to know why men resort to such a brutal solution when we know its truth: each conflict merely leads to another and each terrible loss will find itself revenged in yet more grief but, time and again, it is the path we choose.

The tension in the room, borne out of sleepless nights and too many plots, was as thick as the tapestries that lined the walls, tapestries that depicted virginal maidens taming unicorns whose placid faces had nothing in common with the frown that knotted Margaret's brow.

'Parliament will never agree to such demands, they will not countenance them. You are setting yourself up as Protector; no woman can do such a thing.'

Thomas Kemp put the papers down and ran a hand over his face. He looked tired, careworn and there was a tremor in his fingers; Margaret knew she should not weary him further but she did not have the luxury of time.

'Why not?'

She pointed to the papers spread out in front of her, papers she had pored over.

'There is precedent: my grandmother, my mother both ruled kingdoms when their husbands could not and, here in England, Eleanor of Provence acted as regent for her husband, Henry III and the people praised her for it. Why can't I do the same for Henry, for my son?'

'Because it is not the same, Madame, it is nothing like the same.'

Kemp was too tired of the constant arguing to soften his tone.

'What is done in France is of no consequence in England and what was done 300 years ago bears no semblance to today. Eleanor's Henry was alive and well, fighting abroad; she was clearly seen to be nothing more than his mouthpiece carrying out his will, while your Henry is...in truth, I do not know what he is but he is clearly incapable of acting as the source of power and you cannot exercise that power without him.'

He waved a warning hand as she was about to speak.

'Do not argue it, Madame: I know the English Court far better than you ever will. And this bill you propose, these articles you would put before Norfolk,' he picked up the densely worded papers again, smoothed them through his spotted hands. 'They would give you the rule of the whole land: you would appoint all the officers of state and all the bishoprics; you would have control of all the benefices and finances of the Crown; you would have sole governance of the Prince. Madame, this is not a regency you propose, it is a rule.'

Margaret knew he spoke with far more understanding than she could claim but she could not allow it. 'And if I do not secure it, that rule will surely go to York! You must support me on this, my dearest Kemp, you must. York has Warwick and Norfolk close behind him, we are without Somerset...'

'And without his man Thorpe as Speaker in Parliament; they have arrested him too.'

Kemp sighed, and twisted the Archbishop's ring with its great seal of Canterbury around his finger as though the burden of it pressed too heavily.

'You didn't know, I thought not. We have been quick to appoint men loyal to you to the Commons but it is York who really has control of it.' Kemp's voice was weary, without the trace of a fight; it would have softened a less desperate woman. 'I will act for you, Madame, you cannot doubt it. I have delayed the calling of this Parliament long enough in hopes that the King would show some sign of recovery but of that, I fear, there seems little hope; unless, of course, you have news I do not.'

He knew the answer well enough: there was no reassurance to give. 'There is no change in him. I have presented Edward to him twice now but to no avail, there is no sign he knows him.'

Or me or anything else, that is the truth of it.

She had laid the child across Henry's knee, held his hand, whispered desperate urgings into his ear but it was as though he were a statue garbed as a man.

He revolts me, he revolts us all. And if I falter he will destroy us all.

There was no point in anything but honesty.

'Henry will not name Edward as his heir, he cannot and York knows it. I have to make this stand. I have to trust that there is enough love for us or enough fear of York to make the Commons see me as the best hope the country has of stability. They brought me here as a Queen who would broker peace. Well now is the time for me to make good on that promise.'

It was a pretty speech and perhaps Kemp would have made good on it, perhaps he could have persuaded Parliament to her cause; she was never to know. Kemp called Parliament, he put forward Margaret's bill and he died.

He died and my voice was lost, it was that simple and that disastrous: it was as if my proposal had never been. For almost two years I had gambled and plotted to secure a future for Henry, for me, for the child who was supposed to be my certainty; it was as if I had done nothing, as if, in truth, I was nothing.

On the 3rd of April, Parliament named the Duke of York Protector of England as though my marriage, my child, my husband's majority had never been. And this was a Protectorate far worse than Glouces-

ter's had ever been: Richard of York did not guard the kingdom for a child, he guarded it for a madman and he guarded it for himself.

***

'Madame, you must come, at once. It is the King.'

The same words, the same wasted hope, the same frustrated tears to follow; she could not bear it again. Month after month, Margaret had sat out the days at Windsor with a helpless child and a helpless husband, watching as York built his kingdom around her, waiting for something to happen other than false alarms. Almost daily a shaking servant brought her news of her husband that would come to nothing except a misguided physician's hopes. This time it was his almoner, Henry Server, who spoke; she did not care, she had no care left.

'I must come, really? I must?'

He recoiled as all the servants did now for her tongue dripped acid quicker than kind words these days. She ignored him, turned her fury at the interruption at Osanna who had entered the room behind Server.

'What is the King?'

Osanna, wary of her mistress now with real cause, had more sense than to respond.

'Tell me, what is he? Is he a new man risen from his bed and appointing officers to the Council who might care about my future? Is he a vengeful knight sending Warwick back to the North with his ambition whipped out of him? Or is he a brave horseman riding out to the Tower to rescue Somerset, perhaps dragging York in chains behind him?'

Margaret could see the tears starting to fall down her companion's pretty cheeks; such a sight could no longer move her or stop her tongue.

127

'No, wait, I know: he is a priest in the Chapel leading Mass and making men believe in a God I no longer think has any eyes for England or its King. Is that what he is? Or is he a breathing corpse, lying like a statue with no more control over his body than a babe and less care of it?'

Osanna was weeping openly now and Seward was twisting his hands in discomfort; they both knew Margaret had refused any call to Henry's chambers for days and would stalk from the room if any physician has much dared to hint at a new treatment. And yet, despite her cruelty, they would not leave and, unbidden and unwanted, some hope suddenly stirred. Margaret sat forward, watching them carefully.

'Is it honestly something new?' And then, as she saw the relief on Seward's face, she realised. 'Dear God, is he awake? Tell me, has the King woken?'

'We think so, Madame, we think so but you must come...'

But Margaret had stopped listening. She grabbed Osanna's hand and together they flew down the halls and out through the courtyard thick with January's heaviest snows to the King's chamber where the physicians must have thought the wife afflicted with the husband's ills, she stood so long in shocked silence at the side of the bed. And, as unlikely as it seemed to everyone present, it fell to Henry not her to speak the first words.

'Margaret, it would seem I am returned to you.'

His voice was thin and shook a little but the words and meaning were clear enough. She sat down heavily on the furs they had piled around him and took his hand; his fingers were as slight as twigs on a winter tree but at least he did not flinch away.

'Henry, dear Henry, thank God you are back with us. Do you know what happened to you? Do you have any memory, any sense of these last months at all?'

She did not know what to ask or what she wanted to hear; there was fear in his eyes as he slowly shook his head and bewilderment in his voice as he answered. There would be no comfort in his words.

'There is nothing, Margaret, nothing. I was awake; then they tell me I was not and now I am awake again. That is all I know.'

'Do you remember about the child?'

Margaret could sense the physicians muttering, knew they were afraid that the question would cause him some distress but she had to know.

'Do you remember that I was awaiting the birth of your child, of your son?' She took a deep breath. 'You have a son, Henry, an heir.'

He looked at her with the innocent eyes of a child himself and she knew she had no choice but to seize this waking moment.

'A son, Henry; Osanna will bring him now and you can see your little Prince. We have all prayed so hard for this day when you would see him and claim him as your own.'

Do not fail me, please do not fail me. Claim your child. Give me a weapon against York.

Carefully she helped him to sit up against the pillows, ignoring the complaints that she was too careless of a sick man, desperate only to put Edward into Henry's arms and see him recognise the child. When Osanna returned, breathless, dragging the indignant wet-nurse and equally indignant baby, Margaret thrust the squalling bundle onto the bed before anyone could protest.

'A son.'

Henry gazed at the scarlet little face staring up at him with obvious bemusement. 'My son.' He smiled, 'I do not remember such a thing but he is here and so are you so he truly must be my son.'

It was done: Margaret burst into such noisy tears of relief at his innocent words that she frightened Edward into equally lustful screams and he was bundled away by the furious nurse.

They think I am crying for joy because Henry is returned to me; it is enough, for today, that is enough.

'Madame, the King must be allowed to rest.'

Bartlett, the most senior of the physicians and the least afraid of Margaret, spoke politely enough but it was also clear that he would brook no argument.

'He is fully recovered? He won't relapse? You can tell me that much?' She was so used to speaking about Henry as though he was not there, she could not break the habit.

'Madame, I do not know...' He continued quickly as he saw Margaret's frown, 'we hope so but we have never known the cause of the King's...of his collapse so it is difficult to know for certain whether there will be a recurrence. I am sorry, I cannot promise anymore.'

She knew how much the warning cost Bartlett; lies would have been simpler.

'Then you must watch him, watch and record everything he does. We cannot lose the King again.'

There was a threat in her words; they all heard it.

From that moment on they all watched Henry as though he were an animal whose behaviour they could not predict and the truth became evident all too quickly: this was not a recovery, it was merely a reprieve. It was not so much that Henry had changed, it was more that he never fully returned. His behaviour, the outward show at least, was all anyone could have wished but he listened to everything that had passed while he slept, from Edward's birth to York's rise, in the same manner, with no question or curiosity. And that was where the fear arose: everything looked right but everything remained wrong. Henry had come back hollow: he reacted to nothing, accepted all that was put before him, was docile and biddable. It was as if he never truly woke from that day until his last and any moments of wakefulness were but seconds in a walking sleep. Despite the King sitting once more on the Throne, smiles were strained that New Year and laughter was an increasingly scarce commodity.

***

'She has beaten you.'

Richard Neville, Earl of Warwick, watched Richard of York carefully, knowing how fast his uncle's temper could turn but enjoying the baiting. 'And it is quite a victory: Somerset is out of the Tower, Henry is back on the throne and she has her son. Clever girl.'

'Her bastard son.'

Neville laughed, 'perhaps, but you can't prove it. Maybe Henry finally succumbed to her seductions and the shock was what drove him to his sleeping sickness; they call her the she-wolf, God knows what lurks under her shift!'

'If I wanted to speak to ignorant peasants, I would go into the yard.' York's words had no effect and his anger subsided in the face of Neville's refusal to bite. 'I may not have proof but I know I am right, that child is not Henry's.'

'Then whose? Do you think Somerset really is the father?'

York shook his head. 'No, you are right: she is clever, too clever for that. She parades Somerset and throws banquets to celebrate his release as though they were lovers but I don't believe it.'

'Is Henry really so incapable? You saw him at Parliament when he resumed power, how did he seem?'

'He was in control of himself if that is what you mean.'

York pulled the flagon of wine towards him, 'he gave a good account of himself. His voice was firm and steady, he thanked me and wished me well, he spoke of his joy in the Prince; it was all as anyone would have wished it.'

'Except you.'

Neville motioned to the servants to refill the platters of cold pigeon as quickly as they refilled the wine; he needed a clear head.

'And now what? Does he think you have gone away to lick your wounds or does he know that you are holed up with me and my father planning your revenge?'

York shrugged. 'She knows what I am doing; what he thinks doesn't matter. I am not popular at Court; there is no point in arguing.'

He waited for a moment as if to allow Neville the chance to do just that; when there was no response, he continued.

'Well I am not and Henry has the Crown. It doesn't matter how much patronage I spread, the Court will welcome the return to the natural order of things and will be in no mind to support rebellious challenges once they see their King returned to them.' He smiled suddenly at his nephew who stiffened.

If he could see that smile as others see it, he would know why he is not popular; there is more warmth in snow.

'Henry's mistake is that he sees the mood of the Court and takes it for the mood of the country. And as for Somerset, all he cares about is making a public show: he has called a Great Council at Leicester and will march the Court there as though it is a triumphal procession or a pilgrimage. They won't call me to attend, or you or your father. They will dangle the King in front of the people like a miracle and the Prince like a talisman and we will raise an army while they parade. Well the country is not the Court and there is dissatis-faction enough for us to show our hand. Somerset can plan a pro-cession, we will plan a battle and let's see who is the winner then.'

Neville watched him warily: he wore his hatreds too openly; it was not the mark of a clever man. 'But Margaret knows? What you say about Henry and Somerset is true: they won't expect or even imag-ine that you are preparing an attack but Margaret will not be fooled, she will know why you left. She will stop Somerset, surely? She will know how vulnerable the King would be.'

York crushed a walnut with the palm of his hand and spread the crumbs across the table.

'And what if she tries? No one will listen to her. Somerset has a clever tongue: he will be able to persuade Henry that his people need to see him. Margaret can stay at Greenwich for all I care; she can be my reward when I have killed her husband.'

***

It was dark. The sky was too thick with rainclouds to allow any sliver of moonlight and the servants had not roused themselves enough to light more than a handful of candles. It was not an aus-picious backdrop to such an early disturbance: Margaret could not tell if it was cold or fear that was making her shiver and fret. Ever since Somerset had spun his plan and marched out with Henry, she had feared the worst. The news that York had amassed an army had come as no surprise, she had warned Somerset but he had dis-missed her fears as the notions of an hysterical woman. To have been proved right was of no comfort.

'How has it gone, the battle at St Albans? We are sick for news, My Lord, tell us what you know.'

James Butler, the Earl of Wiltshire and now Treasurer, had arrived at Margaret's chamber so early on the morning of May 23rd, she could think only the worst. He was a great favourite among the ladies of the Court for his handsome looks and his witty tongue but now they stood about him bedraggled from sleep with no thought of anything but the threat of armies approaching.

'It is done, Madame, it was done quick in truth, in an hour or less.' He stopped as though searching for words; she could have screamed at his hesitation.

'Then how is it concluded? Are the losses high? Are we victorious? Tell me something; your silence begins to frighten us.'

'The losses are not so high, not in terms of numbers of men dead. The fighting was kept to a matter of streets no more, the soldiers chasing each other from house to house. It was barely a battle at all but —'

And again he stopped as though he did not have words. Margaret could not bear it; some of her waiting women had already begun to whimper.

'My Lord Wiltshire, my patience wears thin. There is clearly other news that I must have. Tell it. Now.'

'It is not so much the losses, Madame, as what is lost.'

He spoke quickly now as though he would have it over.

'It was Warwick who got the better of us: he outflanked our army, brought his troops through the back streets and caught the King and his guard by surprise. They ringed them with archers and casualties were high: the Duke of Buckingham was wounded and Northumberland and Clifford, all Warwick's enemies picked off one by one. And then Warwick turned on Somerset, he killed him himself; butchered him. It was cruelly, foully done.'

There was a gasp of horror; Margaret did not know where it came from but she felt Osanna move to hold her.

'The King? What of the King? Is he dead too?'

'Not dead, Madame, but wounded with an arrow to his neck.' His words came out in even more of a rush. 'It is a scratch only, not fatal, he will live. He will be well but he is taken.'

'Taken? I do not understand. Taken by who? By what?'

'By York, Madame. The Duke of York has the King.'

It was his hand now that reached out for Margaret as she began to fall. 'Be calm, please. York does not wish him harm, I am sure of it. He has asked the King's pardon and sworn his allegiance. He brings him back to London as we speak, as his King, York says, not as his prisoner.' And then he hesitated and they all knew the worst. 'I truly think York will not harm him but the King, Madame, the King is not well...'

He did not need to say anything more for it was written plain on his haggard face: the King was lost in more than just his person and York had his puppet to play with how he would.

London and the Midlands: 1456-7

Richard of York and I: we were both destined to underestimate the other time and again. We played cat and mouse over and over while Henry slept his waking sleep, handing victory back and forth, always hating each other. It was a dance to the death.

Greenwich had become a prison. Since she had taken it from Gloucester's family on his death, Margaret had loved it best of all her homes and now it was a prison. She had turned it into her own Palace of Placentia, her pleasant place to live. She had seen to it that the floors were tiled with rich red terracotta, her name-flower engraved into them, and had the pattern repeated across the sparkling glass of the windowpanes. It had been a place of beauty, a source of pride and now she paced the floors and scuffed its tiles and stared unseeing from the windows, waiting for York to come with his armies and seize her child.

'Madame, the Duke of York is here.'

He was in the room before she had a chance to refuse him entry.

'My Lady, I trust that I find you in good health?'

There was a bow but its effect was ruined by the rest of his words and the insolent smile Margaret could have scratched from his face, 'or at least in better health than I left your husband in.'

Katherine's grip had the strength of iron in it; if it held back Margaret, it only encouraged him.

'Margaret, I swear I don't know whether to admire or pity you.'

He sat, without any thought of permission and stretched his long legs proprietarily across the front of the hearth.

'Is that all you have had in your bed, truly? Is that what you would pretend fathered your son? You are a brave woman to spin that story, I grant you that.'

'How dare you speak to me like this,' there was venom in her voice and, this time, no pretence at hiding it. 'I am still your Queen and my husband is still your King. You may have set yourself up as Protector again but that makes you a guardian, not a ruler. You should remember that.'

But York's poison was more than a match for hers. 'Oh I do remember, with every waking moment I remember who has the crown and how pathetically he wears it.'

Suddenly, to Katherine's gasped horror, he had hold of Margaret's hand and pulled her roughly towards him.

'You would do better to remember who holds the cards here and speak a little more carefully; I can make your life harder than it needs to be or gentler than you deserve. The choice is yours.'

It was as if the other women in the room, the servants who stood unsure what to do, were invisible to him. Without warning, the grasp suddenly turned itself into something far closer to a caress. Margaret couldn't help herself: shocked out of her fury she burst out laughing.

'My God, I thought you were arrogant but you are truly ridiculous! What are you proposing? That I tumble into bed with you in the hope of some kindness? That I make myself a whore for you?'

Still laughing, she reached out her other hand, stroked a finger across his lips and, as he relaxed into the promise of something more, slapped him hard across the face.

'You bitch!' He leapt to his feet, his cheek bleeding where her heavy ring had caught him and pushed her hard away.

'You little fool. My whore? Well you have been someone's whore, and trust me I will find out whose, but I would not stoop to make you mine.'

He tore from the room, cursing Margaret and his men and calling for his horse.

'He will never forgive you for that.'

Osanna was shaking and close to tears but Margaret shook her head at the warning.

'I don't care. I know he will make me pay but that was worth it. Believe me: that was worth it.'

***

'Take everything from her. Reduce her household to its bones; remove all her Lancaster revenues; make sure she is forbidden entry to London.'

No one would argue with him in this mood: his secretaries bustled away to turn his fury into legalities, simply grateful not to be the target of his malice.

'What do you hope to achieve?'

Neville, the only one who ever dared speak plainly to him, had watched without comment as York flung orders around; there was little point in trying reason until the mist had lifted.

'Margaret is virtually a prisoner at Greenwich; Somerset is in the Tower; you are Protector. Is this humiliation of her simply for revenge or are you planning something else?'

York looked at him but didn't respond so Neville continued, keeping his tone as light as he could, given the directness of the question.

'Are you going to kill the King?'

'Do you think I should?' The question was carefully calculated and Neville smiled.

'Oh no, you don't get to make this my decision. Kill Henry or don't kill Henry but don't put my head on the block.'

He won't do it; he hasn't got the nerve. And he will lose his moment.

'I should have done it by now; that's what you think, isn't it?'

York waited for the response this time but there was none forthcoming. He sighed, 'I should have done it by now. An arrow wound can run to poison quick enough; the moment was there for the taking. And with Henry dead and Margaret's child so young, I could have taken the Crown without too many voices raised against me.'

'But instead, you do nothing more than Parliament allows you; you don't show the King's feeble state to the world and you have Henry well-cared for.' Neville shrugged, 'so, yes, the moment was there to be seized but you have done nothing to seize it. Henry still wears the Crown.'

York rubbed his face; he was tired, weary of a situation he knew he had created.

'And now? If Henry was to die now, do you think the people would support me?'

'Honestly?' Neville shook his head. 'No, I don't. The fighting at St Albans may have been short-lived but it was bloody and we can't hide that; the townspeople who witnessed it were terrified and their stories have spread. I don't think there is any appetite for more violence or any love for those who unleashed it.'

And there will be more: the more you humiliate Margaret, the more she will dream of destroying you. You are a fool; you have led us to a fight you don't have the stomach to finish properly.

139

There was silence and then York abruptly left the room: he had no answers and no strategy. Within days he sent the sleeping Henry home.

***

For the first time in weeks, musicians were playing in the gallery above the Hall. There were fewer perhaps than in previous days but it was still music and it was soothing.

'He doesn't have the victory he thought he would.'

Wiltshire filled the goblets full with deep purple wine and toasted Margaret with a grin.

'He has won too many men to his side with promises of power and now he can't deliver. Half the Court snap at his heels like hungry dogs. It is very gratifying to watch.'

'I wish I could see it for myself.'

She sipped gratefully at the wine he had brought; York had stripped the cellars bare and left nothing but rough offerings in the depleted kitchens.

'Tell me about Warwick: Alice had heard some gossip that he is becoming a thorn in York's side but she had nothing of substance.'

Wiltshire grinned 'she was right. The talk at Court is that it is Richard Neville not Richard York who is really in charge. Warwick, at least, delivers on the promises he makes, whether he should have made them or not.'

Margaret settled herself more comfortably and gestured for Wiltshire to go on. The news of a threat to York, particular if it came from within his own support, was as warming as the wine.

'There is a rift between the two of them. The rumour is that York regrets making Warwick Governor of Calais but it is too late to curb him: with the wealth it has brought, it seems Warwick's star is starting to rise out of control. And Warwick is not cautious like York: he doesn't seem to care where he lavishes his patronage as long as it buys him loyalty. Some of the traders he is protecting are little more than pirates and what he would call a retinue would be an army to most men. There is something though that worries me...'

'What is it?'

Ever alert to bad news these days, she sat up at his hesitation, sensing an edge creep in to his voice.

For the first time that evening, Wiltshire suddenly avoided her eyes.

'There are other rumours, enough rumours to make it worth listening to them, that Warwick is pushing York to take up arms again in France, to try to regain England's lost lands.'

The lightness in the room had gone; Margaret sat rigid, the wine and the music both forgotten.

'If Warwick could do that, if York could achieve that, it would bring the Crown much closer to him.'

Wiltshire nodded, 'that is why these stories are so worrying. I think there may be truth in them. Warwick is clever enough to give such advice and his uncle is clever enough to take it. York knows he gave up the King too quickly, that it made him look weak. The people may not want a war in England but the losses in France still cut deep into their pride; they would give up this Henry quickly enough if it seemed York might be a new Henry V in the making.'

'And the French Court is no less riven by faction than ours.'

She gestured to a pile of papers scattered across a table in an alcove by the window, 'my father writes often and tells me time and again that France is filled with disaffected men who would willingly aid York if it would serve their own ends. We have to watch him closely, James, and Warwick too: I cannot let him take me by surprise again.'

'He won't.'

Wiltshire was himself again; keen to prove himself the worthy champion. 'He won't. You are not as isolated as you might think. Whatever victory York might claim, not everyone delights in this newly snatched Protectorate. Don't forget, for every supporter York pulls to him, there is another who has lost a father or a son to his brutality at St Alban's. They will still pledge their loyalty to you.'

He warmed to his theme, as eager as a puppy to please.

'Think of who will support you: Henry Beaufort now he has his father's title of Duke of Somerset; Owen Tudor, he is surely no lover of the Yorkists and neither are his sons, the Earls of Richmond and Pembroke; there is Lord Grey and the Percys too. Don't forget them or underestimate their hatred for Warwick and the Neville clan. And there is Rivers: you have kept him close to you and his wife; they have powerful friends.'

Despite the mention of Rivers, which always unsettled her, it was hard not to feel his enthusiasm, not to feel a surge of hope at such a list.

'I think you are right. None of them have any love for York or any hope for advancement under his governing.'

She smiled, grateful to have something to do rather than sit and wait for events to unfold.

'I will write to them and get their pledges. I cannot move around the country now but you can be my mouthpiece in the world and secure their loyalty.'

It was a good plan and they kept to it. Margaret wrote letter after letter and Wiltshire used his charms and easy manner about the Court to see that every word was read and remembered. She had an answer from everyone on that list in those dying months of 1455 and Wiltshire was proved right: at least while she had the King, her support was strong.

And so Margaret became once again the one keeping secrets, keeping her counsel, gathering protection around her while York played with power and all the while watching her husband like a hawk watches its prey for the one moment of lucidity which would tip the scales again and restore Henry to the Throne. Despite all York's prayers, it came.

The Midlands:
1456-58

There are days in a life that run so quick, that turn events in a moment and years in a life that must be slowly-paced, whose importance is not always known until they have passed. Part of writing a life is to judge the different moments in it, to make sense of the slow passages as much as the quick, because they cannot be judged when they are lived.

'Do you see the people Edward, do you see them wave?'

Margaret pointed to the crowds lining the streets on the approach to Leicester; her men had done well to encourage such a crowd to come and, even if it was coin that tempted them there rather than loyalty, they would still cheer loud enough.

'They have come to see you, their little Prince. You must smile and wave back and help me give out the presents.'

As soon as the re-awoken Henry had taken up the Crown again, she had taken him out of London. The Protectorate may have ended but the danger was barely tamed and time, she knew was borrowed. The City was too visible a place for Henry now: he could manage little beyond the gentlest conversation and spent much of his time looking absently away into some life that was more real than any palace he found himself in. But if Henry could not be seen, Margaret could and so could her son. So she moved the centre of Court to the Midlands where her holdings were secure and the people had felt the benefits of her patronage. Where there was, more pertinently, little love for York. And she had seen to it that, when the royal party moved, it was done with great procession and with a great show of largesse wherever they rode out. Tutbury, Sandal, Leicester, Kenilworth, Coventry, they visited all of them, entertaining the local nobility, endowing places of learning and healing as they went. She was creating the illusion of power again but the part she loved the most, the part the people loved the most, was showing off Edward who always rode the final stretch of any journey sitting solidly on his little white pony, as fat as a barrel beneath his determined rider.

'Can I give out the oranges, Mama? They like the oranges?'

His baby lisp was beginning to fade and his attempts to engage the crowds who flocked to him in earnest conversation had them calling him cherub and angel.

'And the ginger; put that in the basket too. See how pretty the green looks against the fruit.'

The basket was too heavy for him but Margaret knew he would refuse any help and the crowds would adore his toddling efforts to please them.

'It looks like treasure; they will think I give them treasure!'

And they did. With skill learnt from the pageants she had witnessed so many times, Margaret made the people see how well the Crown was worn. Everywhere they stopped, she made sure to distribute gifts that would not be so generous as to show undue extravagance (she had, at least, learnt that lesson about her subjects) but that would bring some little luxury to their lives: soft white bread, velvety-smooth red wine, the best capons, oranges like jewels and fragrant green ginger. And everywhere there was Edward, with his sweet nature and his ready smiles and his excitement at the tableaux and speeches so carefully staged to honour her as the embodiment of a virtuous wife and mother.

'Will Father the King come out to see the people here?' Edward's face was so trusting, so open.

Your father barely acknowledges you beyond a pale smile but you always ask the same hopeful question; surely it would be easier if you had a memory to mourn rather than this phantom we pull around with us.

'No my love, the King will not come out today. But everyone knows he is here and they will be glad to have had a sight of us and of their little prince.'

Always the same answering smile, always the same carefully chosen words, what else could she do? She could not let the crowds see Henry: she could not let them see the pale wraith of a man he had become but, more than that, she could not risk him speaking, blessing them the way he would, like their priest not their ruler. Henry kept to a closed litter. Margaret rode out with her ladies, wrapped in their finest cloaks and kept Edward always near so that he charmed everyone with his sweet nature and his ready smiles but Henry was kept invisible. And it worked: the crowds did not need the man, they saw what they wanted to see, the Crown in all its glory. As for York, he stayed away in his own estates, waiting for his next moment and, Margaret knew because she orchestrated it, very well-informed of her every movement.

The show was one thing but it was also a time to build alliances and to build a Court that shone in a way new to the English Court. The royal advisors, straight-laced and serious to a fault, may have found Margaret's notions fanciful and born of too many romances but she had a dream to create something special: a Court that would be seen as the centre of power, of intellect, a place truly fit for a king, where the quarrels of faction would have no place. So she wrote letters and sent invitations to her uncle's court in France and to the court of Burgundy where learning was prized in everything and encouraged the thinkers and the artists to come to England. And, for that brief time, they did. She wove a golden age around her and draped the finest artists she could find in it.

Jean Fouquet, whose paintings were more beautiful than anything the Court had ever seen brought his talents and left a miniature of the little prince that never left her side. Robert Morton came and played music beautiful enough to even rouse Henry from his distracted state. And while she cultivated the gentler face of her Court, she did not neglect to strengthen its bones: Waynflete became Chancellor, Salisbury Treasurer and Booth Keeper of the Privy Seal; the Duke of Buckingham was her man as was Shrewsbury and she bound them tight with marriage treaties that served their families very well. It was a carefully built construct: her household and Henry's so intertwined none could really say where the power lay and Edward's household tucked inside with all the appearance of the King's control. And it was appearance and no more: Henry spent his days now in prayer or in his twilight world; nobody could trust that he would ever fully return but nobody could admit the truth of that so Margaret ruled and everyone looked the other way. It was a delicate game, to make belief that the King held power when everyone knew it rested with a Queen but the tissue held as long as they all willed it.

And yet, no matter how strong I built my base, no matter how fairly I wielded the power I had, the shadow cast by York and Warwick was an ever-present taint.

'You do not keep faith with London. Every time you call Parliament outside the City, London feels insulted. You refuse to try to understand them.'

A constant refrain, from Buckingham, from Somerset, from Booth. She would not listen: she could not forgive London the slights she held against it; she did not trust Henry near it.

'They will grow to hate you and your Court. They will flock to York and to Warwick. You must leave the Midlands and go back.'

More words, more warnings to be ignored. Until York's meddling in France bore the wrong kind of fruit and she had no choice but to return the King to London.

***

'Does your word carry no measure of influence at all with any member of your meddling family?' Salisbury flung the letter down on the table where Margaret had been helping Edward practice his letters, startling them both with his lack of manners as much as his evident anger.

'Nurse, it is time the Prince was put to bed.'

She stilled the protest that sprang immediately to Edward's lips with a kiss and sent him grumpily away with a promise of a later visit to his nursery before turning to her Treasurer.

'Whatever the cause, the child does not need to hear it.'

He reddened although the rebuke was gentle enough.

'I am sorry,' he did not sound it but Margaret chose not to comment. 'It is these French raids on our coastline: they go too far and I am tired of paying the price for York's trouble-making. I thought that you had told your uncle that it was York who wanted war in France, not us.'

Again she chose not to comment on his tone.

'I have told him, many times but he doesn't choose to listen. To be honest, I think my words sound very hollow when judged against my obvious inability to control York and Warwick's plotting and the mischief-making clearly going on at Charles's court.'

It was true, they both knew it and so did the French: no matter how many letters Margaret wrote, she could not do a thing to stop Warwick's ambitions in France.

'Have the raids on the coast worsened?'

Salisbury nodded. 'It is no longer a matter of raids. We are used to French raids on English ports: they do it to us, we do it to them; that has always been the way of things. Plundering like pirates on both sides and no real harm done. But not this time.'

He pushed the letter across the table.

'There have been reports for a while now that the French were gathering a fleet far larger and more war-like than their normal raiders. Well now they have struck and the reports of the attacks on Sandwich and on Fowey are dreadful: bloodshed and wanton cruelty on a scale we cannot deal with lightly.'

It was true; the letter was so full of atrocities, so detailed in its descriptions, Margaret pushed it away.

'It is a warning. My father's hand might not be in this but my uncle's is: he wants us to remember that France is an enemy we should not ignore, that they will not tolerate any thought of winning back French provinces to English control.'

Salisbury thrust the letter back again. 'It is worse than that, read on.' His continued abruptness was so unlike him, she did as she was told but stopped again, this time more puzzled than horrified by its contents.

'The Council is accusing me? Saying I had some hand in the attacks on my own country?'

Salisbury shook his head. 'Not some hand, no: the controlling hand. And they do not believe that you really think of England as your country. York has placed the blame for the attacks firmly with you. He has positioned himself to the Council as the voice of England and aligned you with the vengeful fury of France.'

He sighed.

'You have never made friends in London, despite everything we have said to you, and York has taken advantage of it. Look at what he has done,' he pointed to a paragraph she had not yet read. 'He has persuaded all these panicked lords that Warwick should be granted a Commission to keep the seas safe. Can you imagine it: a pirate to keep the peace? It would be amusing enough if it did not mean more power granted to a man who would destroy you.'

Warwick is the threat? I have been watching York so closely: have I been watching the wrong man?

She would have asked Salisbury for his council but there was little point, there was only one possible course of action.

'I have to go back. I have to go back with Henry and recall Parliament, even though I cannot keep York and Warwick away from it.'

The thought of it was enough to set her hands to shaking.

'If I keep Henry here, he will be safe but we risk becoming ever more isolated. If I go back to London, we risk him being seen for what he really is. But what else can I do? I have to go back and break York before he breaks me.'

I have to set a trap and march myself straight into it.

Salisbury did not respond; there was nothing to say.

London and the South: 1458

I did what I had to do: I returned to London, persuading Henry that he had to go because the people needed to see their King in all his strength and majesty. Had I known that I was setting the scene for a humiliation that still can burn when I think on it, I may have taken my chances and stayed well away.

Once again Greenwich's chambers rang with the sound of the Queen's fury and servants cowered in the corners, hoping not to be called and bear the indiscriminating brunt of it.

'I will have no part of it! A procession for peace? Dear God, if I hadn't believed he was mad before, I surely must think it now!'

'Madame, forgive me but that is no way to speak about the King.'

Poor Bourchier must have wished himself safely back in his Canterbury palace but she was in no mind to address his discomfort.

'I am only voicing what you and every man around you thinks. This Loveday, is that how he names it? It is a nonsense. No, it is worse than that: it is a dangerous conceit. Well he has charged you and Waynflete with making this ridiculous masquerade work so you must persuade him from it.'

'Madame, it is for me to do the King's bidding, it is not for me to pass judgement on him.'

'Well someone must!'

Osanna, knowing Margaret's moods better than anyone, thrust a goblet of wine into the Queen's hand. Its red surface mirrored Margaret's furious face but sipping it allowed her to calm myself; Bourchier was pious even for an Archbishop and she knew he would not countenance any more outbursts against Henry. With an effort she tried to speak in a gentler tone.

'My Lord Archbishop, you must forgive me for my sharpness; it is only concern for the well-being of the King's subjects that makes me speak so plainly.'

She tried to smile but it was more fearsome than winsome and did nothing to settle Bourchier's ruffled feathers.

'Surely you must understand my fears? The whole country is disordered, our borders are threatened and now we allow the most powerful Lords in the kingdom to march into London with retinues that look more like armies when we can do nothing to control them. How must it look? The streets are full of armed men who need little excuse to find a quarrel and the citizens think we have turned their city into a battlefield. They fear another St Albans!'

She knew her voice was rising and took a deep breath; her more controlled tone did not fool Bourchier but the set lines of his face relaxed a little.

'You need to help me. I know that Henry talks of nothing but peace and reconciliation but how can his great plan for this procession do anything other than fan the discontent? He makes fools of all of us but he cannot see it.'

She put a hand on Bourchier's arm as though to invite a confidence.

'It is already becoming dangerous. I have heard rumours that there was an attempt to ambush York and Warwick as they came into the City. If we cannot at least make a show of protection around our greatest subjects, surely all we do is set the stage for war and I cannot believe that is something you of all people would want.'

Bourchier too had taken refuge in the good red wine Katherine pressed upon him and was watching her now above the goblet's rim with eyes that were a little too knowing.

'I am sure the Duke of York would be most flattered to hear of your regard for his position and your concern for his safety. It is true that tempers are running high and an ambush, of sorts, was attempted. But all is well and calm is restored, although, perhaps, you were hoping for a less favourable report?'

Her instinct was to take refuge in anger but there was something rather engaging about being recognised and mocked, something too few men would dare to do; there was a hint of something like amusement in his eyes and, for a moment, he reminded her of Beaufort. With the quick turn of mood that so often confused those around her, she laughed and the room settled.

'My dear Thomas, I think you know me too well. So the ambush came to nothing?'

'To nothing. Northumberland and Clifford were behind it, there is little doubt of that, and probably Percy and Lord Egremont had a hand in it if Warwick was intended as the prize. York and his sup-porters are furious but the King has refused to permit any punish-ment and has somehow persuaded York not to retaliate. Henry promises much from his Loveday and, for now, whether you like it or not, the Lords are prepared to listen.'

His words did little to reassure her.

'No matter if they do; the day is ill-named and ill-judged.'

Why does everyone want to believe in Henry's foolish schemes? Why will no one but me recognise his delusions?

'Seriously Bourchier, tell me: how can anyone believe it will work? We are all to walk together in a joyful procession promising peace and pardons while we pretend that there are not armed followers on every corner? Tell me, please, how is a pageant going to stop the Nevilles and the Percys ripping up the North and making leagues with the Scots against us? How will masses and prayers persuade York to renounce his claim and accept my son as rightful heir?'

153

She threw herself into a chair, suddenly weary of the battle to be heard.

'I persuaded Henry to come back to London by spinning stories of all the pardons he could grant. I never meant it. I am sorry I ever mentioned pardons to him if this is truly what he plans.'

Bourchier had drained his glass and waved for another.

'You need to understand that this is more than a plan; this show of reconciliation is an order and he will stand no discussion of it. The King has prayed for guidance and the King believes God has ordained this path. And he truly believes it will work. If you heard him speak of it, Madame, you would hear the joy in his voice; it is as though he has found a new purpose.'

There was a sudden enthusiasm in Bourchier's voice; she heard it and knew there was no ally here. 'It is quite astounding; he has every detail thought of. York, Warwick for his Neville clan and Salisbury are to endow a chantry at St Albans where masses will be said for those slain in the battle there and they are to pay annuities to the Somerset and Clifford families as a token of their repentance. Egremont will be bound over to keep the peace on behalf of the Percys and fines will be paid by all of them. They must all accept the part they have played in the divisions which now threaten the country and they will; they will prove their repentance by walking hand-in-hand together through the streets of London. They will all swear public fealty to the King and so every rift will be healed. The King decrees it and the King believes it. No one will refuse him.'

'And I must partner York; I must hold his hand and smile, all the while knowing he would have me and my child dead in an instant if he were man enough.'

Margaret drained her glass in turn and signalled for more.

'Well, perhaps luck will be with us and Henry will relapse. Then there will be no more talk of Lovedays and such nonsense.'

She thought Bourchier might anger again at that, not that she cared, but the wine had softened him. 'No, Madame; that would not be luck. There are too many armies surrounding the City: if the King was to fall ill again so publicly, York will move and move far more cruelly this time. Besides, the King truly seems to be well and, perhaps, we should thank his great idea for bringing him strength not fight against it.'

She heard the plea but ignored it.

'But how can it work? How can it? Can you really believe that these promises Henry would have us speak will hold beyond the day? Because I cannot. The promises will break and so will the King and nothing will change'

The look he gave her then had a challenge in it she had not reckoned with.

'Whatever happens to the promises and to the King, that last, I fear, is not true. Change must come and, if you cannot clear the way to it, then it will come by harder means. You know the real truth whether you will admit it or not: there will be no reconciliation until we allow York and Warwick to play a full part in the governing of the country. It is York's right and it may serve to keep his more powerful ambitions in check for nothing else will. You know it, Madame, you always have; whether you will allow it, that I cannot tell.'

She shook her head, 'I care nothing about York's rights, I never will.'

He sighed and signalled for more wine. 'Then, Madame, we will have our Loveday and then we will have our Civil War.'

***

If I had imagined that the day would be hard to bear, I had not imagined it enough. He taunted me every step of the way. Every step from Baynard's Castle, through Ludgate Hill, to the towering spire of St Paul's Cathedral. Henry may have led the procession but

155

he let York play King and the man revelled in it.

'It will be the most wonderful day, Margaret! How can it be any-thing less when we are to hold our celebration on March the 25th, the Feast of the Annunciation?'

Henry laughed, a sound so rare she almost believed in the myth he was creating.

'We will make Lady Day a Loveday and have the Virgin as a symbol for our peace. God and his blessed Mother will turn their joyous gaze onto our humble pilgrimage and it will succeed in all its aims.'

Bourchier spoke the truth: Henry has found a new purpose. Noth-ing is overlooked except the pointlessness of the whole conceit.

'No one will fail to understand your message, My Lord. It is clever-ly, perfectly done.'

She could not argue with him, his purpose was too firmly set. In a gesture she barely recognised, he grasped her hand and pulled her towards the table which was littered with lists and sketches.

'Let me show you how I have designed the procession at last; it is quite perfect, I know it.'

The plans seemed to change daily; Henry's thoughts and ideas spread across sheaf after sheaf, his writing becoming tinier and ti-nier as his vision grew.

None of us can make any sense of what he wants, of what he thinks will be the result and yet we still indulge his fantasies.

He pushed the latest page towards her: he had drawn the proces-sion across it and labelled every player. There were all laid out: Henry first, then Margaret would follow hand-in-hand (for Henry would have no movement on that) with York, then would come Som-erset with Salisbury, Warwick with Northumberland, all the masters of the great families dancing across the page in visible harmony just as they did in his imagination. She wanted to rip it to pieces.

'It is wonderful Henry. It will be like a moving tableau, a symbol of peace. The people love such spectacles and you have created one they will remember for all their lives.'

She smiled at him as though they shared the same vision.

'It is a shame that so few people will see us move through the churchyard and into the nave but those who do will talk about it and the story will grow. I am proud of you: it is very cleverly done.'

It was, in that at least she was honest. Margaret had envisioned an assembly in the churchyard, a brief walk in their paired humility through the cathedral's heavy doors and along the nave, surely long enough to bear witness to their great intention, and that would be all. Henry's plans had, however, run beyond her reluctant imaginings: this was to be a truly public show to rival anything she had ever staged and he had no conception of what he was creating. When he looked up, she could see he had a light about him; a certainty that what he did was so right that it gave him a restless, inexhaustible energy. It was unnerving to see.

'But it won't only be a few who witness this, my dear wife; that is why it is so wonderful!'

He pointed at the paper and she saw a map sketched carefully below the figures.

'Here is the route: we will begin our procession from York's palace on the river and go to the Cathedral from there.' He clapped his hands like a delighted child, 'It will be such a great show of faith for us to assemble within the walls of Baynard's Castle with all York's men armed and around us but posing no threat. How clearly will that show my trust in him?'

'Dear God, you cannot be serious!'

It was out of her mouth before she could stop herself. 'You will make York too important: he will revel in it too much. You are letting him welcome us, welcome all of us, all the nobles of the Court into his great home as though the Crown was already on his head. You cannot put him so high!'

But he did not understand at all and merely smiled his gentle smile.

'But that is what I must do. I must show him that I recognise his importance; he must see my humility and he will know that there is nothing meant for him at my hand but preferment and trust. It is the act of a Christian.'

It is the act of a madman, why can he not see it?

Before she could say anything else, he had run on, his fingers skimming across the papers, tracing out the route.

'We will make the journey from Westminster along the river to York's home and then we will all walk together along the streets of the city so that everyone will see us humble and united. There will be no litters, no horses, no one man set higher than the other.' He carried on describing the day but she was no longer listening.

He would not be swayed. As the day approached, he barely slept and assumed a wakefulness as disturbing to watch as his sleep-walking absences. He wrote and rewrote his plans, prayed over them constantly and summoned Bourchier and Waynflete at every hour of the day and night to discuss prayers and music and sermons. He wore them to shadows but would not rest and would hear no objections to anything he proposed. Margaret had never seen him like it before and would see nothing like it in him again; it was as though he poured a lifetime's energy into those few weeks. His innocence was as frightening as his obsession: Henry truly believed that he was walking his country to peace.

***

The sun had come up just high enough to cast its rays across the turrets and towers of the castle and turn them to liquid gold. It was the perfect backdrop.

'Watch her come. Watch her climb up towards you and never forget it. This is what she will become, what we will make her become: a woman who looks up to the House of York, who knows and accepts where the real power in this country lies.'

York looked at the family grouping he had so carefully arranged in show around him: his wife Cicely and their children, seven of the thirteen she had born him still living. He knew Margaret would mark the contrast with her own precarious family as he fully intended her to do; the smile of satisfaction at her discomfort that settled on his lips would do for family pride.

He heard the trumpets sound the fanfare that signalled the arrival of the royal party and motioned the children into stillness: this would be a tableau as real as any royal court. He imagined Margaret's face as she began the climb up the great double-arched bridge which swept up from the river stairs to Baynard Castle's imposing gateway and the forest of towers that surrounded its double courtyard as though it were fortress and fairytale palace combined and felt a pleasure almost physical.

As his guests came into view, his smile widened but he made no move forward and said nothing until they were at the top of the steps and finally at his level.

'Your Majesties, you are most welcome to my home. My wife and I and my children are honoured by your presence here.'

Margaret saw the bow and heard the words; more than either, she felt the mockery.

And Henry sees none of it. He sees only what he wants to see; he does not feel the hatred that fills every word dripping from your poisonous mouth.

159

With a practiced gesture, York motioned his family forwards. One by one they curtsied or bowed. The daughters were lovely, all of them, but it was the boys who drew Margaret's attention: Edward, Edmund, George and little Richard, as small and dark as his brothers were tall and fair but no less confident in his position or his bearing.

We parade our children like prize trophies when they are nothing more than threats: you would kill mine as I would kill yours without a second thought.

'Your Majesty, let me take the Queen's arm; it will be good practice for our procession.' Henry smiled in delight at the gallantry. Margaret had no choice but to comply.

'Did you admire my children?'

The voice barely above a whisper was too close, his breath too warm on her neck. 'It's what I am good at, don't you think? Giving my wife children and such a pleasant duty to have to perform.'

She tried to pull away but his grip was far too strong.

'And not just for me. Oh I make sure my wife has learnt the pleasure in it and I have taught her such clever things to do with her mouth, with her fingers; I swear I could place her in a brothel never mind a nunnery if I ever sickened of her.'

This time she did pull away, stopping suddenly in the entrance hall, 'you are sickening, you disgust me.'

He stopped, making a play as though something in the wall tapestries had caught her eye.

'Keep walking my dear or people will think you are not so in love with today as your pitiful husband.'

He took her arm again and steered her forward.

'Such a sweetly innocent response. Can you really be so easily shocked? Surely you must have had some enjoyment at your son's getting or was our beloved King asleep through that as well?'

She could not speak, could not risk a scene he would have enjoyed too much, so she drove her fingernails hard into his palm. She saw the rage rise in his face and yet he kept on walking, fooling Henry with every step.

Throughout the endless day that followed, she wondered if the crowds were as fooled. They cheered loud enough, perhaps they were. And the mood in the Cathedral was as solemn as even Henry could have wished it as they filed past the great shrine of St Erkenwald, along the endless nave all patterned blue and red with the light from the great rose window, to the golden chalice containing the Host where they all swore aloud to live in peace as Henry had charged them to do. It surely must have seemed as though the words were meant and the vows would hold. But the worshippers did not see how Warwick's face tightened with distaste as he rejoined hands with Northumberland and the crowd did not hear the poison York poured into Margaret's ear from behind his traitorous smile. Constant taunts: of Henry's prowess as a husband, of her son's parenting, of all the lovers he judged her to have taken to bed. And the best taunt of all? That she would be his mistress. That Henry's next collapse was certain in everything but its date, that her child was nothing more than an irritant to be discarded and that he would use her until he was happy to do the same. It was the most solemn promise he made that day: that he would humble her, break her, teach her to obey.

A Loveday: was anything ever so badly named? My poor deluded husband meant us to leave that day and build the peace; I left to build an army.

London:
October 1458

Why, when we are watching and waiting for an expected attack, does the blow always come from a different direction? I had my eyes firmly trained on York, yet it was Warwick who lit the fuse which blew the Loveday's fragile accord to the skies. Some will tell you that the fragile peace our Loveday promised held from March until October, that it looked like holding longer and it was my fury, my ambition that broke it. Some will tell you that and some will believe it; it is not the truth. The peace that Henry gambled on lasted but six weeks until Warwick's French meddling destroyed it in a day.

The rain had worsened. All day its heavy drumbeat against the window had been a constant irritant, a physical reminder of their confinement inside a palace that was too crowded, too busy. It seemed that every noble in the country had come to Court to be close to the King's commission of enquiry into Warwick's conduct and Margaret was heartily sick of all of them. The sight of the new arrival in the Hall, pushing a dripping hood away from her face and looking around for somewhere to warm herself, did nothing to improve her foul mood.

'It has been too long, Jacquetta, it is good to see you returned to Court.'

It was not true: Margaret had argued against Bourchier's choice of Rivers to lead the commission but he had ignored her and Henry pretended none of it was happening. She had hoped the wife would not accompany the husband but that prayer, like so many others, had gone unheard.

'I am not here from choice.'

Jacquetta's tone touched only lightly on courtesy. 'My husband was summoned and I did not want him here alone: the Court is a troubled place, I think, with too many whispers and conspiracies.' That barb she was permitted, but not the next. 'How is the King, is he well? We hear such strange stories of him.'

She needs to relearn fear.

'Stories, Madame? How interesting, tell me have you come here with gossip about the King's person?'

A smile, a calm tone; it needed nothing else.

'He is the King; surely he is always well or is it lately the custom that we allow anyone to speculate about his health? Wouldn't such questions be treasonable? But perhaps I mistake you. Perhaps you merely have some potions you wish to offer him against the winter chills?'

A pause for gentle emphasis. 'You still meddle with such things I hear.'

No one watching would have seen a flicker on either face but Jacquetta heard the threat; it only now needed the slightest underlining.

'I hear my own share of gossip and some of it is about you, about you and your husband to be more precise. Perhaps there are other reasons why you don't trust him at Court alone?'

Jacquetta's face paled, 'there is always gossip about husbands and wives, why should I care about this?'

'Because it upsets me, Jacquetta, and you do not want that.'

Margaret was aware that the room had quietened as Jacquetta's discomfort became increasingly apparent. Her unexpected arrival alone was enough to warrant interest; the possibility of an argument that would prove the rumours of an estrangement between the two women was turning too many heads.

'Come to the window with me where we can talk with less chance of being overheard.'

She motioned her to seats in a quieter nook of the room with a hanging acting as a partial screen. 'We need to speak plainly. It is not just idle talk: there have been rumours for weeks that you and Rivers are no longer the happy couple we are used to seeing and now the Court buzzes with speculation about quarrels over lovers and mistresses.'

Jacquetta smiled bitterly at that, 'as it is wont to do when any rift between a husband and wife is played out on a public stage and nobody knows where the fault lies but all are desperate to find it.'

'That is as maybe but the talk is all that you fight constantly and that your tongue has grown a little over-sharp for his taste.'

Margaret looked at her rival closely, seeing the tight lines newly etched around the older women's mouth and eyes. 'You don't look well. Is it true?'

'Yes, it is true.' The words were spat not spoken. 'Of course it is true, how can it be any other way after what you had us do? You were supposed to take a child, not my husband! Why do you think I returned? Because I could not trust him near you and your whorish tricks!'

Dear God, she thinks she has lost him; she will betray us. If she loses her belief in him, I have no more hold on her.

Her voice was rising; people were beginning to look without any pretence.

'Jacquetta, for God's sake, calm yourself.'

Margaret forced a laugh as though her raised tones were some kind of jest.

'I don't know what you mean and I don't want to know. There cannot be a rift between you!'

Margaret moved closer and took her hand, forced her to stillness.

'Jacquetta, there cannot be a rift, do you understand? It would harm us all. You need to be a loving wife, whether you feel it or not, and make him a loving husband. He is nothing to me, that business is done.' She meant it: the days she had dreamed of Rivers were long gone and the rumours had unnerved her as much as the thought of having them both returned to Court.

I cannot give air to gossip; any public split in the marriage could make one or both reckless.

She drew a deep breath and arranged a more welcoming smile on her face: it would not be enough to fool Jacquetta but I might be enough to lull her.

'Jacquetta, forgive me. We are old friends and deserve to reacquaint ourselves with a little more grace than this.'

Margaret rose and drew her back to the wider circle, trusting that the balance of others would soothe the mood.

'Sit here with me and our old friends and tell us all about your family; I have missed your stories of their exploits and you were always my favourite storyteller. Perhaps an afternoon of memories would be a warming pastime in this October chill.'

She was conscious of how stilted she sounded but no one commented and Jacquetta, at least, still knew how to play her part. Warming to being placed firmly at the centre of attention, she raised a smile as the other women bustled around, fetching cushions and calling for honeyed fruits and cakes like children themselves.

Margaret sat back, aware how much her circle needed a diversion: Westminster had been a tense place for the past few days and she had been a tense mistress once again. She had set the trap against everyone's advice and against Henry's pleas that Warwick be ig nored not summoned to defend himself against the charges of piracy and aggression laid against him by the outraged French. Everyone knew that if ever there was a man less suited to being Captain of Calais and commander of the seas it was Richard Neville: a cutthroat pirate parading as an admiral. She would have stripped him of the title as soon as Parliament had been re-called and given it to any man with sea-legs and an ounce of integrity but Henry would countenance nothing, believing in the oaths men had spoken as he believed in his Bible.

She had argued the case so carefully: Warwick had destroyed a Castilian fleet to save England from a threatened invasion that did not exist and the people celebrated in the streets as though he had beaten a great French armada; the looting he had unleashed against the Hanse Towns only furthered his reputation as a man of action; the name of Henry V was on too many tongues and all the time York stood waiting behind him, fanning the whispers, drawing the King's name into a comparison that could only weaken him. Warwick's wings had to be clipped: he was becoming too much the people's favourite. She had worn down the arguments and so, she thought, she had won.

She had demanded the enquiry, she had gambled that Warwick would be caught and crippled by it; she was beginning to fear that all she had done was turn the Court into a powder-keg and given a stage to a master performer. Warwick had not come to the Commission like a penitent: he had come like a conquering hero with a retinue 700strong; his men swarmed every corridor and cranny of the Palace like a cloud of scarlet locusts, leaving her and her women confined to their chambers for propriety's sake. Anything that brought entertainment, even if it was a brittle afternoon with Jacquetta, was a welcome respite.

The atmosphere did soften but it was to be short-lived: Margaret had barely begun to be irritated by Katherine and Osanna's squabble over who had eaten too many of the candied violets when the chamber door flew open.

'Madame, you must not leave the room. Not one of you.'

It was Wiltshire on the threshold, a sword poorly concealed behind his back so it would not appear drawn in the Queen's presence.

'Warwick's men have run to fighting through the kitchens and cannot be confined; they have attacked your servants and there are brawls everywhere. You must stay here for safety until we restore calm.'

It was clear from Wiltshire's lack of his usual mannered courtesy and extravagant manner that he took the threat seriously; Margaret, unable to switch so quickly from a calmed threat to a new one, found it hard to believe that Warwick would mount an actual attack within the Palace walls and could not hide her scorn.

'My dear Lord Wiltshire, is this some new way you have of trying to engage my ladies, by frightening them and then acting the gallant knight who would rescue them? You have tried it before and it does not work.'

He would not indulge her for a moment.

'This is not a game, Madame, I mean it: you must not leave these rooms.' He would have left as abruptly as he had come if she had not challenged him, conscious as she was of the paling faces around her.

'Then if it is a real cause for concern, you must tell me what has happened and tell me properly. Surely Warwick can control his own men? I am sorry, but this is too hard to believe.'

'Warwick can control his men but he will not; it is Warwick who started it.' Wiltshire's fury was clear in his brittle tone. 'Warwick has nothing but contempt for this commission we have called him to. He made a mockery of it from the start.'

You warned me he would do this; you warned me but you won't accuse me of failing, you are too loyal.

167

'He refused to answer any questions. All he has done is hurl accusations that I will not repeat in your hearing. He is a barbarian and we were foolish enough to treat him with the courtesy due to a nobleman.'

Wiltshire shook his head. 'As unbelievable as it sounds, there was a brawl in the hearing itself, blows exchanged within the Painted Chamber and this spilled out into the retinue crowding the outer rooms. Oh Warwick went quick enough to attend to it but he won't stop it, he encourages it; he repeated the slanders and had all his men echoing them...'

But then he paused and reddened. 'It is no matter what he repeats; I must go and assist in...'

It is my child, Warwick has named him as a bastard; dear God, what if he has accused Rivers?

'Repeating what? What has Warwick said that all his men would repeat, that leads to such behaviour in our royal palace?'

Margaret was on her feet, not caring now who heard her. 'If you care for my safety, you will tell me Wiltshire, or you will watch me leave this room and question others less delicate than you.'

Her safety was too important to him; he knew her too well to ignore her threat. 'Then at least let me be quick, I am needed. Warwick was told by Lord Rivers that he must resign his command of the seas by order of the King. Warwick refused: he said the King was in no mind to give such orders so the demand must arise with you and he would take no orders from a slattern or the fool she cuckolded. And then he shouted that he might consider withdrawing if the little Prince was renamed not for the King but for his true father.'

There was a gasp, from Jacquetta Margaret was sure but she could not bear to look.

Wiltshire continued, clearly not trusting his nerve if he were to stop.

'At that, a fight broke out and the man most insulted struck Warwick a blow. Warwick would have hit back but the noise of the men brawling outside took him away.'

'Who struck him? Who thought themselves insulted?' As she spoke, she felt Jacquetta's hand take her arm: if Rivers had been the one to fight, it was surely over with for all of them. But Wiltshire looked confused, as if she should have known.

'Why Somerset of course. Warwick looked right at him when he said it; it was the old insult about Somerset's father.'

Margaret gripped Jacquetta's hand tight, willing her not to give them away, willing herself to sound more commanding than she felt.

'Of course; it is such an old and worthless slur, I had forgotten it. Well it is clear: Warwick slanders his King, his Queen and his Prince and allows his men to draw their swords in our palace; these are the acts of a traitor and they will not be borne. Go; see that the fighting is stopped and that any man known to be involved is properly punished. Do not disturb the King with this.'

Wiltshire was once more her champion. 'And Warwick? What would you have done with him?'

She willed herself to stay calm: it was her moment of triumph; it had to be carefully done.

'He needs to be taught a lesson. Have him arrested and taken to the Tower and, when he has cooled his heels, then we will have a proper trial.'

She thought she had him; for a brief, beautiful moment she thought she had him but she was too late. The cry went up to capture Warwick but he had already fled, gone through the kitchens and out to the Thames like a common thief. By the time a reward was offered, he was on a boat and safe to Calais with the next tide, parading the bruise he got from some miss-swung spit as though it were a mark of honour and decrying Margaret for a murderess who would have taken his head. And that she would have done. He had behaved like a traitor and run like an outlaw with York's protection at every turn and it would take her another year to have them named and accepted for what she always knew they were.

London and the Midlands: 1459-60

Thirteen years I had been a Queen, five years I had been the mother of an heir and still I looked over my shoulder at every turn and knew no peace and no comfort. Henry gave the appearance of health perhaps but it was a fragile state that a moment's passing could lose; here was no real King to hold his country strong. So who broke the peace? In truth, not one of us for there was never a peace to be broken, there was simply a waiting, a reckoning to come. I had thought my son would make me safe; I was wrong. Henry had thought a game of peace would keep us safe; he was wrong and I had been a fool to let him have his mummery. And York watched our senseless charade and thought he had the Crown so close he could grasp it.

'Give them their badges my pet and smile, remember, smile at every one of them.'

Margaret gestured to the men drawn up before them and put an encouraging hand on Edward's shoulder, not that he needed one: he loved pageantry as much as anyone and was slowly beginning to understand its importance.

'It's my badge isn't it? They're all going to be my soldiers.'

She had to mask her smile at his serious little face, 'yes, your badge and your men. They are fighting to protect the Crown for you, for their beloved little prince who will one day be their King.'

Edward nodded, 'like Father, I know.' And then his next question all but disarmed her with its innocence. 'Is Father a good king? Some people say he doesn't rule the way he should.'

Out of the mouths of babes; my grandmother was right.

'He is a very good king, as you will be one day, but you will be a different kind of king that is all. Now go and practise being a soldier!'

A short answer, a light tone; nothing that could play into her enemies' hands.

He needed no more persuasion and toddled off towards the waiting men, a basket filled with silver swan feathers clutched tight in his chubby fist. More spectacle; more show. It had been a deliberate choice to decorate the soldiers not with Henry's badge but with the silver swan's feather that would evoke memories of the standard carried into battle by the great Black Prince. Such a fearsome name but he lived on in the men's hearts with the same fervour they still felt for Henry V and Richard the Lionheart, their heroes of legend.

And they will feel those echoes when they see my Edward's badge. How can they fail to have hope for the future when they saw their little Prince carrying symbols they associate with the great kings of their past?

He was the sweetest sight: handing out his sign to battle-hardened men with such a solemn little frown on his baby's face they had to bite down their smiles so as not to hurt his feelings. They loved him and cheered his name and his mother watched their hopes settle round his little shoulders like a cloak.

'I wish the whole country could see this; maybe York would hold less sway if my boy could weave his magic everywhere.'

Margaret saw Somerset smile and had the grace to blush. 'I am a fond mother, I know but he does win their hearts.'

And yet I have no one to replace him: where I have one, York has four and maybe that is all that matters in the end.

As if he read the too dark thought, Somerset smiled a kinder smile.

'He does. He acts like a king and fills the soldiers with hope; you cannot want for more than that. We have repaired palaces and re-armed the guards, recruited men everywhere that are loyal to the King and sometimes I think that is all we need to win' he gestured towards the cheering men. 'Prince Edward with his sunny smile, inspecting the troops on his little pony.'

It was a fiction and they both knew it but it lifted the clouds for a while.

***

'Is this was we waited for? Is this what we waited for all through spring, all through summer, this?' Margaret could no longer tell if it was rain that lashed her face or tears, whether it was the knife-slash of the wind or something too close to fear that made her shake but she could not bear it. 'Answer me, someone! We have waited and watched and prepared through a summer so hot I thought the sky itself would boil. We have made our soldiers wait while the crops in their fields wilted faster than they could be cut and the rivers turned to paths of dust so that their families went hungry. Did we really make them wait through so much for this?'

But no one would speak, her commanders were as lost as her; she could not forgive them for it. 'Look at you, dear God, there is not a man left among you. How can this have happened? We knew York was coming, we knew he planned to meet the Earl of Salisbury's forces at Ludlow and take the attack, even when he lied about his loyalty. We knew all this but what good did it do us?'

'It did nothing because they knew more than us.' It was Clifford who finally answered, his voice dulled by exhaustion.

'What do you mean? Audley promised me that he would win, he promised me that this would be our revenge for St Albans...'

'And Audley is dead so what did he know? Our great commander is dead and his body beheaded on York's command. And Sefton and Carrington and Welles and Hesketh and God knows how many men, 2,000 at the last guess, so I think you should forget his promises.'

Clifford's exhaustion had turned to a fury to match her own.

'Madame, you ask whether this was what we waited for, look at it and before God don't ask that question again. We did all we could but York was better, that is the truth of it. His archers were better, his spies were better; he knew the direction the charge would come from almost as soon as we did and he knew better than to charge across a river like Audley made us do...'

'Enough; enough.'

His words were shaming, the sight before her was shaming. She stood on the mud of what had once been Blore Heath and saw the truth of his words in every corpse strewn before them, in the river so full of blood it ran with an unearthly red as though Hell had split open and sent its fires spinning through.

'The Yorkists accuse me of bloodlust, of wanting this war; they are mad. How could anyone want this? Perhaps if you are young and foolish with something to prove or old and drunk with only memories to cling to, you might find combat glorious but this...'

She shook herself, aware from the blank faces around her that men who had fought in what she could only witness had no interest in her revulsion for what they had had to do.

'What of York now?'

'He is long gone and took the carnage with him.' Clifford shrugged, 'we should have wished for another St Albans. This battle saw cruelty beyond anything that Warwick unleashed that day. York showed not a moment of mercy: he chased the men down like blood-hungry dogs attack a dying fox and slaughtered them without a thought.' Clifford stopped, too numb from defeat and too battle-weary to continue.

'He will pay for this; I will make him pay so dearly for this.'

She spoke the words more to herself than to any of the broken men about her but she meant them to her very soul. At that moment, stood on that battlefield, deserted by everybody but the dead, she hated him as she had never hated him before.

'We will all pay for this.' Wiltshire's voice was as blank as Clifford's. 'We will all pay and carry on paying because the divisions across this country are too strong to mend.'

He paused as though she might rebut him but she had neither the heart nor the belief. 'And the country is divided because the centre is gone. The crown sits on a head without the strength to wear it and we will all push and snap around it like dogs quarrel about a bone until someone snatches it up.'

And then you will turn on him. We all know the truth but none of us will admit it: the Crown is an empty prize which destroys its wearer; once you have it, it is already lost.

'So what is your answer?'

She had to challenge him; to admit he was right would be to lose, to let the malaise of defeat infect them too deeply.

'Do we stop? We can see the cost in front of us, so do we stop? Do we let York have the Crown and trust he will let us sit out our lives on the sidelines, swapping stories of who we used to be?'

She looked around her; no one would meet her gaze.

'You are right, this will continue and we will all pay while there are sons to replace dead fathers and families enough left to care where their loyalty lies. So I ask you again: do we stop?'

Still no answer.

'Then we will pursue him.'

A simple order given on a battlefield that rang the death knell for so many men; given without any sense that there might be a choice. 'We may have been outplayed here but our forces are stronger, they are greater in number and now our men will be more consumed with anger than his. We will pursue him.' There was not a voice raised in dissent; she did not expect there to be.

So the army marched and victory, which had faded to a dream, suddenly danced back into view. York's men could not be trusted to stay loyal once they knew victory was uncertain and the tide of men and favour began, it seemed, to turn towards Margaret's suddenly growing forces. As they swept towards Ludlow through a rain-sodden October, hearing stories of turncoats and deserters, she thought again she had them both. York and Warwick were so close, so outnumbered, she could feel her hand tightening its grip on the crown with every mile they advanced. But the moment slipped past before they caught it in its pirouette and the prize eluded her again.

York had learnt what Margaret had not: when to fight and when to flee. As the Lancastrian army assembled, York was already skipped back to Ireland, one son with him and one son sent safe to Devon and Warwick had taken ship for Calais. Henry gave thanks for a battle averted; Margaret took refuge in curses and rages that had her women scurrying from her faster than her quarry had fled. She was clever enough to keep her anger for private show; in public she made their retreat look like a triumph. She paraded her army through Ludlow like conquering heroes and, if the soldiers were too free with the wealth of the town, then she counted it as a useful lesson for those who dared to harbour the King's enemies. She was grace itself with York's wife Cecily, left cowering in Ludlow Castle with the youngest of her children and expecting imprisonment or worse. She called Parliament, had York and his followers attainted at last and their estates forfeit, had every lord and bishop she could summon sign an oath of loyalty to the King, to the Prince and, by default, to her. It looked like a triumph; it did not feel like one.

All I had truly built was another Loveday, another show; nothing now would feel like a triumph until York was dead.

***

'My dear Lord Wiltshire, it seems that every time I see you, you are crashing through my doors as though every fiend in Hell was on your tail! What are we all supposed to do? We expect a dashing courtier and all we see nowadays is a ruffian! What on earth has happened this time?'

James Butler had once again burst into Margaret's rooms in a dishevelled state and her tone, kept light for fear of frightening Edward who was curled up reading at her side, belied how disturbed she was at his appearance. She was beginning to too closely associate him with bad news.

'Osanna, take Edward to Lady Alice. No, no protests my pet.'

Edward's lip had pulled and his stare had grown quite mutinous at the mention of his nurse, poor Lady Lovell, who he considered himself quite too old for and who he was constantly leading a merry dance.

'Mr Ashby will be with you next week, just as I promised you.'

She patted the book he had been picking his still stumbling way through.

'Look how clever you have been to read his book with all these descriptions of how good little princes should behave so they grow into wise kings. I know you have taken note of his advice which is why you will be a very good pupil for him and then there will be no more need of nurses.' She shook her head as he quite clearly latched onto her last words as the only ones of interest. 'But until then, Edward, you have to do your duty: Lady Lovell has been kind to you and you will be respectful to her. If you have truly studied his lessons carefully, Mr Ashby will expect no less of you.'

The frown had gone before it could settle: nothing could cloud his temperament for long and he was gone with a smile and a kiss and a promise of candied violets later if his increasingly fraught nurse's report of him was good. Wiltshire, meanwhile, had been settled close to the fire with a cup of spiced wine to keep out the January frosts but it was clear that his mood, at least, had not lifted. Margaret held her voice as light as she could but he would not be easily softened into smiles; the unease in the room was becoming palpable.

'James, what has happened?'

His handsome face was too drawn, the dark circles under his eyes too pronounced. She reached out a hand but he either did not see or could not respond to the gesture.

'I know nothing ails the King so I can only think that it is York who has made you look so fierce. Is that it? Is he returned from Ireland?' Still no response; he stared into the fire like a man who would never get warm again.

'Is it Warwick then? Is he still playing the pirate out of Calais? If not them, what is it? Please don't tell me that something has happened to Somerset.'

The attempt to keep the mood steady was clumsy and her voice was rising. She was aware that Wiltshire, along with most of the men around her, had thought little of her decision to allow Somerset to take the command of the seas against Warwick. She knew herself it had not been well-considered, that it was based more on the memory of the father than the ability of the son. News that her attempt to send Somerset to Guines where he might at least hold Warwick a little at bay had been a failure would not have come as a surprise. Wiltshire, however, shook his head.

'Nothing has happened to Somerset, but he has done little to help himself or anyone else.' He sighed but still did not look at her.

'Forgive me, I must appear to talk in riddles but I have ridden hard from Kent and taken little rest.'

He shook his head as she started to speak.

'Let me tell you as best I can even if it is not as clear as you might want. There was an attack. Warwick, or at least his man, Sir John Dynham, has struck at Sandwich and captured the entire fleet that Somerset intended to use to regain some control of the Channel. Dynham's fleet was so quick that no warning was given, there was simply no time.' Wiltshire rubbed at his roughened face and continued almost as if he was talking to himself. 'Dynham must have had spies and help, there are surely enough Yorkists in Kent who would have stopped any attempt to raise the alarm; perhaps we should have moved against them sooner but we didn't see the danger. No matter, it is too late now. They have done their work; the raiders got into Lord River's lodgings so easily, I can only think that they must have had men in place for days.'

At the mention of Rivers Margaret set her cup down quickly lest the wine spill over. If he noticed her shaking hand and the matching tremor in her voice, he said nothing.

'You do talk in riddles and you need to talk much plainer. What of Lord Rivers? What do you mean? Was he on board ship? Was he captured with the fleet? What raiders in his house? You make no sense; tell me simply what has happened!'

He was not looking at her but Katherine was. Margaret saw her frown and knew her companion at least had noted the loss of composure, had seen the way Margaret clutched at the arm of her chair as though she would fall from it. Wiltshire, still acting as if he spoke without an audience, continued as she had asked although his voice was a monotone as he laid out the facts of the raid.

'Lord Rivers had not sailed: he was due to go with the fleet to Guines on the morning tide and had remained in his lodgings. But someone must have warned Warwick of the plans: the raiders seemed to know Rivers' every step. The raid came the night before:

Rivers and his son were sleeping but Dynham's men seized them from their beds and have them under guard already in Calais. They would have taken Lady Bedford too but her husband pleaded for her and she was allowed to stay. It was she who raised the alarm.'

So Jacquetta, at least, was safe but not Richard and not Anthony. Margaret could barely breathe: she might trust Richard not to betray her but she feared what Jacquetta might do to save her beloved son. If she was to bargain with Warwick and tell him the truth, they were all lost.

'Why do they take him, James? What is Warwick's game?'

There was too much fear in her voice: Katherine's questioning stare was now quite open.

'It is not a game. Why has Warwick taken him? Simply because he can. There has been no reason given: they have been held for two days now and there is no word of a ransom. They haven't been harmed; we know that much from the sailors who witnessed their capture.'

Wiltshire's voice was as dark as she had ever heard it; there was little trace now of the dashing courtier.

'We have been waiting to see what move the Yorkists would make and they have finally shown us. What else can Warwick be sending us but a warning, a sign of what he can do, of the true extent of his power? I think it is clear: the waiting is done and we must prepare for an invasion.'

He was right in everything he said.

***

'There is nothing to be had in this Court but rumour and I am heartily sick of it!'

Margaret threw the embroidered cloth she had torn more than

sewn on the floor.

'I don't want to hear one more word about slanderous songs fools are singing in taverns or preparations for battles we don't even know will be fought.'

She kicked the brocade across the floor and flung her embroidery silks after it. Her women, inured now to her fits of temper, barely registered the mess.

It had been another tense spring. All the support she had thought she could summon to stop Warwick parading his power up and down the Channel had disappeared like mist on a summer morning. Her Lord Admiral, Henry Holland Duke of Exeter, could have had the Earl as an open target as he sailed back to Calais after weaving plots with York in Ireland but Warwick had kept on sailing unmolested as Holland's men mutinied against the order to attack and he could do nothing to command them.

Everyday brought new reports of ballads pinned to city walls and sung by anyone who could find a voice at the bottom of a tankard that named Margaret as a whore and Edward a bastard. The slanders were worse in the South and were shouted down quick enough in Coventry when she rode out but their poison was being felt in every corner and she could feel the people slipping away. And all the while Henry was moving back into his shadow-world, the whole Court could sense it. Blore Heath had made him fearful and the Yorkist flight had done nothing to settle him. When Francesco dei Coppini, the Papal Legate, had declared his support for York, Henry did not speak for three days.

At Margaret's outburst, Katherine stopped whispering to the little circle around her but her face was mutinous. Her women were wary of her now and Margaret knew they gossiped; their closeness was gone and now they watched her, Katherine worst of all, and watched Edward too as though they might see some truth of the rumours in his face and bearing. Her only comfort was that he favoured her: she played on it, calling him 'my little Anjou' and mak ing much of family likenesses no one could argue against. Everywhere there was talk of war and the waiting had everyone's nerves stretched and everyone's temper frayed.

Still she did not expect Katherine's complete refusal to change the subject.

'I don't think this is idle talk, Madame, but something you should hear; they are saying in the streets that Coppini gave York a papal blessing and now all the men in London are flocking to his cause. They think York will come to the City and they will welcome him.'

There was a certainty in her voice that stopped Margaret unleashing her anger and had her shouting for a servant instead.

'Get Waynflete, now. If these stories are true I want to know from my Chancellor, not from Court gossip.'

The squire's return was quick as he had run to obey, but his face was fearful. 'Archbishop Waynflete is not here, Your Majesty.'

This time the waiting women instinctively backed away as Margaret leapt to her feet. 'Where is he? He cannot have left without my permission. Who told you he has gone?'

The boy was almost incoherent now, his voice shook so much.

'His secretary. He said, he said that, that the Archbishop has resigned. I know nothing more, I swear it.'

They are deserting me; I am losing before the battle has started.

'Send for Wiltshire,' she waved the boy away; there was nothing to be gained from questioning him further. 'Send for him now and you had better all pray that he comes or I will make you all pay.'

It was a day and a night before he came: by the time he arrived, Margaret was stretched to breaking point and most of the Court was feigning sickness to avoid her.

'It is war.'

His usual blunt delivery, nothing dressed up to ease her feelings. 'York's son, the Earl of March, has sailed into Sandwich with Warwick, Salisbury and Coppini in his train. There is no pretence this time of saving the King from false advisors. It is war.'

'So there will be no more waiting, they finally play their hand.'

The first real declaration of a fight for the Crown: it was almost a relief.

'Then we will win. A king is still a king and his office is a holy one.' She had heard it expressed often enough and seen how people would continue to kneel to Henry even when there was precious little left of the man; it had to be true. 'The country will rise for Henry and we will have this matter finally done.'

But Wiltshire laughed, 'you would be very foolish to believe that. The people of Sandwich threw open their town to March as though he were a conquering hero; they celebrated and feted him and cheered him through their town like a God become a man.'

She shook her head, his words made no sense. 'Because they are tired of the raids, surely, and merely relieved that they are over.'

'If it was just Sandwich then perhaps, but it is not.'

Wiltshire paused as though weighing his words.

'It spreads, this feeling for York and his brood, like a disease. Even Bourchier has prised himself out of his Canterbury comforts; he led the clergy of the county in a welcome for March as though he was royalty. And Lord Cobham has promised March every able man in Kent for his army and has already made good on his word. Madame, March has swept unchallenged through to London where the City fell at his feet like a dazzled bride.'

'What shall I do?' She could not think, could not comprehend what he was saying. 'Is there no one left loyal to me? How has this boy captured their hearts when the father never could?'

Will it always be my fate to look in the wrong direction for the fight? I thought York was my enemy; how can this boy have become some mythical hero, as though the sun itself shone through him, when the father cannot make anyone love him?

Wiltshire reached across the table and took her hand, a gesture so intimate it would normally have startled her but she was too lost to mind him.

'I don't know what it is about the boy, I swear I don't. His progress through the countryside was just as swift as Warwick's mocking progress across the seas: our men had no more substance before him than snow in sunshine and they disappeared as quick.'

His grip tightened as though he would anchor her back to the world; he could see it was slipping away.

'Margaret, I am sorry. I wish I could tell you that there are men who remain loyal but I don't know who they are. Bourchier has left us; Beauchamp, the Bishop of Salisbury and Waynflete. Even Lord Say has thrown in his lot with the invaders, even though his own father was murdered by Cade's rebels. The boy bewitches all of them.'

She groaned and shook her head but he carried on reciting a list of those who had suddenly discovered Yorkist blood in their veins. Nowhere went untouched. And, gradually, as he spoke, she became consumed with fury.

'They have given up on me like the worst kind of cowards.'

There was a darkness in her eyes that made him recoil.

'I should take their heads, all of them. I will, I swear it. I know what they think: they are weighing up a broken king, a French whore as a queen, and an heir they do not believe in against the promise of a man surrounded by sons with a fertile wife who knows her place and a pedigree steeped in England.'

Her eyes were black against the stark whiteness of her face; it was all Wiltshire could do not to cross himself.

'Well they are fools. Do they think that a crown can be surrendered? Do they think I will give it up like some bauble I am bored with?' She did not see him, he knew it and she would not be argued with, no matter what was to be unleashed. 'We fight.'

It was as simple and as deadly as that.

**

It was deadly and it was swift.

The Yorkists moved as fast as Wiltshire knew they would: through Kent and into London and, by the 4th of July, they were swinging North as fast as Margaret's army could muster. Twenty, thirty thousand, maybe more and, every day, more men flocking to join them; no matter how much Margaret pretended the opposite, she was truly afraid. What did she have to offer? A king who shook and cried at any mention of the battlefield.

She tried. She demanded to take the lead and ride at the army's head with Edward at her side but the clamour of opposition was deafening and could not be countermanded. The soldiers would follow even the weakest, most hopeless man if he wore a crown before they would ever follow a woman and there was nothing she could do to change it. Yolande's long-ago lessons had all been true and all the raging in the world could not change them.

She marched out of Coventry. She had no choice; she had no real support. No Somerset, no Exeter, no Northumberland: they were all too far away and could not be called in time. She rode out with an army motivated too much by hate and fear rather than experience and hope. An army that sacked Northampton and put it to the torch and drove too many men to the Yorkist banner who might have fought for her. It was a pitiless act, the first of many but she was becoming too used to the hatred whipping up around her to care.

***

'We have to leave, now. Gather whatever you can carry but we need to go.' Margaret whirled through the room, grabbing cloaks and hoods, anything that might hide them on the road.

'What has happened?' Osanna's dark eyes were like pools of pitch in her white face.

'We have lost the battle.'

Alice, ever the more practical one, immediately sprang to her feet and began hustling Edward into his boots and cloak.

'We lost the battle because we were betrayed and now we must run before York finds us.'

'God save us, he will burn Coventry and all of us in it.'

Osanna was in tears in seconds and at the sight of her frailty, a luxury she could not afford, something in Margaret snapped.

'Perhaps he will; I could hardly blame him if he did but do you really think God will save us if he tries? If you do, you have a far stronger faith than I.'

Osanna screamed as Margaret pinched her hard.

'Wake up woman and look around you: this is what reliance on God has brought us to, fear and flight. If Henry's endless prayers have not reached Him, I very much doubt yours will. I would rather put my faith in strong horses so take what you can and move!'

It had the desired effect on her speed if not her weeping but that was more easily ignored.

'What did you mean, Madame, betrayed?'

Alice was bundling Edward towards the stables, ignoring his protests at being so hurried, 'and why are you riding out without a guard or without waiting for the King?'

'Because my guard is all dead and the King is taken.'

The words were too blunt; Margaret saw Alice start to shake and knew she had to calm her tone. 'Alice, please don't fail me. You are the strong one, if you crumple, they all will. I will tell you everything once we have the horses ready, I promise but you have to do as I ask now.'

It was enough: there were no more questions until they were saddled and on the road out of Coventry, even then Margaret could give her only the barest details as their pace quickened.

'We were betrayed by Lord Grey of Ruthin: he took York's side and turned the battle. Our losses are truly dreadful: Buckingham, Shrewsbury, Beaumont, Egremont, they are all dead.'

'And you know this for sure?'

'For sure.'

She tightened her grip on Edward who rode in front of her for the sake of speed. 'The soldiers who came to warn us gave me too much detail for me to doubt it.'

Alice looked across at Edward but he was paying no attention: what was a frightening escape for them was an exciting adventure to him.

'And the King?'

'York has him.'

What more could she say? When the news had been brought, she had cried and shook and feared for her husband's safety; now she had no tears left to shed and the only person she cared about was her son.

York would be a fool to let Henry live a second time. He is as good as lost, there is nothing to do but run and save his heir.

Alice knew it as well as she; they rode the rest of the way, out of the Midlands to the safety of Owen Tudor's grim fortress at Harlech Castle, in silence. Wales where York was too hated to pursue her; where Edward would be, for a time at least, safe.

Wales, Scotland and the North: 1460-61

'They do not want him.'

Henry Holland nestled himself into the cushions of the chair as though he had just arrived home safe from a crusade rather than a ride to London and back, and grinned. 'They do not like him and they do not want him. Poor York, so close to the Crown and yet he cannot grasp it, it is almost pitiful.'

'Not to me. Poor York; what nonsense.' But Margaret had no real anger in her for all the pretence of a stern tone and Holland knew it. 'Shall I tell you all about his humiliation then or would that be too much of a bore?'

He dodged quickly to avoid the cushion and laughed at Edward's surprised delight. 'Your mother has quite an aim, young man; I might need your protection.'

'You will if you don't tell me everything!'

Margaret smiled with a warmth she had not felt in weeks and reached out a hand to Edward, 'come and sit here and listen to the way the people treated York and all his silly ambitions, my pet. We will beat him yet, you will see.'

'Do the people hate him?' Edward's face was so serious that Holland softened his exuberance.

'No, I don't think that they do but I don't think they could love him and you have to love your King.' He was talking to all of them but his attention was on Edward. 'When York first rode into London, with his son...you do know who he is?'

Edward nodded, 'the Earl of March, the one they say is as golden as the sun; the one Mother fears more than his father.'

Holland laughed at Margaret's gasp of surprise and Somerset's snort of amusement. 'Very nicely said. Well, when York first rode into London, the people cheered to see him. He had his other sons with him, Richard and Edmund and George, and they made quite a splendid sight.'

'And Father the King, was he there to?'

Holland's face clouded but he answered honestly. 'Yes, he was; they had him in a carriage and in chains. It was very sad to see and many of the people wept at that but more cheered and that is the truth.'

He stopped but Margaret motioned him to continue. 'So the crowds were pleased to see York and he must have thought he could have the Crown easily enough.' He paused again, 'I did not want to go to London as your Mother well knows: I thought the Parliament that York summoned was a trap and I wouldn't come back from it.'

'Then why did you go?' Edward looked at his mother, 'if it was dangerous, why did you send him?'

She shrugged, 'because I had to know what was happening in London. I couldn't go so Holland had to and I knew I could rely on his loyalty.'

After much persuasion, I could rely on his loyalty: Holland was reluctant, Somerset flatly refused to countenance the idea but I made Holland go because I could. As one day you will make people do things for you that they would rather not.

'Anyway, it was a triumphant entry to the City.'

Holland picked up the story before Edward could ask anything else. 'York is a clever man: he didn't march under his Yorkist badge but with banners which showed the arms of Lionel, Duke of Clarence who was the third son of Edward III.'

Margaret had not known that, 'so he finally uses his royal lineage in public. He must feel very confident of his claim.'

Holland shrugged, 'perhaps he did but his appeal to history did him little good. Oh he is clever enough at the pomp and the pageantry. I have never heard such fanfares as the ones that preceded him into the Palace of Westminster; it was as though a Roman Emperor conducted a Triumph. And his swagger as he approached the throne and laid his hand on its embroidered cushions as if they were already in his possession was quite something to behold.'

Ever the story-teller, Holland stopped to see how well he could hold his audience's attention; there was not a murmur in the room. 'York stood there and demanded that the Crown be placed upon his head as though every noble in the place would come running with it and fall at his feet and what do you think happened?'

He looked to his audience as though for an answer but they were like children waiting for a treat. 'Nothing!' He burst out laughing. 'Absolutely nothing. There was a silence deeper than this one and he waited and waited for a voice to be raised in support of "Richard Duke of York, King of England" and not one came! He didn't know what to do.'

'What did he do? What happened?' Edward was breathless now with excitement.

'Nothing, there was nothing he could do.' Holland grinned at him. 'There was nothing he could do because there is already a king on the throne. Archbishop Bourchier broke the silence and requested that York go instead to fetch the true King and bring him into Parliament; he was like steel, unbending, and York could do nothing. They don't want him, little Prince: they want your father and they want you.'

Edward laughed and clapped with delight and everyone followed him, Margaret loudest of all.

'He cannot have expected such a response: not one voice raised in support of him. That must have been a silence to deafen him!'

But once the laughter had died down and Edward, giddy with amusement, had been quieted and put to bed, she sent her ladies away and sat with Somerset to consider what the news really meant.

'His failure does not mean my victory, does it?'

Somerset shook his head, 'no, it does not. York will wear them down; it may take time but he is determined and he will do it.' He watched her carefully, 'you know that it is your son who is really at risk, not your husband: there might not be the mood to depose a king but deposing an heir, well that is much easier done.'

'I know and I feel utterly helpless. No matter what plans and strategies we make, the truth is I do not know which way to turn and I would value your counsel.'

Margaret looked around her at the solid grey walls that let barely any light through. 'For all Wales has been a welcome refuge, it has become a prison in these last weeks. I cannot not risk a return to London to plead my family's cause but who will plead it for me when all my knights are dead or unable to act? Holland cannot return to London and I know you will have no part of any Parliament York presides over. Wiltshire is in sanctuary: if he comes out, Warwick's men will do to him what they have done to Lord Scales and behead him without trial. Rivers is lost to me.' She could not go on but she did not need to for Somerset understood.

'And the Lords and Bishops summoned to Parliament will act as they are charged to do, in the interests of the country and its peaceful governance: they will defend the King, for that is what is right, and they will debate and discuss and weigh the merits of York against Lancaster and they will pore over the details of the law. It will all be properly done but nobody will truly speak for your son.
'

He sighed and looked away. 'Can you blame them? What man ever wants a child on the throne except those who see it as a way to seize power for themselves? And who truly wants a war that would rip a country apart? This is a Parliament with swords raised at its back. Its members will not see Edward as we do: as the boy who inspired the hopes of the soldiers, a boy already bearing himself like a Prince, a true heir to a true claim. They will see a child who cannot rule, a child, moreover, governed by a meddlesome mother whose loyalty is questionable and with a father whose sanity none would swear to.'

He stopped as though he had strayed too far but there was nothing she could say against him: she knew that rumour would swiftly start; she did not know why York had not already spread it. They would question Edward's bloodline and the shadows it cast. It would be carefully done so that no ill-word was spoken against the King but they would mark the pedigrees of the father and the grandfather and think the boy too close to the taint of madness. She knew it and could disprove it and could not speak it. That was the bitterest pill.

'Madame,' the urgency in Somerset's voice could not be ignored. 'Madame, you cannot stay here. You are not safe; Edward is not safe.'

'I know. I know. I have known from the moment we left Coventry that we could not stay here. Why else would I have been sending envoys to the North, to James II in Scotland if not to find out where real help may lie?' Her tone was harsh and he shifted uncomfortably under it but he did not bend.

'The North is loyal and the Scots will be as happy, as ever, to meddle in English affairs. There is a ship made ready for you to sail whenever you will command it but you still delay. If you know the danger, Madame, why do you stay?'

'Because if I leave without knowing how matters stand in London, it will be too much like a defeat!' She was on her feet, pacing the narrow confines of the room. 'Do you not see? While there is any hope that Parliament might uphold my child, I cannot leave and ally myself to what would be seen, I know, as an invading power.'

But Somerset shook his head, 'that is a foolish dream. You cannot influence anything, it is past that now. Your only hope is to find an ally and fight. You have no choice, Madame, no choice.'

***

The room was silent as it had been since the servants left, relieved to be dismissed. The remains of a meal no one had taken pleasure in were strewn across the table. An observer would have needed strong persuasion to believe any bonds of family existed between the two men facing each other from their pushed-back chairs, no matter the similarity clear in the hard lines of the their faces.

'You are a fool.'

The tone was pure contempt; son or not, York would have drawn his sword without Warwick's restraining hand.

'You are a fool and you know it.' Edward, Earl of March, watched his father's face darken and paid no attention whatsoever. 'Warwick knows it too, don't you?'

'I know that you owe your father more respect.' Warwick's tone was measured: he had no interest in taking sides, it was not his way. March laughed, 'really? Why? We have only achieved what we have because the people love me, not my father.'

He looked across at York whose rigid arm was still firmly in Warwick's grasp. 'Do you think that if I had stood in Westminster and claimed the Crown, the archbishops would have told me to go and fetch Henry?' He made a mocking bow, 'they would have fallen to their knees with joy; you know it.'

'You arrogant bastard.' York knew his son's words were true; it made him hate him even more. 'I have the Crown, what more do you want?'

If he had hoped for an apology, he was disappointed; March shook his head. 'No you don't and thinking that you do is why you are a fool. You don't have the Crown; you have the promise of a crown. You have made yourself heir when Henry dies, what does that matter? You have no more now than you did when you walked out of Westminster with your tail between your legs.'

'What more would you have me do?'

York stood up and shook Warwick off, crossing the room towards his son who simply sat and watched him come. 'I have disinherited Margaret of Anjou's child; everyone has accepted that, everyone has accepted me as the rightful heir. What else could I do?'

'You could have killed them.' The answer was so coolly given and so evidently meant that York stopped abruptly and stared at the boy's smooth face.

'What, you really never considered it?' March laughed. 'Then you are an even bigger fool than I thought. You should have killed Henry when you first took him; you should have demanded the child be given to you as Protector and killed him to. You aren't man enough to do either are you? That is why the people will never choose you and why Margaret of Anjou will keep fighting: you can be beaten, father, you can be beaten.'

And you cannot.

Warwick watched the two men; watched the father weaken as he saw the depths of cruelty in his son's eyes, depths he did not have for all his pretence of it.

Margaret of Anjou does not know what she is facing; March will destroy her and he will not do it for his father's reasons, however deluded they might be. March will not fight her for the good of the throne and its safekeeping, he will fight her for the sheer pleasure of power and he will not stop, at anything.

***

'Your Majesty, she arrives. I think your fortunes may finally be turning.'

James Lindsay's smile was as warm and comforting as his welcome had been since Margaret's bedraggled party had first arrived at Lincluden Priory. The Provost had shown them nothing but kindness, giving Edward, to his delight, the run of the stables and treating Margaret with every royal courtesy. It was much needed for their departure from Wales and arrival in Scotland had been less than auspicious. Their ship had sailed at night in weather as filthy as Margaret's temper soon became and landed at a Scottish port whose name not one of them could pronounce where the lodgings would not have pleased the meanest garrison. The beds were filled with fleas and the ice in the wind which howled through their chambers was fit to freeze the bones. They had woken after a dreadful night with the prospect of a hard ride through driving rain to be greeted by the terrible news that Margaret's ally James II was dead, killed at the siege of Roxburgh Castle and his young son now sat on the throne. Scotland, it seemed, was in no better a shape than England.

When they finally clattered through the gates of Lincluden, where Margaret had been promised safe lodging, she was close to breaking and near collapse. And yet she was furnished with such a welcome, she could not give into despair: Lindsay spoke only of the belief Scotland had in her cause and saw her furnished with writing materials, put messengers at her disposal and encouraged her to write messages of hope.

He refused to see me as anything but a brave queen with a noble cause and gave me the strength to be just that. He truly was the kindest of men.

At his urging, that first night she kept to her room and refused any company, instead writing letter after letter to anyone she thought she could still call friend: to Somerset, to Thomas Courtenay, the Earl of Devon, to Lords Roos, Clifford and Greystoke and to James's widow, Mary of Guelders. That was the longest of the many letters she wrote in those long cold hours and was a truly heartfelt appeal from one mother to another, a more truthful letter perhaps than any she had ever written.

And it seemed that Lindsay was right: she was not forgotten. Every day brought a new response to her fevered messages, a new promise of forces being amassed and men on the move. And finally, Mary herself sent word that she was on her way and would meet; would, in her words, 'let our sons build a friendship that would sustain them when they both became Kings'. It was a small light of hope that had left them both, mother and son, almost giddy with excitement.

'Is he really so close to my own age? Will he ride with me? Will we truly be friends?'

Margaret looked at her son who was so usually closeted with tutors, so increasingly and so obediently wrapped up in matters of state and duty, she had not thought how much he must long for companionship of his own age.

'He is nine to your six my pet which is not so great a gap and yes, his mother and I would very much like you to be friends. But he is a King, Edward, and he has newly lost his father; you may need to go a little gentle with him.'

But there was no need for any words of caution: within minutes the boys had discovered a mutual love of horses and fled to the stables, all thought of crowns and mourning forgotten. It was a heartening sight and lightened the mood for everyone.

'They will be friends and so will we; we will follow their example.'

The Scottish Queen, with her blonde hair and sparkling eyes all light to Margaret's dark, was all smiles and charm and grace: it was hard to resist her and equally clear that she knew it. The steelier side that stopped her ever granting a favour unless there was a reward to be had was well-hidden when she first drew her captives in. And they were different in more than just appearance; Margaret saw that quickly enough in the week they spent together at the Priory and the longer days that followed at the Scottish Court. Mary adored clothes and jewels in a way Margaret had only ever played at to keep her dressmakers happy; she loved court gossip and could spend hours poring over the latest romantic entanglements involving her women; she said whatever came into her mind as though she dared anyone to contradict her but in so playful a way, nobody would. And she had no thought of discretion: her dislike for her late husband was readily and often expressed, to Margaret's amusement and Lindsay's pretended disapproval. She was surrounded always by knights who seemed to think they were in some chivalric romance, their only role to rescue her. The Earls of Douglas and Angus, two of the biggest men Margaret had ever seen, with beards as wild as haystacks, were reduced to simpering maidens around her.

I underestimated her of course; she might have played at being the romantic princess but her silks and velvets hid iron. She knew exactly what she would give and exactly what she would take.

'How many men for your army, my dear Marguerite? How many would you like? Name a figure and they are yours.'

As quick as that she turned the conversation one night as though delivering such a force was nothing to her; as if it could be as easily conjured up as grains of sand on a beach. And if she wanted the stronghold of Berwick in return, if she demanded the garrison town of Carlisle as reward, how could she be denied? The borders between England and Scotland were ever-moving and those towns changed hands so often that their ownership was of little concern to Margaret when there were bigger prizes to be gained.

Perhaps I should stay, live out my life as the mistress of a Scottish laird; perhaps I will be happier, safer.

A constant thought but never a real one. She could not stay: Scotland was too wild for her, too far away from the power she craved.

She might be safe but she would only ever be an after-thought and there was nothing for her son; she watched the Scottish lords eye him like the wolfhounds they favoured circled the meat flung from the dining tables and knew it was only a matter of time before someone valued their money chests over their loyalty to Mary.

The promised army came and grew and, if she still felt any concern at re-entering England with an enemy force in her wake, it was no longer the time for such scruples. She could not stay because all her spies told the same tale: York was moving, his armies growing and he was heading North through the snow-covered December countryside to choose the battlefield; remaining where she was would give him an advantage she could never again allow.

***

'He is dead.'

Three short words.

'He is dead.'

Three short words she had waited an age to hear; she could not comprehend them.

'Can you swear it?' Her voice, her hands were shaking: so much rode on the answer. 'Do you have proof? Do not tell me such a thing unless you have proof.'

Sir Andrew Trollope, Margaret's commander in the field, would not sit although he looked grey with fatigue. The battle against the York-ist armies who had massed near the little town of Wakefield had barely been over for a day and it was clear that he had not yet slept. Margaret too was exhausted. After such a long march from Scot-land, she had been desperate to see the enemy for herself; she had wanted to ride out amongst the lines and let Edward charm and inspire the men who would fight his cause but neither Trollope nor Lord Clifford would hear of it and had left her in no doubt that they would have her carried from the field if she ignored them. With no other choice, she had retreated a few miles to Pontefract Castle where she had paced the rooms, refusing to eat or retire to bed, driving herself and her retinue to distraction as she waited for news before finally falling into a fitful sleep in a chair drawn close to the fire.

But if the news was true...

Sir Andrew's tone was as weary as his face but, as he spoke, some of the light of a battle well-made came back into his eyes.

'I am your proof. I saw him die myself, Madame, and watched his corpse get its beheading. And not just the father but the eldest son too is gone; Clifford put young Rutland to his own sword so there was no mistaking it and no chance of mercy even though the boy begged for it. Clifford demanded revenge for his father's death and there was not one among us who would deny him that. And Salisbury too, he was caught and killed not a mile from here. They are all dead and their armies routed. Your enemies are beaten. But if proof is what you need, well we brought you the spoils, Madame, and arranged them for your viewing. Let me show you.'

Still not truly believing him, she followed Trollope outside the main gate.

'There is your proof.'

The soldiers had indeed brought the spoils home and had festooned the heads on the castle walls as though they were holly boughs to welcome Christmas. Edmund of Rutland, barely a man, grizzled Salisbury and in the middle, a paper crown thrust on his bloodied filthy hair, Richard of York himself.

'Do not let Edward see this until I have schooled him how to behave. He has to see this like a Prince.'

They should have let me perform the coronation myself; I would have smeared his blood across my face like a pagan war mask.

'It is over.' She looked at the armies stretched around her, weary yes but victorious and ready to march on through the country to London and sweep the rest of the Yorkist threat away. 'We have them beaten.' 'No.' Trollope shook his head. 'No, we do not. He had other sons and they will not forgive this.'

But she was not listening: Richard of York had always been the prize and Richard of York was dead. Nothing else mattered.

***

She could not control her army: it was charged against her often enough and, even though she pretended otherwise, it was the truth. She could not pay them and she could not control them. The Scots are wild when they are in battle and wild when they are out of it and they have no love for the English; she knew it, she chose to ignore it and she as much as anyone paid the price. They looted as they swept down through the country to meet with Wiltshire's men; they looted without mercy after the second battle at St Albans.

I was a French Queen at the head of an army comprised of every demon that London and the South could conjure up; I breathed life into every damning story ever told about me.

The stories of outrage moved faster through the country than even her men could and every wrongdoing was built a thousand times as the stories of the approaching hellish legions moved from village to village. She could blame Yorkist tongues and simple minds who would turn any soldier searching for bread into a thing of nightmare; she could rage that monks have ever liked to make their chronicles fanciful. She did all that but she knew the truth: her army stole wherever they could and whatever they could be it food or women and they burnt whatever they were in the mind to burn. It did her no service for, as the stories grew, the barbarians drove as many men to the banners of Warwick and March as flocked to Margaret's side.

I claimed my victory and York's destruction too quick: it was one battle and I judged it as the whole war.

She had thought York's death was the answer: it was the spark that fired the real flame.

There was still a son to avenge his father; a golden shining man-boy who, or so his stories would have it, was a favourite of the heavens and not of Hell. Edward of March, now Duke of York in his turn had taken up his father's cause and, as Trollope had warned her they would, the people flocked to him like flies to dung. Late at night, when there was no one left to fool, she faced the truth: if the people had ever loved the father as they loved the son, her campaign would have been a short-lived one. She listened to the gossip about this new York even if she pretended it held no interest for her: that he was fearless in battle; that he was far more experienced with women by the time he was eighteen than many men achieve in a lifetime; that he commanded loyalty and could hold it. She listened and she knew: this Duke of York was a force far worse than the one whose death she had too loudly and so misguidedly celebrated.

***

'Your Majesty, there is a messenger. You need to receive him without delay.'

Lord Clifford's face was grave as he entered the chamber where Margaret was dining quietly with her women, all of them longing for some measure of rest and comfort. It seemed they had done nothing but ride since leaving Pontefract in January, spending weary days in the saddle and uncomfortable nights with whichever supporter would open their gates; reaching Kenilworth in the early weeks of February had been a blessing but, if they had hoped for some brief days of respite before they continued the march towards London, it was clearly not to be.

'What is it My Lord, do we get no peace? Tell me it is news of Wiltshire and Pembroke and great armies advancing to meet us and I will gladly admit him. It is such a cold night; we could do with something to warm our spirits.'

But Clifford was grave and would not be thawed by any attempt at lightness. 'He has news of them and their armies but it is . . . Madame, you need to hear this direct, there is nothing I can do to soften it.'

There was no choice but to agree. Margaret had little stomach for bad news: the tales and complaints of her army's excesses were enough and she had heard a pack of them. Wiltshire had landed in Wales and joined forces with Jasper Tudor: she knew that they were marching towards her, she had been waiting word of them for days. The boy who was brought in, however, was young and trembling and clearly no bearer of good news.

'Who has sent you?' Margaret tried to smile but he could barely meet her eyes.

'My Lord Wiltshire, Your Majesty.'

He was alive at least; that was something.

'Then your news must be important and you must tell it. Quickly now, tell me what makes My Lord Clifford's face so long.'

And still the boy would not smile or raise his glance. His voice was flat and quick as though he had practised what he would say and hoped for no question or interruption.

'There has been a battle, Your Majesty. The Earl of March that was, the Duke of York I should say, fought against your army in Wales and he has defeated them. There are thousands dead, thousands. My Lord Wiltshire has escaped but Owen Tudor is dead, chased seventeen miles from the battlefield and his head taken. Those who survived have fled, some to find you, some...' and then he faltered but she had already interrupted him.

'Dear God! Why must every victory we win lead straight to a de

203

feat? Why is it that for every one of that family we despatch, another rises up to torment me?'

There was no answer, how could there be. But the boy was still trembling and it was clear there was more. She turned her anger on Clifford; it was pointless to attack the messenger.

'Why didn't you tell me this yourself? Why would you leave this to a frightened child?'

'Because you need to hear the way he tells it. Finish your story, boy, and tell the Queen exactly as you told me. Tell her about the battle.'

'It was at a place the locals call Mortimer's Cross, in the Marches of Wales. My Lord Wiltshire had joined his men with My Lord Pembroke and was trying to bring them here but York would not allow it.' Again she interrupted him. 'Your master would not have wanted a battle there but he had strong men about him. So why did we lose it, boy? Are they so much better soldiers, these men who fight for York, than any we can command?'

Her tone was sharp now but his fear seemed to have gone: for the first time he looked at her properly.

Dear God, he looks possessed; that light in his eyes, it is unnatural.

'I cannot answer that, Your Majesty, but the soldiers think that God fights for York and that has made their side much braver than ours.' She was so shocked, she could not find the words to question him; she would have had him beaten for insolence or worse had not Clifford stepped in.

'Tell the Queen what you saw lad, do not try to find a meaning in it. Better heads than yours will look to that.'

The boy was no fool: he took the warning in Clifford's voice and dropped his gaze to the floor but he could not hide the awe in his voice.

'There was a sign before the battle, everyone saw it. Three suns appeared in the sky at the same time above York's army, all blazing and golden with light around them like you would see around the heads of saints. It lit him up like a fire came from him, we could all see it. Then the Duke of York fell on his knees and gave thanks to God; he said it was proof that his cause was just and that Heaven smiled on him. Everyone was staring and praying as though they were witness to a miracle. What else could it be if it were not a miracle? And now he takes a new badge: three suns to remind any-one who challenges him where God's favour truly lies.'

Clifford hustled him away then before Margaret's fury could be unleashed on his stupid, witless, enraptured head. She chased ev-eryone from the room as the fear began to flood through her. A sign: of course they would see it as a sign no matter what trick of the light it must surely have been. Soldiers before a battle, there can be no more superstitious group and Edward of York had played their simplicity with such a clever hand. With one simple gesture he had drawn up the battle lines and pitched Heaven against Hell; it was a masterly stroke.

***

She lived in a world where the old courtesies were gone. No one requested an audience any more, no one deferred to her. Every castle she settled on echoed to banging doors and running feet; she was a queen who could barely remember what it was to be a queen.

'Warwick is on the move and he has the King.' Clifford was barely through the door before he delivered his news.

'Where is he?' Margaret caught Osanna staring at her and quickly amended the question, 'and how is my husband? What news do you have of him?'

Clifford sat before he answered and drank deeply, he was dusty from the road and there was a tension in the lines of his face that did not bode well.

'Warwick marches out of London to meet the Duke of York. He has a sizeable enough army it seems, drawn from London and Kent and every southern county that fears these northern hordes we have unleashed. As for the King' he shrugged, 'there is no word except that he rides with Warwick.'

'Then Warwick must be stopped.' She moved the flagon of wine out of Clifford's reach. 'Do you hear me? He will dance Henry in front of the people like a puppet; we need the King under our banners, not adding to York's spell.'

'What do you need us to do?' Somerset's steady voice, less hot-headed than Clifford's.

'We need to move.' She looked at her councillors and it was obvious from the gleam in their eyes that they were in agreement: this wait for battle was stretching everyone's nerves as thin as gossamer.

'We need to gather our armies and take the battle to Warwick and' she smiled at them and saw the answering savagery on their faces, 'and if we meet him at St Albans then that would be a fitting place to revenge ourselves and end this challenge. Without Warwick's strength, York will be easy to break.'

Trollope laughed: 'it is not if we meet at St Albans: that is where we will choose to fight. Give me the command and I swear the second battle there will sweep away any memories of the first.'

'It needs to be properly finished this time. Do you understand?'

'It will be properly fought and properly finished, you have my word.'

Trollope pulled out one of the maps lying on the table. 'We will move the army down through Grantham, Peterborough and Huntingdon into Dunstable; that is 13 miles outside St Albans and Warwick will expect us to make camp there ready for a daytime battle.' He grinned. 'Except we will march through the night and attack at first light; we will be in the streets of the city before they have broken their fast.'

'That is too much to ask the men to do; they will be exhausted.' But Trollope waved away Somerset's objection.

'Providing we let them have free hand in the towns on the way, they will do whatever we ask. Unless you object to that, Your Majesty?'

She shrugged, 'what are a few more towns that hate me? They will forget soon enough once we have beaten York and rewarded their citizens.' She pulled the map towards her, tracing its outlines. 'Do whatever you need to as long as you keep your promise and end it: Warwick dies, nothing else will do.'

Battles are fought on belief as much as they are fought on men and arms. We had been the losers in this at Mortimer's Cross, now we were the winners.

It seemed, at first, as though Trollope would be as good as his word. Warwick did not believe the army would reach him so quickly; he did not believe Margaret could field so many men; he did not believe the attack would come from the South, he expected it from the North. He did not listen to his commanders, or his men or his brother, Lord Montagu, who all read the battle differently and all judged it better. By the time Warwick had the evidence that everything was quite the opposite to what he had expected, it was too late: Lancaster had the advantage and Warwick's men had lost their faith. They would no longer obey any order he uttered, no matter that he finally gave the ones they wanted. The runners who crowded Margaret's tent told everywhere the same story of confusion and betrayal: Warwick did not realise the seriousness of the attacks on Montagu's position and did not send the reinforcements pleaded for; Yorkist forces had seen the truth of what would come and were deserting in their droves, the ranks simply would not hold. By nightfall it was clear that the battle was hers and the name of St Albans would no longer be one full of shame.

And yet, for all Trollope's fine promises, my victory was tainted.

Warwick had escaped and there was not a man left with the energy to pursue either him or the sizeable army he still commanded. He could ride to meet with Edward of York and there was nothing more to be done. Despite the knowledge of victory and the relief at losses far lower than they expected, the mood among Margaret's captains was a sombre one: the capture of Warwick would have been something solid to show the soldiers, they would take it as a sign that the cause they fought for was just, a sign to rival any heavenly portents the Yorkists might claim. What followed then was a shock to all of them.

***

Margaret could feel the velvet of her robe too thick around her neck: it had gathered so much dust it was as though the cloak had grown another collar. She longed for a warm bath, clean linen and hair that smelt of scented oil not mud and rain; things she had once taken for granted and expected, things that now felt as scarce as hen's teeth. She sighed and forced her attention back to the reality of the over-crowded, pungent tent.

'The men need food and wine. They are exhausted and we must reward them properly for what they have done today...'

Margaret broke off, it was clear that no one was listening and that everyone had turned towards the back of the tent. 'What's happening?'

And then she saw the cause of the commotion and almost dropped to her knees as half the men around her had already done. 'Henry? Dear God, husband, is it really you?'

She walked uncertainly forward to where he stood, unannounced, a hand raised in blessing, a vague smile on his face. About her, men knelt as though they were in church, faces wreathed in smiles.

We have conjured a phantom.

Still nothing; his smile was unfocused, his eyes quite blank.

'Henry, it is Margaret, your wife, your Queen.' She placed a hand lightly on his arm.

He does not know us. He does not know any of us. It is the nightmare all over again.

She was trapped in some frozen tableau of Hell with no way to break the spell; sensing her panic, rising to the surface as the seconds ticked past, Edward pressed closer into her side and turned his face into her skirts.

'Madame,' it was Clifford who spoke; she turned, desperate for a lifeline. 'The King is not...' he hesitated, 'he is not himself. I think it may be some time before he can speak to us.'

He is himself; he is completely himself.

She suddenly realised that Henry had not entered the tent alone but was flanked by three of York's champions: Sir Thomas Kyrielle, Lord Bonville and Lord Monatgu, Henry's one time chamberlain. It was clear from their demeanour and Clifford's furious expression that they were not there of their own choosing.

I have to take control of this before his spell traps us all.

'My Lords, I am surprised to see you here. Are you an escort? Or prisoners perhaps, which is it?'

Her voice sounded calm but she kept one hand lightly on Henry's arm as though to tether him and kept Edward behind her with the other. If this was a trick, she would not let her son be caught by it.

'An escort, Your Majesty; an escort for the King. We wanted to see that he was brought safely back to you.' But Bonville's wheedling tone and Clifford's snort of laughter told the opposite story.

'They are only an escort because they were caught.' Clifford was brief and factual as was his way. 'They were found pretending to be the King's guards but I have no doubt this one,' he gestured at Montagu with unmistakeable contempt, 'had only returned to snatch the King and ride after Warwick in hope of a reward.'

'Is that true?'

Margaret tried to smile at Henry, hoping he might react to kindness, 'were they protecting you or holding you hostage?'

Nothing, a blank stare; there was no sense to be had here.

'If the King will not condemn you then I must decide.' She turned back to Clifford. 'What do you advise My Lord? You saw them and you clearly do not trust them; do we treat them as the King's gaolers or his liberators?'

Clifford shrugged, 'why would we keep them alive? They are traitors; it is no more difficult than that.'

'Not Montagu.'

At first Margaret did not realise who had spoken; she thought for a strange moment it was Edward but he was still behind her, standing in silence, his eyes wide as he realised the enormity of what was happening around him.

'Not Montagu.'

It was Henry: something had pierced his trance, some bond of affection that ran deep enough to stir him.

'Do you want the others to live? Is that your wish?' Margaret tried again to encourage him but he had gone back to wherever was more comforting.

I cannot do this; I cannot bear this blankness; he will drive us all mad.

'If that is what the King wants, so be it: spare Montagu but kill the others.'

Weary of it all, she waved a hand and it was done: they were dead within the hour. She saw Edward's eyes widen at her cruelty but she had neither the energy nor the inclination to pretty-up her words; he would learn harder lessons before they were done.

'Henry,' she turned back to her husband, 'Your Majesty, we are all so grateful that you have been returned to us. Look, your son is here, he has been waiting for this for so long.'

She pushed Edward forward but there was no point: the father did not see the son and the son wanted only to hide from the father.

And so we will fall back on pretence. I cannot do this again. Why didn't York kill him while he had the chance? Why didn't Clifford?

'The King needs time to recover from the strain of his imprisonment. He will greet the troops and then he will retire.' More false words.

'Your Majesty, is that wise?' Clifford stepped closer so his words were private. 'Look at him; he is in his shadow world again. He will do as we tell him but we will be back to praying or silence if he is not led round like a child. Do you want the army to see that?'

Margaret's voice was as low as his but, where Clifford was full of fear, she was made of fury.

'Of course I don't but what choice do I have? Do you think I can't see him? He is a shell but a shell can wear a crown well-enough to convince the simpletons who gaze on him and want to see a king.' She shivered, 'I wish York had killed him.'

She heard Clifford's sharp intake of breath and shook her head. 'So do you, you are just not honest enough to admit it. I wish he was dead and that we could ride into London with Edward as the King but we cannot. We have the King back with us and we will get to London before York; we have to parade Henry and hope it is enough.'

211

***

Jacquetta Woodville sat in the quiet Hall, alone with Richard Lee as he had requested and wondered if she had misheard everything that had just been explained to her.

'The decision whether she enters London rests with me?'

The Mayor of London, smiled, 'not yours alone, there will be more negotiations I imagine but your view will be listened to, yes and you will deliver the final decision. Your family is well-respected, Madame, and your husband has been a good friend to the City, if he was here...'

Jacquetta shook her head, 'It still makes little sense. I have no authority with the City of London and I certainly have none with Margaret of Anjou. Why don't you deal with her directly?'

Lee pursed his lips, 'I will meet with her for form's sake but it is awkward. If it was the King who summoned me, that would be one thing but to make treaties with the Queen...'

'Let the women deal with women.' Jacquetta smiled, 'and then you can blame us if the decision you take is the wrong one. It's a good strategy when you don't know which side to pick.'

He bridled. 'That is not the issue. Besides, you know her; you will be able to tell if she is speaking the truth about her intentions.'

Whatever the reaction he expected, it was not the gales of laughter that greeted his statement. He had heard rumours that Jacquetta Woodville could be strange at times, he was beginning to believe it might be true.

'The only thing you can be certain of is that Margaret of Anjou never tells the truth. If you knew...' she stopped suddenly. 'Well it doesn't matter what you know as long as you know not to trust her.' Lee sighed, 'you might be right but I need to be careful. She has the

King, she has just had her son made Prince of Wales; she clearly feels that she is in a position of strength...'

'And she is close to London and York is not.' Jacquetta finished the sentence for him. 'She wants a triumphal return to London with her Edward at the head and you do not know which way to bet.' She smoothed her skirts and rose to leave.

'Send the women if that makes everything safer for you, it doesn't matter to me. If we let her into London and York triumphs, I will simply say you forced me to do it.'

'That is your right.' He shrugged, 'we all have to find our way through this in a way that keeps our heads on our shoulders.'

Jacquetta smiled. 'I am glad we agree on that at least. I will meet with her and I will do the right thing, you can trust me.'

And Margaret of Anjou and her bastard child will never enter London.

***

Another darkened room, another weary soldier with news that added to the gloom. She was even beginning to wish for Jacquetta and some nonsense about potions to conjure up luck and love.

'They are frightened of you. Frightened of you and frightened of your army. They will not let you pass, Madame; London's gates are closed.'

Trollope, newly knighted but still nursing a wounded foot from the battlefield which did little for his temper, gazed at Margaret levelly across the chamber as though challenging her to defend the rabble who followed her, a rabble who had become the watchword for evil across the country. She would not pretend she could. Neither would she accept defeat.

'Then, Sir Andrew, we had better be cleverer than the citizens of London and persuade them that we can be trusted. Give the people some proof or promise of our good intentions.'

She thought for a moment. 'We need a proper, formal approach: get Dr Morton to write some clever words and wrap them up in the law so that the City has a document, a legal pledge; that will appeal to their aldermen. I cannot believe it is all lost: the citizens are providing supplies and money to us so there must be some hope. We must work a little harder to convince them, that is all.'

But it was clear her words had no audience with him.

'They provide nothing. The supply carts have been turned back at Cripplegate by angry crowds and the provisions have been shared among the citizens. And as for the money? That has disappeared into thin air.'

'Why is London always my stumbling place!'

The crash of her goblet against the hard floor and the pool of wine that resulted brought the servants running but she chased them away.

'They made such a show of their great love for me when I first came to this Godforsaken country and yet they have blocked me at every turn since. I am tired of it! We should storm their walls, take their city and teach them a lesson in manners!'

'Which is exactly what they expect you to do. So much for your promises of good intent.' Somerset's drawling tone was as laconic as ever and his response to Margaret's furious oath at his impertinence was a dismissive hand.

'My father said you didn't listen to the people and he was right. Do you think anyone in London truly care who wears the Crown? Do you think that their adoring cries at your bridal procession had any real substance? They will follow whoever can control the armies they all fear and promise them protection and they will cheer anyone who can charm their hearts. Edward of York can do both and it seems you, Madame, can do neither.'

He is right. I have mistrusted the City from the start and made no effort to woo them and I have refused every word of advice on the matter, from his father or anyone else.

She could not argue with Somerset's honesty; the fight left her as quick as it had come. She needed London and this was not the time to be headstrong or proud so she calmed her tone and put herself at Somerset's and Trollop's bidding. If they were surprised, at least they had the grace not to show it.

'Then what would you have me do? You are my commanders, command me and I will listen, I promise.'

'I share your sentiments, Madame, and your frustration but Somerset is right: we cannot attack the City; that would be an act of madness.' Clifford, who had held his counsel until now, smiled, a little grimly perhaps but there was at least some warmth in it. 'Your first instinct was a better one. Reduce your demands and calm their fears. The Londoners are terrified of your army so don't try to take it into the City. Ask only for admittance for yourself, the King, the Prince and your immediate retinue; they cannot deny that. And then prove that your word holds good: travel to Barnet now with only those you have specified, leave your army here at St Albans and swear that any soldier who commits any form of attack against the citizens here will suffer the severest punishment. Make them believe you: publish the words of your pledge around the walls of the town if needs be. Then they will see that you are to be trusted.'

He waited to see if she would argue; when she did not, he continued. 'It can be done swiftly, Madame, and you will not lose face. There is a delegation from the City already here: London's Mayor, Richard Lee is outside, he is a good man by all account and will welcome this solution, I'm sure of it. Tell them that you will listen to their fears and seek a peaceful solution for all; it will be a gracious move.'

She did as he counselled and was delighted that his instincts seemed to be right: Lee and his sheriffs returned to the City with a promise to take her pledge in good faith and deliver it to the Council. Margaret left that day for Barnet with her hopes high: London, it seemed, was in her sights once more.

***

'There is news.'

'From your expression, it is not what I want to hear.'

Trollope was once again the unsmiling messenger: she was becoming increasingly weary of his stony face and grim demeanour.

He shook his head. 'The Earl of March, the Duke of York, whatever we must call him now, has finally combined his forces with Warwick and marches towards London. They are only days away.'

'And days too late!' She would not have her mood broken. The weather had finally warmed and she had spent a happy enough morning playing with Edward and a puppy he had somehow discovered or wheedled from an indulgent servant. She was sick of battles and gloom especially when there seemed so little need for despondency.

'Smile, Sir Andrew: while you were away, the delegation from the City arrived; we will be inside London's walls before our new Duke even makes St Albans. Come with me to greet them, thank them for their kindness and smile!'

The manor house adjacent to the Church of St Mary's where Margaret had set up a court of sorts was small and cramped but she swept down its little staircase as though it were the finest of the palaces she expected shortly to have returned to her. And then the smile faded on her lips as she saw the waiting group. The aldermen she had expected were crowded there, hats in hands and nervous smiles in place, but they were clearly just the backdrop to the three women who now dropped deep curtseys: the Duchess of Buckingham, Lady Scales and, smiling her most insolent smile, Jacquetta.

Why her? What trick is this?

Margaret halted abruptly and tried to match their gracious show with a friendly welcome: it felt as hollow to her as it must have sounded to the company.

'Ladies, I confess, you are not the party I expected but you are most welcome.'

She gestured to them to come into the smaller inner parlour. 'Make yourselves comfortable and I will call for refreshments. The kitchens here are small but surprisingly good at honey cakes and I know My Lady Rivers at least has a sweet tooth.'

'That is kind, My Lady, but there is no need.' It was Jacquetta who replied.

She does not use my title.

'I hope our presence is not unwelcome even if it is surprising to you.'

She is insolent: her voice, her manner, everything.

'Well, if you won't sit, then I will.' Margaret tried to keep her voice light but there was an edge; Jacquetta's smile did nothing to ease her misgivings.

'The Lord Mayor would have returned in person but he felt it would be more suitable to send us women.' Jacquetta paused and the smile became ever more mocking. 'Unless, of course, the King is able to meet with him?'

I have lost. Dear God, I have lost and I have no idea how or why.

Jacquetta's smile was broad now but as cold as frost in the cruellest winter; she was enjoying herself, it was plain to anyone.

'He is not?' She nodded. 'Well I am sure my meaning will be plain enough for you. The City thanks you, Madame, for your pledge of good conduct and your promise that the people of London would feel only your kindness. The City also hears your request that the royal family be admitted to begin again the process of your government.'

She paused then as though the matter weighed on her when clearly it did not. 'They have listened to your pledges and yet it seems that they hear no truth in them.'

Again she paused as though wrestling with her conscience, it was quite a performance. 'I have tried to speak well of you Madame, of the Queen I have known so closely for so many years but, I am sorry, it has not proved enough. The citizens fear that your words are words alone and do not have the substance to guarantee their safety and so, Madame, the City cannot admit you.'

The final pause, the sweetest smile. 'London remains closed.'

'Leave.'

No one moved.

'Leave. Now. All of you. I would speak to Lady Rivers alone. Go!'

They did not need telling again. The room was empty in seconds.

'Why Jacquetta? Why are you doing this?'

The time to flatter the woman's vanity was long past; plain speaking was needed now.

'The City would admit us, you know that they would: our guarantees are good and my army is nowhere close. If you have so much influence, why would you treat me so carelessly?' Margaret shook her head, 'no, this betrayal must be your doing. You came to refuse me, not to discuss terms; why? What do you stand to gain from such a stance?'

This time the smile that brightened Jacquetta's plump face was as lazy as a cat's on a sunny wall. 'Why would I plead your case with care? Why would I plead it at all? Do you understand nothing?' And then she stopped and Margaret saw the hatred, felt it pour from her like molten lead, heavy and thick and all-consuming.

'I do not want you, or your husband or your mockery of an heir anywhere near the City. What an opportunity! The aldermen are afraid and they are confused: you are their Queen yet they don't know how to behave towards you. But they know and respect my husband and they think I am your friend; don't you see? They believe that I will try to find a fair solution for everyone. And so they are happy to believe me when I say that you cannot be trusted, that you will unleash your army and destroy them. In truth, they want to believe that anyway; their hearts are cast for York not you.'

She was all but spitting the words now. 'Which is exactly as I wanted it. You think you can control everything around you, well you can't. I have been offered a far better prize to keep you out of London than anything you could offer to let you in.'

'Warwick. You have traded me with Warwick.' Margaret was suddenly exhausted.

'You have betrayed me to win your husband back.' She was grateful for the chair: her legs would not have held her.

'And my son, do not forget my son, Madame. You know what it is like now to be a mother with a son to protect. What would you do if you were me?'

But her words were not intended to establish a bond and Margaret would not allow any common ground between them.

'And are you a Yorkist now? Will my brave Lord Rivers ride against me?'

For a moment Margaret thought Jacquetta might strike, there was such malice in her eyes.

Her husband's name in my mouth is still salt in her wounds.

'You are not the one to speak of betrayal. You have no right to ask what we will do and no right to command him in anything anymore. We will do what keeps us alive and you would be minded to do the same.'

She turned and left without a further word; with a shaking hand, Margaret drew the bolt behind her.

I am beaten, I am truly beaten.

She sat alone in the room for hours, ignoring every knock on the door. When she emerged it was to face publicly the truth she already knew: London was closed, her army was without provisions and becoming more mutinous by the day and Edward of York was at her heels. She made great speeches to her commanders that night about the virtues of regrouping, of moving North and gathering her most loyal countrymen to her cause; it was all lies and they all knew it. Their departure at first light was a flight, a flight from certain defeat; a flight and nothing more.

Towton:
1461

*I thought I knew everything about battles; I thought I knew every-
thing that they could be, that I had witnessed all the horrors a battlefield can deliver. I knew nothing.*

It was such a hard winter: even in February the snows were still
falling heavily from a sky that seemed to have been leaden for
weeks. There was no thaw, no break as the Lancastrian army moved
away from London towards the North, avoiding York by a matter of
days as he swept his forces down into the City. And what a reception their stony hearts gave him. Margaret knew that the messengers who brought the description of his triumphal entry expected
her to scream and rail; she was simply too exhausted, too outplayed. All the times she had used tricks and tableaux to win sympathy and support or to make the story of her family far greater than
it was. She was a novice compared to York and his advisors.

*He knows so well how Londoners love the look of a king and he
gives them everything they could have dreamed of and more.*

She sat in silence, her stomach churning, as she listened to the
messengers fight to keep the awe from their voices as they described how York rode in splendour through gates now flung open
with abandon and wreathed in flowers to greet a golden god on his
huge charger, and how the people cheered themselves hoarse at
his coming.

*No matter he is as vicious in battle as any commander of mine; no
matter the soldiers they welcome with smiles and wine could be
just as dangerous as mine. They do not see it. They see the show-
man and love him for it.*

Every man who stood before her elaborated on the tale. They were
almost breathless by the time they described the great rally York

held on the 1st of March, with food for all and work forgotten, and the triumphal procession he made to St Paul's, the solemn ceremony that followed it a few days later; a coronation in all but name. She listened in mounting dismay but could not stop herself asking for every tiny detail. How he had the City Criers summon the people in great crowds. How he had long lists of Henry's failings read out by Bourchier, resplendent in his Archbishop's robes and matched them to equally long lists of his own virtues, these loudly declaimed by George Neville, York's handsome Chancellor. And again at the Cathedral: the same charade of the strong man versus the weak but this time with York's great royal lineage spelled out so even the simplest commoner could catch it and scream for joy at this King of miracles they were offered.

My efforts were like a child playing make-believe with a paper crown compared to this.

And all through the telling, the same refrain: what a difference to his father's poor misguided efforts. This York could not have thrust the crown away even as pretence, the people would have forced it on him. It was all so perfectly done. Everyone applauded the title of Edward IV, looked at the furred robes, saw the sceptre and the crown, attended the lavish banquet and truly thought they had witnessed a coronation when it could be no such thing. Margaret could not match him, she knew it: all she had was a hollow-eyed man, his crown a mockery on his empty head, and a child who would be snatched from her if she stayed still too long.

She could not capture hearts but, in that at least, she and Richard of York had been evenly matched. Now she faced a gilded paragon of nineteen with a laugh as loud as a lion's roar and a golden mane to match, framing a face that made even the matrons around her go giddy. Put a crown and an ermine on him and it was as though she was pitted against a storybook hero to defend a cause that seemed suddenly to have no more weight than a butterfly's wing.

And yet I cannot stop. I cannot accept defeat. I cannot let him win.

She was afraid, her advisors were afraid: to continue meant war, war to the death, slaughter unleashed. And to stop? To surrender? That was fear of a worse kind, fear that caught at Margaret's throat and kept her without any rest, turning over the same questions night after night. What usurper would ever allow another anointed king to live? What usurper would ever allow a child who would become the focus of every rebellion and discontent and misguided plot to live? War might be a death-sentence for them all but surrender was a death-warrant for her son.

***

'Why can't London treat me like this?'

Margaret waved again and again as the citizens swarmed through the winding cobbled streets of the city of York to rain down cheers on their little prince.

'Listen to them: they call after my beauty as though I were still a girl and look how Henry seems to enjoy the applause.'

She gestured at her husband who was managing to sit astride a horse and wave blessings on their heads.

'It is a good reception. There's no love here for Edward IV whether he takes the city's name or not.' Somerset smiled at a young girl waving flowers at him and grinned even wider as she collapsed into blushing giggles.

'It is a homecoming for you and a good one but you would never get this in London, you know that. The North, the Midlands they will be loyal to you but not the South; you have lost any claim there.'

'They will learn to love me. I just need better envoys to help me win them over than the last time.'

Somerset laughed again but at her not at his adoring audience.

'Perhaps if you made the thought of loving you sound less like a threat you might have more success.' And then he shrugged, 'you might at least have the chance to try and persuade them again. If Trollope is right and 19,000 men truly have rallied to our banners, then numbers alone would seem to call themselves for Lancaster.' Margaret turned her face to the sun.

'I was so afraid but I honestly think it goes in our favour this time. Think about it: our troops are already pitched together. Edward might march towards us but Warwick hasn't reached him yet and everyone says Mowbray is a sick man in need of rest, his army is nowhere close to joining forces with York. We should be able to command the place of battle; Trollope has sworn he can do it. Perhaps all my fears were unfounded.'

She sounded confident and she meant it. They had been moving about the countryside for weeks, both sides gathering men and support in almost equal measure: two kings and one Queen in a curious game of chess played out across snowy fields and fearful villages, but the advantage looked like it was falling to her. The three prongs of Edward's army were scattered and the Yorkists had to march through lands where her armies could hold and ambush them: the river crossing at Ferrybridge was one they could not avoid but one the Lancastrian commanders had already begun to strengthen.

'Every omen the soldiers cling to calls the victory mine.'

And yet we did not win. If battles were fought on figures and plans, on paper not on battlefields, then the world would be a very different place but they are not: they are at the whim of weather and stray arrows and men's fear or belief or lack of it. And a battle once begun is a beast run out of control. When I next saw Somerset there was no confidence, no cheering crowds, just horror piled upon horror.

***

It was dark but it was anything but quiet. The noise of battle preparations would not stop: outside the tent restless horses and restless men, inside the tent a restless queen as highly-strung as any soldier facing his first fight.

'Give them an extra ration of ale.'

'Your Majesty, do you really think that is wise? The men are unsettled and already drinking too much...' but Trollope stopped arguing quick enough when she turned on him in fury.

'I know they are restless, that's why they need more ale and we need to pray it leads to sleep not flight!'

Margaret knew it was wrong to cross her leading commander and so publicly but her nerves were stretched as taut as the bow strings massed in front of her and she did not care.

'What else can I do? You have spoken to them, Somerset has spoken to them; Northumberland, Exeter, you all give rousing speeches but still their fear spreads through the camp like a deadly disease and I cannot stop it.' She glared at Trollope who was equally as furious. 'You should have let me address them, or the Prince; none of you have a common enough touch to make the men rally to you.'

She had pushed him too far.

'And you think you do, a French Queen? Or that a child could make them ready to die, because that is what they believe will happen?'

His rage ripped through her, as uncontrollable as his army.

'Dear God, are you really so blind? They want their King! They have to fight a battle on Palm Sunday of all days against a man they think can produce signs of God's support in the heavens on a whim and they need a king who will mount a charger and lead them, a king who will shout a battle-cry and give them something solid to fight for. And where is Henry? Safe behind the lines, cloistered in the abbey at York, reciting masses like a monk, unable to fight or rally them. That is the poison, Madame, and you can try and counter it with speeches or drink all you like but you will fail unless you can produce a king worthy of the title.'

It was treason but it was the truth. There was nothing to be gained from fighting him.

'Anthony, I am sorry.' Suddenly she had no strength and sank into the rough chair they had provided for her use.

'Why is it going wrong?' She gestured to the battle plans littering the table. 'We should have held them at Ferrybridge; we should have held them there and taken Warwick's head and instead we lose Clifford to an arrow in the throat and the Yorkists swept through as though our forces were made from mist. How could it have happened?'

It was not an accusation but a plea for reassurance and he heard it as such; his anger subsided as quickly as it came but, even then, he could be of little help.

'Madame, I swear I don't know. You are right: we should have had them beaten before this. I have planned every step of this so carefully, we all have and yet we have failed to hold them at every single point.'

He pulled a map towards him. 'Look at our position.'

Margaret knew it well enough, she had been consulted at every stage but still she looked again as though they would find some magic answer on the paper as yet unseen.

'There are our armies, grouped on the plateau above the River Aire.'

She followed his finger, too tired now to question him.

'It was a good strategic move. It put our forces above that muddy plain which is the Cock Beck.' He ran a hand across his grizzled chin, 'I didn't think the Yorkists would get this far, they had to fight their way through bridges and crossing-points far better defended than Ferrybridge and yet, against every calculation and every expectation, they have managed it.'

He was right: each crossing had fallen before York's forces like blossom in a summer breeze and their army had been in place almost as soon as hers had made camp. Margaret's army had thrown up their banners on the 27th of March, after days of marching; days in which the tension was almost tangible, a charge as though of lightening in the air. As the Yorkist armies came ever closer, her men were straining to have it done; every one of them, from the simplest foot-soldier new to the field to the battle-hardened veterans who had fought in campaigns across the Continent and understood both the prize that was at stake and the likely cost. And finally, when it felt that every straining sinew would snap, they had got to the little village of Towton and seen that the enemy were at last come close enough. The victory was there on the plans but it was not there in the tent and Trollope and Margaret both knew it.

She shivered: the night was growing colder and snow, which had begun almost as soon as they set camp, continued to fall thick and silent outside the thin canvas of the tent.

'I am becoming as superstitious as the men. I am looking at plans and papers as though for magic spells and I don't know what to do.'

'There is nothing you can do and you must leave.'

Trollope shook his head as she opened her mouth to argue. 'You have to leave, now before it starts; the men do not want a woman here.'

He laughed suddenly but there was such bitterness in it, it made her shudder more.

'If they could see the fury on your face, I think they would believe you could lead them into battle but they will become more afraid if you stay. You cannot be a king to them so you must sit at the Abbey and pray or shout at the fools who won't see your strength or

227

cry. I don't know, Madame, what to tell you to do apart from go.'

He was right; she did not argue. She rode the ten miles back to the Abbey to her sleeping son and witless husband and paced the night through until she thought she would lose her reason. And when Somerset finally came, accompanied by a bloodied and silent Exeter, she could have envied Henry his detachment and wished she too could hide her mind as easily from horror.

'Saddle their Majesties' horses and give the Prince to me; there is no time to take anything.'

'What has happened?'

She clung to his arm as though she were a beseeching peasant not his Queen but she was too terrified to care.

'I have seen them, the soldiers coming from the battlefield; they were running as if the hounds of hell pursued them but they were too bloodied and it was too dark for me to make any sense of it and I dared not approach any of them for fear of discovery.'

'Thank God at least for that.'

Somerset shook her off, brusque and deliberate in his movements as he grabbed the sleeping Edward from his nurse's arms and pushed the uncomprehending Henry towards a horse. 'Take as many furs as you can and go. I will tell you what happened as we ride but, I swear, if we don't leave now, you won't be alive to hear it and neither will your child.'

It was enough. They were saddled and gone within minutes, the furs doing little to protect them against the unrelenting snows. She rode well, she always had, and kept pace with Somerset who clung grimly to Edward; the child was wide-eyed against the sudden shock of the departure but made no protest. Henry had followed meekly with Essex and had already started to slip deeper into his shadow world; Margaret could sense it but could do nothing to help him and had to trust to the care of the few servants still loyal that he would survive the ride.

'You must tell me what happened.'

Her words echoed through the snow; for a world so newly turned upside down, that had seen horrors she knew would soon be hers to weep over, it was strangely quiet and peaceful.

'We have lost and lost badly.'

He paused and she wondered for a moment if that was all he would say but then she heard the horror in his voice as he began to unfold the events of the battle and knew he did not want to relive what he had seen.

'We lost the battle in the first hours and I don't know how or why.'

His voice cracked but he continued and she did not interrupt him or look at him, the effort the retelling was costing him was too obvious.

'We had control of the position; we had the bigger force; we had commanders with courage and experience. We had all that but we did not have the weather, we did not have fortune on our side. All the little snow flurries that had powdered the men as they prepared their arms disappeared by morning; it became a blizzard, a wall of white arrows which swept up the hill and stung the faces of our men until they could see nothing of the enemy forces or of their own.'

He paused and still she was silent but the tears ran down her face unchecked.

'And then the Yorkists unleashed arrows, arrows in such a swarm; I have never seen such ferocity or such accuracy. Our men, panicked, that is the truth of it. Against the force of such a double assault they collapsed into confusion and all our carefully planned advance came to nothing. The left, the right and the centre forces swept out in disjointed waves with no cohesion of thought or com munication, and no way to correct them. Somerset and Northumberland were left with no choice but to support men who could no longer be stopped. It was chaos.'

There was disbelief in his voice, the disbelief of a soldier who has planned and prepared and thought everything under his control when nothing was. It was a hollow, desperate thing to have to hear but she could not let him spare her, or himself, anything.

'What have we unleashed?'It was a question he did not want answered.

'This is a battle men will remember for the longest time but not for great acts of bravery, they will be lost somewhere in the telling. Neither will they talk about winners or losers, they will remember this for its savagery, for the barbarity men will do when it is kill or be killed, for the sheer physical horror of the slaughter we have unleashed.'

'That I unleashed, Edward of York and I.'

Margaret's voice was as dull and shocked as his.

'There is no blame here on you or on any of my commanders. If there has been slaughter here, it is because York and I demanded it.'

Somerset did not respond, how could he? Before the battle began, both she and Edward had proclaimed that no prisoner would be taken, that no quarter should be given and that these orders must be obeyed with no mercy. That was not the way of war in England and enough of her nobles, Somerset among them had baulked at it, but she would listen to no advice.

'Why did you do it?'

There was no blame in his voice; she wished there had been for that would have been easier to bear than his despair.

'Why demand such a thing when you knew it would leave York no choice but to do the same?'

'Would you believe me if I said that I was so convinced we would win, I did not think our men would be the ones to suffer for my words?'

'Would it be the truth?'

She did not know how to answer him. He deserved honesty, she knew that much; for everything he had seen and done that day, the least he deserved was honesty.

'In part, I think. I know what battlefields are like: I know that any soldier will hack and chop and stand on piles of corpses with no sight of what he does if it wins him a chance of life. I did not want the Yorkists left alive.'

Somerset slowed his horse a little and grabbed her reins, pulling at it so that she was forced to look at him.

'In the battle yes, I will grant you that in the heat of battle. But your orders meant that the slaughter went on long after the battle was won. Dear God, Margaret, you do not know what no prisoners taken has meant for us.'

She wanted to shake him off but he would not have it.

'That single order, "no prisoners taken" has left 42of your knights captured and executed on the battlefield. The ferocity of the fighting has left Dacre dead in the battle and Trollope with him; it has left Northumberland dying and Wiltshire escaped perhaps but with a price upon his head that makes him a dead man. And your army, the men who flocked to your banner? Dear God, they paid for your bravado.'

He was shouting now, oblivious to her tears, to Edward's frightened whimpers.

'There were thousands butchered in flight, their corpses plied so

231

thick along the boggy land of the Beck, men are already calling it Bloody Meadow. Even more at the crossing point where the bridge was broken and the river forded instead by bodies drowned and crushed. Thousands and thousands of good men slain and the York-ist losses as high as ours. And do you know why?'

He had pulled his horse to a stop now and hers with it, his eyes black with fury as he spat his damning verdict through the frozen air.

'Because of your pride; your stubborn foolish pride. You wanted your army to see you as their Warrior Queen whose cause was so great, whose cause was so just that they would follow you blindly into any danger, make any sacrifice for you. We saw it and we tried to warn you but you would not listen. You wanted them to love you for your courage and your fearless belief in your right to the Crown in the way York is loved by the crowds who will cheer him to the throne. Well you have failed and you have sent your men into Hell; I will not be the only one left sickened by it.'

He said no more for the rest of the journey but his words burned and burned and she knew the truth of them.

I have lost the battle and so much more. How can the people not hate me for this? Every women who lost a husband, a son, a father; every man who lost his child; how can they not hate me for this?

The thought that they would hate York too, that they might take him as their King and drive her into exile but surely hate him for this as much as they hated her and see that no one who aspires to King-ship is fit to be trusted was of no comfort when measured against the horror she was now mistress of. The world was a lonely place that night.

***

We fled of course; what choice did we have but flight? After the slaughter we had witnessed, after the slaughter we had ordered, it was clear that there could be no thought of a nunnery, no exile on offer.

Capture meant death. Somerset and Exeter knew the truth of it as much as Margaret and knew that not one of the blood-stained soldiers who streamed about the countryside could be trusted not to betray them, no matter whose standard they had once rallied to.

They rode for the safety of Scotland and set the horses at a pace that nearly killed them. They barely rested for there were so few even in the North that Margaret could trust and her army was exhausted and broken; the men left standing melted away and she had neither the time nor the energy to care.

This flight was so much worse than the last time she had been forced to run: she saw King Edward's men in every shadow and an assassin behind every tree. And yet the Yorkist army did not pursue them. Edward must have known she had Henry and the Prince safe with her for he rode into York only a day after they fled. He must have known she would have raced for Scotland where support had always been so freely given to her but there was still no pursuit.

Perhaps he thought himself too safe in his great victory to worry about a deluded king and a little boy. Perhaps he was too intent on the real coronation he would soon demand and felt the ceremony would be enough to put the crown secure upon his head. Perhaps he was simply 19 and thought himself invincible. She did not know but, whatever he thought, he let her go.

It could not last. No matter the triumphant processions he could order and the cheering crowds who would greet him, Edward IV had won his crown through violence. He left a bloody country soaked in fear with too many men who would soon start to seek revenge or demand power in payment for the support they had lent him. Throughout those dreadful days of flight, Margaret was certain of only one thing: the Crown was surely no firmer on Edward's head than it had ever sat on Henry's. And, when he saw the truth of this, then she knew he would not overlook her any longer: he would see her son for the threat he was; he would come after him until he had a corpse in his hands not a challenge in his future.

What would be left to her then, when the scales dropped from King Edward's eyes: a life of hiding or a life of exile? She could not permit either, for herself or her child. Edward thought the battle was over. Perhaps if the only claim that she could have fought was Henry's, then he would indeed have won; perhaps if the danger was to Henry alone, then, perhaps, he would have won. She knew there was nothing she could have done or would do to make her husband King again. But her son? That was a different story. She would have him alive, she would have him safe and she would have him crowned.

Edward of York, it seemed, underestimated me as much as his father ever did: he was a fool to let me go.

Scotland and France:
1461-1463

I did not want to return to Scotland. I did not want to return to France, especially France. To go back to France, to leave England with nothing to mark my claim, with every sense that my cause was lost, was the very last thing I would have chosen to do. And yet, by the winter of 1461 I was that thing above all that I never wanted to be: a desperate exile.

Despite the friendship she was shown there yet again, Scotland remained the bleakest, coldest place Margaret had ever known: even in April the wind whipped through the walls of Linlithgow Palace as though they were made of mist and turned the furs she wrapped herself in as thin as silk. Snow still clung to the banks of the loch and patches of ice sparkled round the shoreline, mirroring the frost that patterned the inside of her casement every morning.

The welcome was warmer than their lodgings but she had the measure now of Mary of Guelders and knew any support from her would carry a substantial price and would not be easily won. So it proved. The Scottish Queen did not come herself this time; she kept a far more wary distance. Mary sent messages which promised love and affection but they also made her interests very clear: she demanded that Margaret make good on her earlier promises and secure the full surrender of Berwick and Carlisle, a promise which had remained merely words. Margaret knew it was a fair request. She also knew that, if it was delivered, it would prove that she still had a hold on power; it was a test she could not afford to fail. So she sent out her orders, she sent out Exeter to the city of Carlisle with an army to enforce her words and demanded the surrender but it seemed she was no longer heard. She knew she should have expected it: what real strength could her authority have after the disaster that was Towton? The people of Carlisle knew as well as anyone that the new King would turn his attention to the North as soon as he was crowned. They were not about to ally themselves with a cause too few believed in and so Exeter returned empty-handed. It was a humiliation and it left her weak.

Nevertheless, Margaret was summoned to Edinburgh, where she was met by Mary's ministers with all the appropriate courtesies: she was housed in the great grey Castle whose tapestried walls at least seemed to hold more warmth than Linlithgow and welcomed daily to the Court. Mary acknowledged her as her sister Queen (Henry would venture no further than the chapel and seemed to have little sense of where they were or why) and was smiles enough in public but her smiles rose no higher than her mouth and she no longer sought Margaret's company through the long evenings as she had in earlier days. The little household was much alone and, no matter how much Margaret might try to push them together, their sons were not the playmates they had once been.

There was no hostility from Mary; she remained too skilful for that. She appeared to engage with every plan Margaret had and laughed with what seemed like genuine pleasure when she proposed that Mary's little daughter be betrothed to Prince Edward; she even spoke of what pretty children they might have. And yet there was always now a reticence about her, a sense of waiting. Margaret guessed the reason easily enough; it was the cause that eluded her for the longest time. Mary had been well-schooled in the ways of diplomacy: she did not know who would triumph, the new King or the old, and would make no firm treaty with either until she could determine the safer course. That much Margaret knew and accepted. What she could not know was that Mary was already being courted by others whose voices dripped with a far more honied flattery and that in this, as in so much, it was Warwick who lurked in the shadows.

***

'Why is it smiles everywhere and yet no army? Why am I told of half-hearted border raids as though these are some sign of Scottish support when no one will talk to me of a real invasion? I am tired of talks and treaties that never move from the planning to reality.'

Margaret pushed away from the table, another meal untouched, ruined by more disappointing messages that soured everything she tasted.

'Do the Scots really think I have no support? Don't they understand that the North will still rise for me? With a Scottish army behind me, with a French army in support, don't they see that I could take the Crown from Edward before it has barely settled on his head.'

Every night the same litany of questions and never any answers.

'Why will Mary not see it? She talks so much of friendship, does she not see how much it would profit her to have a true friend on the English throne?'

Endless discussions that lacked any sign of resolution; she was exhausted from it.

'She already feels she has such a friend and a far more powerful one than you could ever be.' Exeter closed his eyes. 'I need a victory as much as you do, we all do. Do you want me to tell you that everything will be alright? Shall I lie and say that being defeated at Carlisle was not so bad? Shall I pretend that you didn't weep for two days at the news of Wiltshire's beheading, that none of us were shaken by it?' He shook his head. 'I can't, I won't.'

He sighed and drank too deeply of the wine that he turned to far too quickly these days.

'Why should Mary believe that the North would rise for you? What proof is there? Carlisle and Berwick wouldn't, why would any other town, any other Lord do different? Don't argue, please, I have no more patience for it.'

He had seen the retort spring to Margaret's lips and was in no mood to countenance it.

'I know there is some support for you still but it is hard to find and

Mary has been too well-persuaded that it will never come.'

'What do you mean, "too well-persuaded?" What have you heard that I have not? I swear no one tells me the truth anymore.'

'Why would they? You shout like a demon if anyone delivers news you don't like and sulk like a petulant child when people are too scared of you to speak.'

It was an insolent response but the words were softened with a smile that bore a trace of his old charm and she could not deny the truth of them. Reluctantly she sat back down and waited for him to continue.

'I have heard some gossip but this time it is gossip from a good source. It seems that I am not the only man partial to a drink.'

He nodded towards the cup he had refilled again.

'I see your mouth tighten every time I reach for the wine, well perhaps you should take some comfort in the fact that I have always been one who can sup and listen at the same time. Do you remember James Kennedy?'

She nodded, 'The Bishop of St Andrews, the one who was so kind to take us in at Linlithgow.'

He had been kind and very vocal in his support, treating her like a welcome guest when she arrived rather than an exile in flight.

'I remember how sure he was that we had done the right thing in turning to Scotland for help. He promised us that Scotland would always support the claims of the House of Lancaster against any upstart from the House of York, I remember he used those exact words.'

Essex smiled at the memory, 'He did and more than once. Well it seems our dear Archbishop spoke with too strong a sense of his own importance and too much pretence that he was the Queen's confidante; he has been reprimanded like a naughty schoolboy for that and in public to.'

He filled his goblet again and raised it in a mock toast.

'That hurt his pride and badly; he was more than happy to spill his anger to a willing listener with a plentiful supply of wine and to reveal the truth of the game his Queen is playing.'

He took another deep drink, smiles all gone.

'Madame, I am sorry, but she is keeping us happy and that is all she will do. Our dear Queen Mary has other, stronger powers that she must listen to, that we cannot compete with. She will not take sides in any English dispute; she has been forbidden to by the Duke of Burgundy who is furious at her friendship with you and will not have her meddling, as he so delightfully calls it, when Burgundy's sympathy should more naturally lie with the House of York.'

I have been caught too long in England's politics; I have forgotten to look wider at the world and I will pay for it.

'What matter is it of Burgundy's? Why on earth has Duke Philip involved himself?' She tried to sound careless but it did not fool him.

'Do I really need to remind you?'

He began counting his responses off on his fingers as though she was a child who would not pay attention to her lessons.

'Because the issue of who holds the English throne is not a matter for England alone; when has it ever been? Because Scotland has a child King and is vulnerable no matter what his mother might pretend. Because Philip wants to remind Mary where her allegiance lies if the French come calling with marriage treaties and, more to the truth of it perhaps, because Warwick has convinced him that your cause is over.'

'Warwick?' That was not the response she expected.

239

Exeter, seeing how pale she had become, motioned the servant to pour the jug of wine into her goblet this time and did not continue until it was full.

'Yes: Warwick. The man I swear holds the real power in England no matter where the Crown chooses to settle. Kennedy told me clear enough: after Mary came to your aid the last time, Warwick wrote to Philip, making threats and promises both about what would happen to Scotland and to relations with Burgundy when the Lancastrians lost the throne, a possibility he made seem a certainty.'

He was watching her closely as though for a reaction she was not yet ready to give.

'It is truth not rumour. Kennedy has seen the letter; he was in Flanders when it arrived. Our dear Archbishop has very little conscience for a man of the Church and will take his rewards wherever he can. He was supposed to speak to Mary in support of Duke Philip's cause in his never-ending disputes with France but was persuaded by the French King to speak against Burgundy, for an even more sizeable purse I imagine as that seems to be all that commands his loyalty. To be honest, Kennedy's tale became somewhat confused and my patience with him somewhat stretched. Yet one thing seems true: the Scottish Queen listens to everyone, smiles at everyone and simply does nothing. She will not ransom her kingdom, Madame, by picking the wrong side. If we stay in Scotland, we will be a court in exile not a court in waiting and we will grow old and tired with it.'

Until they grow tired of us and start looking for a ransom to repay their generosity.

He spoke the truth, she knew it; every day at Mary's court had shown her that. It was a pretence she could no longer collude in.

'I cannot let that happen. If that is the game that Mary wishes to play, then we will smile and act as though we play along but we will out-manoeuvre her. Forget Burgundy; forget the Scots; we need to plead our cause to France.'

She shook her head.

'The English have always thought of me as French. They have called me a French Princess not an English Queen and hated me for it no matter how much I felt and protested my loyalty to them. Well then, I shall be what they hate.'

She sounded warlike and fierce; Exeter knew she was merely betrayed and tired but he did not argue.

'It matters little anyway: any army that I lead, any army that wins us back the Crown will surely be seen as an invading force and the English will hate me for that as much as they did when we led the Scots against them last time. I can't make them love me, that much is clear and if they fear me, then so be it. The English have always thought that I would make them a province of France. Then let us give them what they have always feared.'

'So be it.' Exeter raised his cup again. 'To the Warrior Queen.'

If he was mocking her, she did not want to know.

***

So much information and yet so little knowledge. Letters, spies, informants, gossip. Margaret mined every seam of information she could find but could not know that every source was flawed, that the truth shifted from day to day and from recount to recount. Her understanding of the world did not extend to the shadows where the real stories were being woven; everything was at once true and false.

Rene was her first mistake. Time and again her father wrote that the French would always see Margaret as their daughter and would provide whatever she needed to regain what they felt had been stolen from her. She read the words and believed them because she longed for them to be true but Rene never changed: he lived too much still in his own imagination and was better at fancy and make-believe than the reality his daughter needed. For all his clever words, he failed to tell her that her Uncle Charles was ailing, was, in fact, near death and her cousin Louis, who had little enough love for his father never mind her, was hovering to take his crown.

Louis. She would have taken far more care if she had known how close to the Crown he was when she was in such need. She knew the gossip: people called him l'aragne, the spider, for he was always at the centre of a web of intrigue, spinning plots and lies. He hated his father and King Charles hated him, had chased him away from his court and left him to brood and fester at Duke Philip's court in Burgundy. But Rene gave her no warning that power was about to shift and that her plans to woo the French were already wasted. As soon as she had the measure of the Scottish Queen, she sent Somerset and Whittingham to France to ask for men and money, all the things her father assured her were hers for the taking. She was swift to act and she was too late: Charles died while her envoys were aboard ship. Louis had the crown before they could land and her men were left like paupers at Dieppe, refused an audience and ignored.

It was not just France that slipped through her fingers: she was blocked at every turn. Louis would not treat with her and she could not persuade him. In England, Edward had his coronation and now formally styled himself Edward IV. He was in progress around the country making all his subjects swoon like maidens at the sight of him and she was attainted along with every one of her supporters, her cause broken at its root.

He had wasted no time, this new boy King. He had called Parliament as soon as the Crown was on his head and laid out his claim as far back as Henry III and Richard II in the most meticulous detail with one hand and charged Henry with breaking the 1460 Accord with the other; it was then the simplest thing to remove Henry's rights from him and disregard the child. Margaret was breathless at the speed of it as the new King systematically and ruthlessly attainted her, Henry, Prince Edward and one hundred and thirty of their followers, swelling his coffers with forfeited estates while she sat at one increasingly indifferent court waiting for scraps to be thrown from another. His actions struck at her resolve like a physical pain. And all the time, in the background and hidden from direct attack, Warwick was meddling: encouraging the Scottish lords to rebel against Mary unless she rid her court of Margaret while promising allegiance and all manner of truces to her if she would do the deed herself. And it worked: Mary was all courtesy and smiles before the Court but she granted Margaret an audience with increasing reluctance in public and never admitted her in private. Margaret knew there was poison but could not know who held the cup.

And then tales began to circulate through the French Court and came rippling through to Scotland that Somerset was Mary's lover, that he had left Margaret's bed for hers or shared them both perhaps. Margaret dismissed the slurs and suspected Warwick's hand but Mary was furious at the slight on her name, blamed Margaret as their author and was barely civil when their paths met. When Somerset limped home from Dieppe, empty-handed with Louis' insults ringing in his ears, she would have had him thrown into a Scottish dungeon without Margaret's increasingly desperate intervention. And there was the final fracture: Somerset swore he would have preferred imprisonment to the furious tongue Margaret unleashed on him and a rift both were too proud and isolated to repair began to snake between them.

'I am leaving.'

When Margaret finally received the audience she had been demanding for days and delivered her news to Mary, it was a relief to both of them.

'It is a good decision. You have family, you have friends; you will be able to plan more carefully.' It was a gracious speech but there was no warmth in it.

'It is a flight.'

Margaret had nothing left to win through diplomacy and no more

243

inclination to try.

'I am going back to a country I left nearly seventeen years ago as a bride, as a queen, with everything before me, penniless and desperate to plead my cause to a man who likes nothing better than mischief-making. I am taking my son without knowing if prison and a ransom might await us. It is not a good decision; it is not a choice.'

Mary shrugged. 'Then leave the Prince, I will see that he is safe. You are leaving Henry here after all.'

Because my husband has no value and I do not care what you do with him; my son is mine.

'Henry cannot travel, he is not strong enough. He, at least, is safer here.'

Mary smiled and waved a dismissive hand, 'no one is ever safe Margaret; you of all people should know that.'

***

She had forgotten how beautiful the tapestries were: six huge hangings alternating black and blue, thick with threads in orange and green, ivory and red and shimmering with silver. As a child she had been dazzled by them, never tiring of the story of the Apocalypse playing out across the sections, fascinated and repulsed in equal measure by the decaying corpse the artist had chosen to represent Death. More than once she had accepted her brother John's dare and crept down to the Great Hall before anyone else was up and moving to see if the figures really did come to life in the dark. They were beautiful and yet she could take no pleasure in them, or in the castle's gardens or the menagerie tucked underneath the walls where the moat used to run. She could take no pleasure because every day she was kept waiting at Angers was another day lost to her cause and to her return to an England she feared had increasingly forgotten her.

'When will he see me?'

Rene put down his book again and sighed: the same question day in and day out as though he could conjure up a new answer from thin air.

'What do you want me to say? When will he see you? I do not even know if he will see you.'

There was no warmth in his voice or on his face; Margaret had expected her return to be strained, there never had been a close bond between them, but she had not expected the strain to run so deep. 'Louis has no place at Court even for me, isn't that obvious? I am as exiled from power as you. I no longer know what he will or will not do. I have sent a message to him as you asked, I have announced your arrival and your wish to pay your respects to him as his cousin and as a Queen but I do not know whether he will care.'

Rene's misery at his failure to please his King was written plainly on his pinched face: he knew Margaret despised him; he no longer had the heart to care.

'Well, I am glad, for one, that you are no longer near him. Louis is a very dangerous man; you should be glad to be safe here at Angers with me and away from that troublesome Court.'

Margaret had not realised her stepmother Jeanne had entered the room; she would not have spoken had she seen her.

How can he put up with her? After so long with my mother, how can this prattling fool do anything but irritate him as she irritates me?

'What I say is quite true Margaret, quite true, you must believe me. The Court is a terrible place these days, really terrible and no place for your father, he is far too gentle.'

The girlish manner so at odds with her matronly bearing, the breathy voice, the constant patting with her plump little hands; one alone would have grated on Margaret's nerves, the combination made her long to scream. She looked to her father to stop the flow but he was smiling as indulgently at his wife as he always did and merely shrugged off his daughter's annoyance.

'Have you heard the gossip? Well how could you not. Everyone says Louis poisoned his first wife because she didn't please him, and his father's mistress Agnes Sorel too because he hated his father so much and would do anything to injure him. You do know don't you that Louis' only comment on the late King's death was to wish it had been more painful. And he is so ugly...'

'Jeanne, please, enough now.'

Rene at least had recognised the warning signs that Margaret's temper was bubbling too close to the surface.

'Whatever you may think, he is your King and it is unwise to speak so carelessly even here. Little Edward, I am sure, would be happier at the stables; why don't you accompany him and we will meet later at dinner.'

She made a pouting face but Rene's kiss made her giggle enough to agree much to Margaret's discomfort. The bustle of her departure and Edward's excitement at the thought of new horses to ride at least broke the tension and Margaret allowed Rene to turn the subject away from Louis to his latest plans for a new chivalric order and the badges and banners he was far more happily occupied with. Had she known that she would sit and wait for weeks rather than days at Angers before Louis finally agreed to see her, listening to Jeanne's opinions on every little matter and at such length, she would have followed them to the stables that day and stolen the fastest horse.

***

'Why should I help you? Edward of York is crowned King of England; he is secure on the throne or so my ambassadors tell me and he promises to be a great friend of France. His man, this Earl of Warwick who makes such a name for himself at Calais, has promised us talks and new treaties which put French interests at their heart. And my ambassadors tell me that no one cares any more for a sick king and an angry wife or a child too young to rule. So tell me, dear Cousin, why should I listen to you?'

Jeanne had told at least one thing true: Louis had grown from an awkward ungainly boy into a very ugly man. He had been puny as a child and now some curving of his spine made his back distorted and bowed and his thin, spindly legs gave him every appearance of the spider he was so often called. But the eyes in his narrow, pointed face were bright and Margaret knew his mind was as sharp as a blade.

'You should listen to me because Warwick is a liar.'

Louis' mouth twisted but he made no move to interrupt and she continued in the confident manner she knew she had to adopt to get any attention from him.

'Warwick will promise you anything to keep you out of English affairs but that is simply all he does: he makes promises. He has also promised his new King that he will bring him France as a coronation gift. You believe what he says but so does Edward.'

She paused for a moment and then lifted the knife.

'Edward is a warrior king; he doesn't spin plans and conspiracies, he acts. And think about it, Cousin, what better way to win his people's hearts and make his throne secure than to take back the French territories they still mourn as England's right?' She saw him shift slightly and knew the blade had struck. 'Edward is not penniless, like me; he is rich with the wealth he seized from my lands, he can afford an army and he is young and full of his own glory. Make no mistake: Edward will attack you and Warwick will keep smiling and promising you his love and loyalty while he does it.'

She stopped and slipped her hands into the full sleeves of her gown: if he could see how much they were shaking, he would be far less convinced by her performance. She breathed far easier when he spoke.

'You are very direct: I thought you would try and seduce me with flattery.'

He continued to watch her as levelly as before but there was a flicker of a smile around his thin mouth that let her fingers untie.

'Well it is a plainer approach, I suppose, than I had expected and more honest than most others try. And I cannot argue with the logic of it, you may well be proved right.'

Louis shrugged as though he cared little but his fingers had knotted in turn and she could sense unease in him.

'I have met the English Earl and I had little regard for him. Warwick is one, I think, who will twist as the wind pulls him and, no, I do not trust his words. I also have no appetite for another war. So, if I was to help you, well perhaps you might regain your throne.' Again he shrugged, 'or you might not, who knows, but the uncertainty would occupy this new King Edward and might prove a diversion for me.'

Margaret could feel him weighing up the potential gains and losses as though he were Treasurer not King.

'But I hope you understand, cousin, I could give you men and I could give you money and we will see what you can do. But, if you want my help, there is a price.'

As I expected but at least you are more honest with me than Mary was; if we are going to pretend to be allies, at least the dance will move out of the shadows.

'Calais.' She smiled as she saw a flash of the greedy boy he had once been. 'You want Calais and, when we recover the throne, as we will do, then you will have it. You have my word.'

'Which is as jewels when compared to Warwick's, Madame, I am sure.'

It is a game to him; he doesn't care who wins or who dies as long as he can play the puppet master. It is enough.

Louis was as good as his word: within days she had 20,000 livres, ships and a thousand men with Pierre de Breze as captain, a man she trusted without question. Perhaps it was not as much as she had hoped for but it was far more than she had left Scotland with and she was content: her cause had champions and life once more.

***

Another ship but this time one boarded not in flight but in hope and sailing in seas whose winds were friendly. Margaret felt the soldiers see good omens surrounding them and for once was grateful for their superstitious murmurings.

'You will win this time, Your Majesty, have faith in that.'

It was Pierre at her side. She had not heard him come to the rail where she watched the rest of the little fleet strung out across the calm October sea, their sales fluttering in the light wind. The skies were clear but cold; she drew her cloak tighter but did not answer him. Undaunted, he carried on. 'Luck is on our side: there is not a single enemy ship to be seen. All those tales of Warwick parading the English Fleet through the Channel and up to Brittany, all those rumours which delayed our sailing and frayed our nerves and now where is he? Nowhere. I feel it: we have luck on our side.'

If his words were intended to lift the chill from her shoulders, they could not. She would smile when the men gave thanks in her hearing for the way God and Fortune smiled on them but she would not pretend in private.

'Do you know how many times we have held the winning cards in our hands only to lose them the minute we began to play?'

She did not turn to address him but continued staring out to sea.

'Do you know how many times we have laid plans that were perfect in every detail and yet they fell to pieces in the execution?'

She paused for a moment, watching the waves rise and fall below them, catching the silvery rays of sunlight like threads thrown across a cloth.

'Are you a gambler, Pierre?'

'A gambler? I am sorry Your Majesty, I do not understand the question.' She turned and motioned him to walk. 'Do you like to play cards or dice?'

'A little, yes, but I still do not understand your meaning.'

He took Margret's arm as the ship dipped slightly and she let him hold it.

He is a flatterer and a flirt and I should remind him that I am his Queen and yet it is good to be a woman for once, to be courted just a little. To remember there is softness in the world.

She smiled, 'when I was a child, my father was a lover of playing cards. He had so many sets and they were beautiful things, all decorated in blues and reds and golds, with menageries of lions and bears, antelopes that looked like a conjuror had thought them up and gods and goddesses wrapped in stars and moons. I would watch him and his friends play tarok and allouette each evening, not understanding the rules but mesmerised by the flashing colours as hands were thrown and dealt.'

She looked at Pierre and smiled again, more warmly this time and felt the pressure of his fingers increase on her wrist; he could not help himself.

'One night when he was quieter than usual and content to amuse himself with his children rather than a fawning court, he taught us all how to build a tower of cards, building each layer with the most delicate touch, barely daring to breathe unless disaster struck. My sister Yolande had no patience for it and would not continue after the first fall but I was captivated and could not bear it when my creations would finally collapse as I tried to build them ever too high, as I saw one card fall and could not catch it before the rest tumbled.'

She stopped and turned to him, 'do you understand my meaning now?'

For all he was a flatterer, he was no fool.

'You fear your return to Scotland will be the same as building your deck of cards: too much left to chance and luck no matter how skilfully you plan it. Am I right?'

She nodded. 'We seem safe now but I do not believe in it. There is so much at stake; I don't think a single disaster will stop us.'

She gestured to the ships bobbing around them.

'I never expected an attack to come from Warwick's fleet, that was a warning nothing more, but I fear mistakes and misjudgements. I am afraid that we will once again meet betrayals and bad luck on all sides that I could no more control than I could make my flimsy cards grow strong.'

The wind blew a little stronger and she shivered again.

'I can only rely on you if you always tell me the truth. I don't want or need pretty words that have no more substance than the water below us. Do you understand?'

'I do.'

He dropped his hand from her arm and she saw the seriousness she had hoped for written plain on his face.

'I will listen and advise and guide as much as I think you need it and I will promise you honesty above all else. I will be your champion, Madame, not your courtier.' And then he bowed and walked away as though to separate the man he would be from the one who had first disturbed her on the deck.

I trusted him from that day until the day he died; he was my friend.

***

There are some betrayals that burn with a flame that only gets hotter over time. Betrayals that make no sense and cannot be argued away with thoughts of a greater good; I have suffered them and they leave a scar that does not heal. And there is never a warning that they will come.

At first it seemed that luck would favour them. The fleet sailed unhindered into Tynemouth and had Alnwick taken from its Yorkist garrison and occupied before anyone on land was aware of the threat. It was such a promising start, Margret felt heady with hope as she disembarked on Scottish soil again. But she had been right to be cautious for that was where fortune deserted them, as quick as it had come. She made some gains and battled on for many months but there was no great invasion, no real strength in her army's attacks; they clawed for any power they could take and held it briefly, if at all.

Margaret had spun such careful schemes and yet nothing was as she had expected it would be except that plans meant nothing. The truth, a truth she would admit to no one but that kept her sleepless and hollow-eyed, was that she no longer understood the country she was so desperate to rule. Exile, no matter how brief, had allowed the sands to shift.

She had thought the men of the North would rise for her as soon as she spread the word of her arrival and yet they did not. What had seemed a reasoned belief when she was far away in France with no real sense of how things fared in England quickly revealed itself as a foolish hope when she returned. Margaret knew they were loyal still in their hearts to Henry, the old families who had always supported the House of Lancaster, but she had failed to understand that a willing heart was not enough; she had failed to grasp the legacy that was Towton. They might hold loyalty for Henry but they would not die for him again, they would not lose their sons for him again.

The country, as she knew it would, had seen the truth of its golden King: Edward was young and vigorous and brave, yes, but he was ruthless too, as ruthless as any man with a love of power, as ruthless as once they had called her and she had, unwittingly, delivered both the proof and the lesson he delivered straight into Edward's hands. Too many letters. She may have learned how to guard her tongue in public but her pen always ran too full of honesty. Then one letter too many: too confident of his support, she had trusted her hopes to the Earl of Oxford and written every detail of her plans for him once she was victorious. The misguided paper had fallen into the wrong hands, or into greedy hands, and the people were quickly shown how their new King repaid any man he considered disloyal: the Earl of Oxford paid with his life for her confidences as did too many of his household. A quick and brutal death with no thought of mercy and a warning to all. So, no, the men of the North would not rise for her.

It was a tumble into misery and defeat. So many things misjudged that sent us spinning to disaster.

News came that Edward was marching towards her with a huge army: it had no base to it but sent her into a panic anyway and chased her army back to their boats and a terrible voyage to Berwick where the winds whipped up and the sea all but boiled. The sailors sent her to shore in an open boat as ill and bedraggled as when she first sailed to England but, this time, with no royal bridegroom waiting. Her ship wrecked fleet was cast like kindling onto the beaches of Holy Island and the men stranded there all slain with no chance of escape.

Plans were made and plans collapsed: the battles and sieges around

Alnwick and Dunstanburgh and Berwick and Norham; all castles that should have held for Margaret and all castles that were lost under the weight of Warwick's army which had finally marched out of London in the winter of 1463 and was an unstoppable force. The flights at night from one beleaguered camp to another, unable to trust anyone, the little money and jewels she had left all lost in bribes and payments for a scant few hours of peace and rest.

Every man I met was a thief who saw our need and took our money to quiet his mouth and the nights we hid in caves and woods were not because love-sick outlaws feted us but because we could not trust a single soul not to betray us to Warwick's men.

Betrayal: the thought of it or the reality of it was everywhere and was always the hardest cross for her to bear. All these defeats, all these losses: they were as nothing compared to the betrayal of men she thought were loyal to her above anything. Night after night, exhausted and haunted and worn to a shadow she screamed the same litany of grievances to her commanders and to her son: there was no trace of glory to be found in war. All the little boys brought up on stories of knights and quests who dream of becoming great soldiers who will fight with honour and loyalty for love of their King or their country become the same beast on the battlefield; every one of them will turn hatred to love if it will save their lives and every one of them will turn their coats until they no longer remember the colour if it would keep death at a distance.

And my own little boy, brought up on the tales of chivalry that would shape his kingship, heard my vicious words and shrank from me but I was too lost in fury to temper them.

Betrayal: she thought she had learnt its every hue but she had learnt nothing until she heard the news no one dared bring her but Pierre.

'Somerset is a traitor.'

She was sitting at the window, quiet for once, letting Edward read aloud some tale of knights and ladies he had become enamoured of and Pierre's cold words made no sense.

'What are you talking about? Who is a traitor?'

'Henry Beaufort, Duke of Somerset, your commander in battle. He has declared for York and delivered his army to Warwick.'

The room tipped. She was on her feet, motioning to Alice to take the Prince before he had finished speaking.

'You are lying! He is one of my closest friends! No, you are lying, at best you are mistaken, why would he do such a thing?' But even as she asked the question, she knew the truth of it; Pierre had sworn her honesty and he had always kept his word.

'To save his head.'

Pierre took Margaret's arm and pressed her back into the chair. The room was spinning, condensed to a scream of pain she did not know if anyone else could hear.

I cannot bear it, I cannot bear it, not Somerset.

'You know him, Madame, he cannot bear failure, he quickens to a fury if anyone tries to lay it at his door...'

'Bamburgh,' she looked up and he could have wept at the emptiness in her eyes. 'I gave him Bamburgh Castle and he could not hold it.'

Pierre nodded but did not speak.

'I gave him Bamburgh despite you warning me that he was the weakest link in my command and he could not hold it. That is the truth of it?'

Pierre nodded again, 'Edward offered him a pardon rather than the execution he had expected and the messenger said that Somerset fell to his knees and wept and his new master swept him up in a great show of mercy and reconciliation.'

'Then he is a fool.'

Rage swept through her; impotent, pointless, burning rage.

'He is a fool and he deserves his fate. Doesn't he realise that he will lose the King's favour as quick as he seems to gain it? Is he so caught up in his own importance that he can't see he is nothing more than a pawn? Edward will keep him alive just to prove that my cause is lost and then he will kill him. Is he so blind he does not know it?'

'Yes, your Majesty, he is vain and self-important, as you well know, and he will believe whatever lies Edward throws his way if it keeps him alive and with a hint of favour.'

There was no malice in Pierre's voice, there never was; in that he was far better than Margaret for her words dripped with it.

'And then, when Edward discards him, if he does not kill him first, he will try to worm his way back to me. He is a snake.'

'And his bite has poisoned you. It is over, Madame, I am sorry but it is over.'

***

'You are going back again.'

It was not a question. There was no invitation to sit, no warmth in her voice, no smile. It was all Margaret could do to remain civil in the face of Mary's complete disinterest.

'I am going back; yet again I have no choice.'

A pause, a hoped for contradiction, nothing.

'No, you don't.' Mary spread her pretty fingers across the heavy brocade of her skirts as though counting out Margaret's losses.

'No army, no castles, apparently no loyalty from even your closest friends and nothing more I can do.'

Nothing you have ever done except look to your own ambitions. You will watch Warwick sweep up from the North and welcome him with all the affection you once showed me; God knows what you will promise Edward once you set eyes on him.

Mary twisted one of her rings, a heavy sapphire, until it caught the light and smiled at it.

'You will take your son with you I assume? I, of course, would protect him as if he was my own but who knows what some of my...' she shrugged as though it was a private joke, 'less biddable lords might do if the purse was right? So Prince Edward goes back to France but what about your husband? Will he make the journey this time?'

'Will you protect him if he stays?'

Mary turned her attention again to the jewels glittering against her slender fingers as though they held far more interest than any king. 'As I said, my lords are not always as honest as I would like them to be but I will do my best, you have my word on that.'

And that is worthless as we both know; as worthless as Henry is to me, or you or anyone else. I will not take him, we both know this pretence of caring is no more than that.

There were no more words and no more audiences to be had. Less than a year from her arrival, Margaret left Edinburgh for Bamburgh and made hurried plans to sail to France once more. It was a sad, depleted party who would return. This time there would be no ships but only four ballingers, flat-bottomed boats more suited to a river than the wild sea Margaret expected and still feared. Pierre insisted that the water in August would be like a millpond and that they would sail in their strange little crafts like kings but her heart was heavy at the sight of them and she shook far more than she would show.

There was some pretence of a royal party, Margaret insisted on at least an outward display, with standards flying and horses decked in the last few trappings left to her but it would have fooled no one: they were poor and bedraggled and it showed. There was no flotilla: Margaret would travel in one vessel with her son and Pierre, Henry Holland and Doctor John Morton and a small guard of French soldiers who would not wear her badge once they saw she had no money to pay them; the remaining army, if a raggle-taggle group of barely a hundred men could be called such a thing, would travel in the others. As she watched the men embark in the grey dawn light, she did not expect to see them all reunited.

Henry she left, safe in name at least, in Edinburgh Castle knowing nothing of events. The sleeping sickness was on him now far more than it was away and had acquired a rhythm they all knew: he was absent for days at a time and as biddable as a babe when awake. She could not believe even King Edward would see a threat in him and could not think about the consequences if he did. She left Henry behind with no great leave-taking and no tears or fond words: he did not know her and Edward would no longer go near the strange man who frightened him with his silences and his ramblings both. It was a relief to close the door on his monastic cell and leave.

I did not know then that I would never see him again beyond a glimpse but I doubt such knowledge would have changed my farewell. He was a shadow to me as much then as he is now, a ghost of a man with only the frailest hold on a world I was desperate to cling to. He was lost to me years before I left him.

France:
1463-1464

So often, it seems, I have been forced to action in a world where only part of the picture was visible to me. I was not the only one who sailed that summer with the hope of forging alliances but that was a twist I did not know. I was little more than a sideshow to a greater power play and my voyage, with its haste and its sorry state, was truly a voyage into an exile that would keep me from England until my son was a man; those things too were hidden from me. Perhaps it is better I did not know how long I would have had to stay away, how hard and lonely my exiled life would be: I do not think I could have set sail. And yet what is harder to bear is that, whatever the path I chose, whether I had been walking down them blind or open-eyed, the outcome would have been the same: my son would not have lived.

France: that was her first thought for sanctuary; it was dismissed almost as soon as the tiny fleet sailed.

Mary's disdain had been enough of a humiliation and Margaret knew that Louis would simply match that with his own scorn: he would mock her failings and meddle from the side-lines without any care for her or her cause. Louis would not do. The only alternative was Duke Philip of Burgundy, whose reputation was far kinder than the spider King's and who had always shown far greater sympathy for the House of Lancaster than of York. Philip's health was failing, that much she knew, but this time she had some hope of both the father and the heir: Philip's son Charles, the Compte de Charolais, was no estranged and embittered Louis and, in public at least, had never shown himself anything other than his father's man. The sights that created her on the streets of Saint Omer were, therefore, as unsettling as they were unexpected.

'The three suns, the white rose, York's badges are everywhere. I don't understand it. Is King Edward here, in Burgundy? It makes no sense.'

Katherine's worries were no more than an echo of Margaret's own. The barely-royal party had travelled almost without stopping from their landing point at Sluys to Saint Omer, carried in the rudest of carts, travel-stained and weary and longing for rest. Leaving Edward with Compte Charles, under the protection of Henry Holland, Margaret had sent messengers ahead to Duke Philip requesting the audience his son had assured her would be immediately granted and yet the town appeared as if it were making ready to greet a very different delegation.

Ahead of them, she could see Pierre on his horse, his face suddenly tight-set as he too took note of the liveried men who milled about the narrow streets.

'It is not just York's men, there are soldiers everywhere wearing George Neville's badge.'

Margaret shivered as she spoke and pulled her cloak tight around her thin shoulders: even though it was only early September, there was a chilling dampness pervading the air as though the marshlands which surrounded the town had seeped into its very fabric. Katherine and Osanna, the only women she had brought this far, were as tense as she and she knew her words would do nothing to calm their nerves at all but they smiled faintly as their mistress continued with a show of confidence they knew she did not feel.

'We should just ignore them. We will go to the Abbey of Saint-Bertin as arranged; Duke Philip knows that we are here and will have sent messages there to greet us; all will be explained once we have seen him and all will be well, I am sure of it.'

But her certainty was not truly felt and was quickly proved misplaced. The Abbot had been warned of their arrival and he allowed them to stay, albeit with little grace, but there was no word from Philip and Pierre's demands for information were met with only a brusque response: the Duke was not there and was not expected.

Margaret had demanded a fire in the meagre room they were

shown to for the damp had filtered in everywhere; the fire had been begrudged but it had been lit and they huddled gratefully around it, waiting to hear Pierre's news from the town. When he returned, however, his words did little to lift the chill.

'Duke Philip did come here but he has left again for St Pol.'

Pierre moved closer to the fire and spread out fingers that were pinched with cold.

'I didn't dare ask anyone if the Duke had been told of your arrival; there are too many men here I would not want to trust with your name. It sounds bad I know but we should try not to see this as a set-back: St Pol is only a short distance away so I suggest we send messengers there and remind Philip that his son promised us an audience.'

He hesitated as though he was unsure how to continue, his voice suddenly faltering. His sudden uncertainty, so unusual, was unnerving.

'Margaret, listen to me: I don't know how safe it is for you to remain here. The town is crawling with Yorkists. Perhaps Duke Charles didn't know or perhaps he is not the friend he appears to be but Neville is here, acting as Edward's envoy and there are emissaries from France everywhere. Louis himself is expected to arrive shortly; no one is talking about anything else. I asked as many questions as I could but none of the answers were welcome.'

He rubbed his hands together, clearly in some pain as the warmth seeped back through them.

'It is hard to get a clear picture but, from what I understand, it seems that there is to be a conference. The talk is that Edward is going to make a treaty with France and Burgundy, an alliance that will safeguard the wool trade and safeguard his crown. I have even heard mention of a marriage between Edward and the French Queen's sister, Bona of Savoy, to settle the peace.'

261

Everywhere I turn, he is there first. He is a poison spreading and I cannot stop him.

Margaret knew her words were tumbling from her mouth, that she sounded too frantic but she could not stop herself.

'Then we must get to Philip! We must go now! We must press our case before such a thing is signed and show him that it is our cause that he must support, not York's. And we must make a wedding treaty ourselves. Louis has a daughter, Anne, I think the child is called: we should propose a marriage with my boy, they are close in age; it would be fitting.'

'And impossible to negotiate.'

Pierre looked suddenly so old and so weary. He was always so bright in her presence, she had forgotten he was well past 50 but now the years showed heavy on his face.

'Margaret, stop for a moment and think. How can we possibly propose a marriage? What do you have to bargain with? Look at us: we have nothing left past the clothes we wear and the loan Duke Charles granted you and that must feed and clothe and house us until God knows when. There are no castles; there is no money; how can there be any talk of an alliance?'

He knows we are beaten; he loves me too much to say it but he knows we are beaten.

Margaret stared around the room, looking for some sign of comfort, someone to reassure her but there was nothing. Her women too had lost faith: she could see it in their downcast eyes and the tears of exhaustion already spilling down Katherine's face. And, even then, she would not accept it; she could not stop.

If I do what they want, if I accept defeat, what will be left?

So she pushed them from their rest and pushed them onto St Pol, determined that Philip would meet with them, determined in her blind refusal to see what was so plain to everyone else: the world had shifted its attention to other players and quietly moved away.

***

Her chair was placed next to Philip's under the canopied dais, a sign of respect she had carefully acknowledged. She looked down at the figured silk sweeping around her in luxurious folds as she settled into the thick velvet cushions. The gold threads of the pomegranate pattern glistened against the rich blue lapis of the underskirt, the black velvet that banded the long sleeves made her fingers look as creamy white as the pearls that encrusted the bodice. Margaret knew she looked more regal than she had in months; it meant nothing.

'The jewels, the gowns, everything you have given me is wonderful...

'But it is not enough.' Philip finished the sentence and there was nothing friendly in his tone. 'Nothing is enough for the great English Queen. Not the gifts we lavish on you, not the fete we throw in your honour, not the medallions we make with your pretty little face on them. You are treated like a felon in your own country and like a queen here and still it is not enough. You are tiresome, Margaret, you and your demands are tiresome and you are wearying me.'

It was a threat: she heard it but she did not care.

'Then stop giving me trifles! If you are so tired of me, give me the men and the money I need and I will go!'

His response was to burst out laughing; she could have slapped him for it.

'What I should give you is a few lessons in diplomacy! You cannot demand, Margaret, don't you understand? All you can do is hope and beg. I swear you will never learn it.'

He looked at her as though examining a toy brought in for his amusement. 'Such determination and such stupidity, it is quite a combination; no wonder the English fear you so much.'

There was a sudden scuffle to her left and Margaret realised that Edward had risen to his feet, furious at the slight.

'You cannot speak to my mother like that, she is a queen!'

Philip turned his gaze on the boy's red face and regarded him gravelly. 'Oh but I can because she doesn't behave like a queen.' He waved a dismissive hand, 'look at how she is dressed, look at how her women are dressed: she looks like a queen with a court but only because I have given her everything she needed. When she came here, she looked like a vagabond leading a crowd of peasants.'

He stopped and smiled calmly at Edward who was almost breathless with fury.

'And yet there is no grace in her, no gratitude. All she talks of is war and politics; all she demands is money and armies. No, that is not the behaviour of a queen and that is not the behaviour of a king. You would do best to mark that.'

If the door hadn't suddenly swung open to reveal Pierre with a face as black as any raincloud, Margaret knew Edward would have struck the Duke and destroyed their fortunes in a second.

He does not see how precarious our position is. He is blind to what I see daily: I am smothered with kindness when I act as a guest and ignored when I act as a queen.

Margaret knew what her son did not: Philip had spoken only the truth. He was never less than generous: he had given her money for all her immediate needs; he had brought his sister, the Duchess of Bourbon, to act as her guardian but he would countenance no talk of war or politics and refused any request she made to return to St Omer and plead her case with Louis. Without his backing, Margaret knew the French King would refuse her and her humiliation would be complete. Edward saw only his mother insulted and act-ed accordingly.

'Edward, wait, this is not the time...' she turned towards the door and gestured for Pierre to join them. 'You look tired, sit down.'

But he shook his head, 'what I have to say is better delivered standing.' Turning slightly, some sixth sense rising, Margaret saw Philip look at Pierre and smile, such a queer knowing little smile that her blood began to chill.

Pierre had also seen the smile. 'I think the Duke knows what I am going to tell you, I think he has known it for a while.' But Philip did not respond. 'Your Majesty...'

He is too formal and it is not for Philip's sake; I do not want to hear this. 'I am sorry to be the bearer of this but I have no choice and I will try to be as plain about it as I can.' He paused but she had no words to help him.

'A truce has been signed between England, France and Burgundy; a truce that recognises King Edward IV as the rightful King of En-gland. Your claim has gone.'

We are yesterday's men, we have been since we landed, we just didn't know.

And then Pierre looked at her properly and she could see that there was something more, something that would hammer down the last nail on her hopes. 'Margaret...'

'No, I don't want to hear it. If you would call me Margaret it must be something so bad I don't want to hear it.'

She was sobbing already, exhausted from months of worry and exhaustion she could no longer hold back.

'Margaret, I must and you must listen. Mary of Guelders is dead;

265

Scotland has made peace with England and King Henry is gone, gone from Edinburgh to Bamburgh and then God knows where. He has vanished from sight.'

There was a strange sound in the chamber, a keening wail as though some animal had been snared and wanted its pain ended.

A blackness descended, a fog that stopped her eyes and filled her mouth with fear. She did not know what was happening. She sensed rather than saw Philip leave the room; she thought that someone hustled Edward away. She did not know. She knew she wept, her face was raw for days, but then a numbness filled her, thick and smothering like a disease.

I became my husband.

She took to her room, to her bed and could barely form a sentence that had any thought in it.

For so many years I had known who I was, I had understood my purpose, my place. For so many years I had battled without cease for a cause I had utterly believed in, a cause I still believed in and, now, it was surely over and what was I?

Her strength left her. She would not leave her room; she barely ate; she refused to talk; she wept silent tears and would not leave her bed. Her women began to fear for her sanity.

I became my husband.

In the end the only one who could reach her was Pierre. He made the arrangements to take her to her father at Nancy, he asked Rene for the help she needed, help he knew she would never ask for herself.

And it was he, in the end, and my beloved Edward who broke my trance, who reminded me of what truly mattered and why I had fought so long. Pierre is long dead now, he died not long after in those early days of my exile but I will never forget his kindness, his belief that I would be restored to a crown he always swore was mine. It saddens me now to think that I never questioned why he was so faithful, that I accepted his loyalty and his kindness but never thought about their cause. After he was killed, fighting with King Louis at Montlhery, Osanna told me that Pierre had been present in Tours at my betrothal, that he was one of the courtiers who had danced attendance on me there. That he had, according to his own words, fallen in love with me then and had loved me ever since. And I do not remember even meeting him: I was a child dazzled by a crown and the promise of a king and I do not remember him. There would have lain a very different life.

***

'Your son does you much credit, Madame. He applies himself well to his studies and is a determined young man. I hope you do not think that I speak out of turn but these have been difficult days and he has come through them well.'

'Your words are kindly meant and kindly taken, Sir John, and I thank you for them.'

Margaret smiled at Sir John Fortescue, so important now in her reduced little household that she granted him a freedom of speech and audience that perhaps would not have come so easily in earlier days. She motioned him to join her at the window where she had been gazing down from the warmth of the chamber to the garden: Edward insisted on continuing his sword practice despite the raw wind that had been blowing for days. Although it was late April, it seemed that spring was still no more than a promise and few flowers had dared, as yet, to poke their heads above the ground. But the sky was beginning to blue and the view was pleasing and she was glad to finally have a place to rest and rebuild her strength.

After Pierre's intervention, her father had shown her more care than any of them had expected, granting her the Chateau of Kouer la Petite near Commercy as a home and an annuity of six thousand crowns to establish her court. And it was a Court: it was tiny, per haps, with less than two hundred and so few knights but they observed the rituals of chapel and mealtimes that Margaret had followed in London and there was a renewed sense of purpose which strengthened her daily.

Sir John, Edward's tutor now, could be gruff in his dealings with anything but the books he clearly preferred to people so his praise was welcome, particularly on days when his charge was tardy to his lessons and his mother was too indulgent. She turned away from the lively scene below and motioned him to sit.

'I am grateful for the careful instruction you give him although I sometimes think he keeps his full attention for My Lord Exeter's teaching.'

Henry Holland had taken charge of Edward's military education and, although Margaret felt he was sometimes too brutal a teacher, her son doted on him.

'He is a lively boy; a preference for swords over books is to be expected, if not encouraged.'

The rebuke was a mild one and she chose to ignore it; it was clear, however, that Sir John had more to say on the subject.

'Although the Prince's enthusiasm for more lively pursuits may be something we should perhaps play down a little for certain audiences. I rather think he frightened the Milanese ambassador with his constant talk of battles and beheadings. I cannot think that report about the Prince will be a favourable one.'

He was serious, she knew, in his concerns but she dismissed his words with a shrug. Edward had found the ambassador to be a pompous man and had delighted in telling his most fanciful tales and riding his little pony far faster than the fastidious envoy thought fitting. Margaret knew she should have stopped him but had struggled enough to contain her own amusement.

'You may very well be right but I imagine my son will not be portrayed in a kind light by many; he is my son and I am the Demon Queen. Edward is doing very well, Sir John and I am happy for all your...'

But her calming words were lost to the sound of a horse clattering through the chateau gates at what seemed a daredevil speed. She ran to the window to see Exeter pull Edward aside with a protective sword already drawn and Sir Robert Whittingham rush out to challenge the rider.

They have come for him! Henry is taken and now they will snatch Edward, they will kill him surely, they won't dare a ransom...

'Your Majesty, it is fine, calm yourself, it is not an attack.'

Sir John's words cut through her panic, forcing to look at what was actually happening: the horseman had jumped down and knelt before Edward, waiting to be ordered to speak.

With an effort she breathed more slowly, calming the trembling she had not even realised had seized her.

'Thank you Sir John, thank you. I might have recovered my health but the fear that someone will attempt to snatch and ransom my child will not leave me.'

Holding the sill to steady her nerves, she watched the scene below, trying to gauge how wary she needed to be.

The interruption was over quickly. There was an exchange of words and a letter passed and then Whittingham was in the chamber, Exeter close behind him, the papers hastily thrust towards her. She could not look at them without hearing some words of reassurance.

'Dear God Sir Robert, what is it? The messenger came as though he was pursued. Are we in some kind of danger? Where is my son?'

She could not hide the tremor in her voice but, when she looked at

Sir Robert, she realised he was smiling.

'Madame, he is safe; he is in his chamber awaiting his tutor and ready for his lessons.'

Sir John left the room without need of direction and Whittingham continued, his smile broadening. 'It is welcome news, I promise you.'

'If from an unexpected quarter', Exeter's tone was as laconic as ever but even he had a light in his eye. 'The messenger brought us news of Somerset...'

'Somerset? Why would I care for news of Somerset?'

She was less afraid now but her interest had begun to wain; she had little appetite for news of traitors, something that Exeter noted and that clearly amused him.

'You will care about this. It seems that our dear brother Somerset has finally realised that King Edward only wanted him alive while he had some use for our little traitor.'

Exeter shook his head. 'You may smile, My Lady, but it has certainly taken Somerset an age to understand what everyone else knew from the start. I don't know why: Edward has apparently had the fool under guard in Wales all this time and treated little better than a prisoner, with daily threats that he would be thrown into a dungeon and left to rot.' Exeter grinned broadly. 'I have no doubt that you would think that quite fitting but Somerset liked the idea considerably less and fled. And not just fled but turned his coat again. Somehow he has put himself an army together and decided that Lancaster is the House with the greater claim or, if not that, the House least likely to kill him.'

'You are finding yourself far more amusing than I.'

Irritated as always by Exeter's habit of turning everything into sport, Margaret turned away from him.

'Sir Robert, perhaps you can give me plain answers rather than riddles. What has My Lord Somerset done now? Are you trying to tell me that he supports Lancaster again?'

Exeter shrugged at her dismissal and pressed his fingers to his lips as though playing at secrets; she ignored him completely, as did Whittingham who spoke with the directness she needed.

'He has raised an army and laid an ambush against John Neville, Lord Montagu, Madame, as Montagu led envoys from Newcastle to Scotland. There was a battle: Montagu escaped but his men were cut to pieces by Somerset's army and Ralph Percy was killed. Somerset pursued them; the messenger believes another battle may have been fought but, as yet, there is no word of the outcome.'

'And you, dear Queen, have another champion.' Exeter's smile was genuinely warm this time. 'It may be that the people of the North have finally risen, it may be that Somerset has won them over. We do not know but, whatever the truth, it is not over, Madame, it is not over!'

***

She had a champion but it was a short lived triumph. There had been another battle fought, on that the messenger was right, and the wait for news was a hard one. When it came, however, there was no joy to be had in it and Exeter this time had little appetite for smiling.

'There is news.'

He said no more, merely flung the letter onto the table where Margaret had picked half-heartedly at another rejected meal.

'And you, I assume, have read it.' She pushed the paper away, 'don't waste my time by making me find the truth in it; tell me what has happened.'

Exeter sat down heavily and closed his eyes.

'It is the worst of defeats.'

His tone betrayed his weariness, his hopelessness; she could have read what had happened in the thick lines creasing his brow.

'Somerset is dead: beheaded on the battlefield and branded a traitor. Most of his army drowned, pushed by Montagu's men into a lake the locals called The Devil's Water and the few who escaped that fate were butchered as they tried to flee.'

'Who else? Who died with him?'

'Robert, Lord Hungerford and de Moleyns, Sir John Findhern and Sir Thomas Roos; they were executed in Newcastle. Sir Philip Wentworth and Sir William Penington at Middleham; fourteen more in front of King Edward at York.'

Margaret shook her head in disbelief. 'Dear God, so many of them to lose.'

And every one of them worth so much more than the fool who had commanded them.

The words were unspoken but hung heavy in the room all the same. She would have cried had she any tears left.

'And they were executed? In cold blood?'

It was far worse than anything that had gone before, far worse even than Towton and the damage would run far deeper. 'Who will dare to rise for us now when they see such dreadful punishment meted out on anyone who declares for me?'

Exeter shifted in his chair, 'there is more.' He looked away as though he did not know how to continue. 'There is news of Henry.
'

'Henry?' Her mind was still dulled from the horrors of the battle-field, she could not understand him. 'What do you mean?'

'King Henry, he was with Somerset.' He spoke slowly as though he also struggled to make sense of the news. 'No one seems to know how or why he was with him but he was. And now...well it seems he cannot be found.'

'Stop talking in riddles!'

Margaret was on her feet, papers scattered to the floor. 'Why can you never explain anything in simple terms! How can he be lost and then found and lost again? You make no sense.'

'I make no sense because the reports make no sense!'

His answering anger was so unexpected she sat down abruptly again, realising she could do nothing until he had given some shape to the story.

'I told you: no one knows why Henry was with Somerset or even how long he had been with him. After the battle, one of Somerset's men told King Edward that Henry had been left at Bywell Castle during the fighting...'

'But surely that would have been a lie to save his skin or earn a reward!' Margaret could not help but interrupt even though she could see it irritated him.

'That was what Edward thought, especially when his men got to the Castle and Henry wasn't there. But he had been,' he waved a hand at her to forbid further interruptions; she had no choice but to bite her tongue.

'The soldiers found his coronation cap lying in a half-packed box in a bedchamber and one of the cooks swore he had seen Henry leave the castle through the kitchen. When Edward's men spoke to some of the other servants, they reported rumours that Henry had been seen wandering in a village nearby, begging for bread in exchange for blessings.'

Exeter looked at her suddenly with more kindness. 'It is not proven but it is likely, too likely to ignore: Henry is lost somewhere and may God help him because we surely cannot.'

'My cloak, fetch my cloak.'

She could not stop shivering, no matter that it was June and the sun was blazing through the casement.

'My poor simple husband, dear God what will become of him?'

Exeter had no answer; her women could not meet her eyes.

'What will become of him, wandering and alone? I would rather have him Edward's prisoner than lost and without help, stumbling through his shadow-world with no one who would know him or protect him.'

They see only guilt. I abandoned him like useless baggage but he is no more than a vulnerable man who could be facing dangers he can no more manage than a babe. And I cannot shed tears for him because not one of them will believe me anything other than guilt-ridden.

Whether she cried or not meant little: there was nothing to be done. There was no one left to send messages to, no one left who would send messages to an exiled queen. And this truly was exile: she was cut adrift from news as though her little Court was of no consequence to the world she had fled. For the first time she felt herself to be what she had always most feared: utterly forgotten.

***

Sunlight, that's what it was. Sunlight.

He had been kept indoors so long he had forgotten the feel of it, the dance of it across his skin.

It is so warm and I have been cold for...for how long?

He could not remember. He could not remember anything, he could not recognise anything and yet...he was not afraid.

Why would you be afraid, Henry, when I am with you?

Henry: that was his name. He remembered now. And the voice, the voice that lived always in his head, that kept him quiet and kept him calm, the voice would guide him as it always did.

Everything was so bright: the flowers, the grass, all so vivid after the grey he had been surrounded with. He sat down and picked a handful of sweet smelling blooms, delighting in the feathery softness of the petals across his cheek.

'Are you alright?'

He couldn't see clearly, the sun was in his eyes, but the voice was gentle and there was a golden light around the head he had seen before in the books he loved so much.

It is an angel; I have been sent an angel. I am safe.

'I am Henry.'

He raised his hand towards the light and bowed his hand, waiting for the blessing.

Bemused, the young servant girl took the cool outstretched fingers in her own work-roughened ones and helped him to his feet. The cloak the man wore was richly woven and far better than anything she owned despite the patches of mud and grass that clung to it but his head was bare and he carried nothing with him.

Whoever he is, he cannot stay here; he has no more sense about him than a child.

Patting his arm gently as though he were a timid animal to be soothed, she led the King quietly down the flower-carpeted path, into the woods and away from the world.

France:
1464-1467

Exile: it is a landscape shaped by waiting and not-knowing; a state of suspension from the world. Life moves on without you in ways you can neither foresee nor control. New betrayals and new alliances form without any warning and foes suddenly become friends whether you ask them to or not. So it was with Warwick, eaten up family jealousies and the monster that is ambition. Hatred makes very strange bedfellows.

'You receive so many letters Mother; how you can claim that England has forgotten us, I truly don't know!'

Edward's tone of mock exasperation was a practised one now and never failed to make Margaret, or her women, smile.

'It is true; we seem to gain more friends with every year although I am not sure they will ever replace the ones we have lost.'

There was a sudden quiet in the room; it was Pierre she meant and everyone knew it. The years of exile may have been years marked less by loss but they were not without it or without suffering. She had lost Pierre to the misfortunes of battle in 1465 and it had been a hard blow.

He was such a kind man, kinder I think to me than any other I have met for his concern was never a cloak for ambition or gain.

'You miss him.'

It was a statement not a question and she acknowledged it as such. 'Yes Edward, I miss him. He was my support after we fled Scotland and managed your grandfather better than I ever could and without him...'

'He died a soldier's death at least. That is something.'

Edward's words were so certain, she could not argue even though she knew he saw only glory not the horrors she knew to be the battlefield's truth.

'That is something.'

With an effort she pulled herself out of her dark mood before it took hold and soured the day. 'Edward you are right in that and everything else today. We are not forgotten, look at these names,' She gestured to the half-read papers piled in front of her: 'Sir Gervaise Clifton, Lord Wenlock, Henry Courtenay and most of the Alderman of London write with news and requests to visit us.' She smiled, 'I think our position is shifting, I really do. We may not be at the centre of things but, at least, we are moving in from the shadows and becoming quite the little Court again.'

'I don't know why you are surprised.'

Katherine smoothed her embroidery out across her skirt, admiring the delicate pansies she had worked across the silver cloth.

'Look at it, it's pretty enough for a wedding gown although perhaps a little too virginal for some.'

Alice and Osanna burst out laughing and Edward looked at them with growing interest, guessing the source of their gossip.

'Did she even get a wedding?' Alice's tongue was sharper, 'no one knows for certain and the only witness to it was her witch of a mother.' Edward was sitting forward now, his eyes shining at the turn the conversation was taking; like everyone else, he had heard the story of Edward IV's marriage to Elizabeth Woodville; how could he not when it was the scandal of Europe?

'Was it really magic that caught him, that made him fall in love with her? I heard some of the men talking and they said she came upon him in a wood, caught in the light of the leaves like a nymph and that he was so...' he suddenly stopped and his youth was obvious in his confusion. 'Well so something, I can't remember what, but she had to threaten him with a dagger. And then they went back to her house and Jacquetta Woodville fed Edward a love potion. Is it true?'

The women were all giggling now at his childlike retelling of what they had all been obsessed with for weeks: no one knew the truth of the meeting between the King and Elizabeth but every tale told about it became the stuff of a romance and all the gossip was that his love for her was a bewitchment arising as much from the mother's magic as from the daughter's beauty. For that was a story repeated everywhere: that Jacquetta was little more than a witch; that a love potion was as much to blame for the King's imprudent marriage as a pair of pretty eyes and that the daughter and the mother shared secrets that no virtuous woman should know.

'Witchcraft and magic: the stories grow more embroidered with the telling.'

And I would be glad to never hear another breath of them. She sails too close that one, too close. So many secrets to hide: what must Rivers think of this new entanglement, of this new son-in-law who would surely kill him if he knew the truth of what the father had done?

Her fingers knotted beneath her sleeves, Margaret smiled at her son who had grown pink with the realisation that there was more to the scene he had recounted than he really knew.

'Jacquetta Woodville is a very foolish woman; whether she is a witch or not, I don't know but I do know she likes to weave a mystery about herself and that is something we can use. This is a misguided marriage, Edward, trust me. Elizabeth Woodville might be the greatest beauty in the land but she is a commoner. A dalliance is one thing, but a marriage for love rather than for alliances and a marriage to someone with no title, no real position? That will make enemies not friends. My letters tell me that Warwick is furious and if he has fallen out of love with his golden protégé, then it can only be to our good.'

'You were close with Jacquetta once, Madame, and then there was such a coldness between you.' Katherine shook her finished sleeve out as though the observation was just that. 'She must feel quite superior to us all now.'

You suspect something, you always have. You watch me so closely and yet you have never challenged me. I do not trust you, dearest Katherine, I do not trust you at all.

'So she must; I hope it gives her some pleasure, I doubt it will last.' Margaret turned to the pile of letters. 'Read through these for me; see if there is anything that needs my attention.'

If Katherine knew the change of conversation was deliberate, she made no sign of it and began to sift through the papers as she spoke. 'It is quite a rise though, isn't it? I know Jacquetta was always meddlesome and ambitious but even she could hardly imagine she would become mother to a queen. Such a rise and such a winding path! King Edward's head really must be turned if he now accepts the Woodvilles as devoted Yorkists, turned or charmed...'

'Katherine, that is enough.'

Margaret's tone was sharp but she did not care and she would rather risk Katherine's petulance at being reprimanded than a slip of the tongue as she struggled to control a temper becoming ever more strained.

How can Jacquetta bear it? Elizabeth Woodville and my Edward share a father; the greatest challenge to her daughter's beloved husband comes from her own kin and the girl has not an inkling. Worse than that she puts us all in danger: enemies will come from every direction, pulling her family apart, desperate to bring down a common girl who dared to become a queen with any piece of scandal they can find. The King's father-in-law father to the boy he usurped. It would be a story to set every hearth alight; it would be a story that could take many heads. Even if she feels her revenge somewhere in her daughter's triumph, surely Jacquetta must be as afraid as...

'Dear God, oh dear God.'

Katherine's stricken voice cut across Margaret's rising panic, snapping her back into the room. She had a letter clutched in her hand; Margaret could see John de Vere, the Earl of Oxford's signature, but no more.

'The letter, it has news of King Henry...'

'Give it to me!'

Margaret snatched it and scanned the close-written lines trying to make sense of words that jumbled themselves as she read them too fast.

'Mother, what is it? Have they found Father, is he alive?'

Edward's face was no longer pink but deathly-white, tears already springing into his eyes.

'He is found and he is alive.'

She could barely take it in even though the proof was there in front of her: after a disappearance so total it was as if the fairies had him, Henry was suddenly found.

This is worse than the news about Jacquetta and I must behave as though it is a miracle.

'He is alive but you must be brave.'

Margaret pulled Edward down into the settle next to her; he nestled into her side as though the years had slipped away from him.

'There is not much here.' She looked at the letter again as though answers might be found when there seemed to be nothing but more questions. 'It seems your father was seen wandering alone in the woodlands that run through Lancashire. De Vere thinks that Henry had been living quietly for some time at a place called Waddington Hall, perhaps known to the family, perhaps not. It says that he spent most of his days walking in the woods where he would talk to himself; he was overheard and betrayed to King Edward's soldiers.'

She stopped: the story might be short but it was cruel.

'I want to hear it all.'

Edward's voice was quiet but steady and she knew she could not deny him.

'He was chased to the River Ribble where he was caught and the soldiers sent him to London. He was paraded through the streets like a criminal, his legs bound to his horse while the crowds were encouraged to shout terrible things at him. Then he was taken to the Tower; he is assumed alive but no one has seen him since.'

And now Edward has his bargaining hand and will pull us back before we are ready to go.

'How dare they, he is the King!'

Edward's voice tore at her heart: childish tears for his father mixed with impotent fury.

'They have no right to put him in the Tower, no right!'

He pushed away from his mother and she saw his face harden, watched the tears stop mid-flow.

'I will not let them do this, I will not. I will get an army and I will go back and I will kill all of them who would insult my father like this. I swear I will do it.'

'And I believe you.'

But I must stop you. We are not ready: I will lose my husband but I will not lose my son.

She did not touch him this time: he was as coiled as a snake waiting to strike and did not want mothering. She had to allow him the desire for revenge but shape it into something she could use.

'This news is hard to bear but there is hope.'

She gestured to the letters again.

'Edward might have the throne but he doesn't sit securely on it, all these reports prove that. There is unrest everywhere: you are upset at what has been done to your father and the people will be to. They don't like to see a king treated like this, no matter they might be paid to insult him and make a public show.'

Edward was calming now, becoming more ready to listen.

'I know you want to avenge your father and that is the right way to feel but we have to act carefully. King Edward has made a fool of himself with his marriage and he has angered Warwick, every letter says so. And they say that the King refuses to listen to Warwick and shows favouritism to everyone but him; he is raising other nobles up to have as much power as his old advisor. That is a foolish way to treat Warwick: he is a dangerous enemy to have; believe me.'

Edward nodded, 'and if he angers, then he will look for other allies. Even to people who were once his enemies.'

She smiled at her son, 'and when he does, we will be waiting.'

***

Waiting. The days were filled with it.

Edward glowered under the weight of the days, chafing against the ties his mother bound round him, desperate for action she could not permit. They were not estranged, they were still too close for that, but she felt him pulling against her and could already sense the day coming when she would no longer be able to bend him. The recent arrival of her brother Jean, the Duke of Calabria, had been a welcome diversion for the whole Court, not least for his ability to keep Margaret calm.

'You have a visitor, Madame.'

There was something about William Vaux's tone that made Margaret look up from her card game with greater interest than his rather dour countenance normally aroused.

'William, you sound very unsettled. What surprise has Katherine sprung upon you this time?'

He had the grace to smile at this for his wife, who could be as much of an irritant to her husband as she was to her mistress, was very fond of playing tricks on her rather more serious spouse.

'I confess that I am a little disturbed but this time the cause cannot be placed at Katherine's door.' He shrugged his shoulders before continuing in a gesture most unlike him.

'Madame, the visitor's manservant will not give his master's name but I have watched him from the window. From what I can see of his build and the garments poorly hidden by his cloak, I think it is My Lord of Warwick.'

'Warwick!'

She was on her feet, the cards spilt across the sunny courtyard floor, 'how can it be Warwick? And, if it is, what has he come for?' Fear gripped her and she reached out a steadying hand to her brother, 'dear God, they have killed Henry and now he is come for Edward...'

'Calm yourself, Marguerite.'

Jean's hand was firm as he pulled her back into the chair and his voice steady.

'If that were true, King Edward would hardly send Warwick alone would he? There would be an army, not a manservant. Besides, you already predicted he might come, this might be what you have been waiting for.'

There was sense and soothing in his words. Relying on Jean the way she had once trusted Pierre, she had shared her thoughts about where Warwick's anger might lead him and Jean had seen the logic in it; his smile now suggested she had been right. But she was still unsure: it was a huge leap from anger to betrayal and one she was not certain even Warwick could make.

'Even if there is nothing to fear, William must be mistaken: Warwick is in England, he could not be here.'

'Actually he could.'

Jean retrieved the cards and began to smooth them out onto the table, clearly giving himself time to think.

'I had heard that Warwick was in France but thought it was a rumour so I paid little mind to it. Then word reached me yesterday that he has been here since May as King Louis' guest and they have been thick as thieves since he arrived. I had hoped to find out more before I told you; I knew you would be unsettled and did not want to give you cause to worry, or hope, if there was no cause.'

'I had not heard any of this.'

And I do not like it. I don't trust Louis or Warwick; the thought of them together is doubly disturbing.

She began to pick at the cards, tearing little slivers from them.

'I do nothing but wait, it is so hard. Now Philip of Burgundy is dead, all the alliances are shifting and, try as I might, I can do nothing. Do you at least know why Warwick has come?'

Jean shrugged.

'Who knows anything for sure when Louis is involved except that there will be plots and meddling. I hear the gossip same as anyone who travels to court as much as I do and keeps confidantes there. Unfortunately, I am seen as being too close to Charles and Burgundy to be overly-trusted by the French and much is hidden from me.'

He looked at her then with an appraising stare.

'Perhaps Warwick comes to tell Louis how he fares in the war he has been waging for so long against King Edward in England.'

Margaret had the grace to redden at that and to bite back the retort that would normally be the response to her brother's critical tone. It was clear that gossip reached him from every corner and she could not pretend she did not know what he meant without making herself appear more foolish than she currently felt. She had been foolish, she knew it and so it seemed did Jean.

Two years earlier in 1465, while trying to win Louis' support, Margaret had written to him stating that Warwick had already risen in rebellion against King Edward and that the only hope for peace in England was the immediate restoration of the House of Lancaster. It was clumsily done and Louis, far more practiced in twisting alliances than she and quite aware that there was no truth in her assertions, merely used her words as a weapon. He fed her lies straight to the Milanese Ambassador as part of his plans to entangle Milan further into French protection and thus strengthen his own network of support. Pierre, politely furious with her to her shame, had reported how Louis had simply used Margaret's letter as proof to Duke Francesco Sforza of Milan, already threatened by Jean's ambitious glance towards his lands, that she was a dangerous troublemaker whose attempts at influence would destabilise the peace Louis was building; that she should, therefore, be ignored. She should have known better than to try and fool Louis, she knew that: it was just the kind of web the Spider King loved to spin and had bought her only further isolation from the princes who might have offered support.

Jean, for once the diplomat rather than the brother, took pity on her discomfort and laid a gentle hand on her clenched one.

'You cannot know, sister, why he is here unless you admit him. And, who knows, with Warwick it may be cause for alarm or it may be a sign that he is ready to look to new alliances; whatever it is, it will not lack interest.'

Taking her silence, rightly, for assent, Jean instructed William to bring the visitor to the courtyard and sent a servant to the kitchens for wine and the spice cake the cook excelled in. Neither of them spoke and the tension that greeted Warwick's arrival was palpable. He, however, seemed amused rather than discomfited by it and smiled at the sight of the hovering servant and the awaiting refreshments.

'My Lady, it is an honour to see you and in far kinder circumstances than when we last met although, if I remember, kitchens also featured rather prominently then.'

He never changes. What would it take to make him lose that arrogance, that belief in his own importance? It is as much a part of him as his breath.

Margaret was conscious of Jean's averted face and his rather poor attempts to hide his amusement behind a cough; her brother had never lost his youthful delight in anyone who could better his sister and would clearly be of little use here. She, however, could not let

Warwick assume a friendship they did not have and there was little answering warmth in her greeting.

'My Lord Warwick, this is a surprising and unlooked for intrusion on my home. I will welcome you as a guest but do not make pretence of any familiarity between us. Tell me why you are here as simply and as quickly as you can tell it so that this meeting can be concluded.'

But her coldness made no impression on him at all: he sat without waiting for permission and smiled, if anything, more broadly.

'It is very heartening to see that neither defeat nor exile has changed you, Madame. Then let me be as direct with you as you are with me. I have come to put the House of Lancaster back on the throne.'

So I had guessed it rightly. There is not even a pretence; I could almost admire you for it.

There was a moment's silence and then she burst into peals of laughter, she could not help herself. 'Oh my dear Lord Warwick, things must fare very badly with you indeed if I have become your hope.'

Her smile was now far broader than his and, as she looked more closely at him, she saw the tension behind his play of charm and the pinched look about his eyes.

So all is not so well with my once so confident Warwick as he would like me to think; let us see who is the better player.

Settling back into the cushions of her chair, she let her gaze linger on him and saw, with satisfaction, the smile begin to fade. She picked out a cake and began to break it into small pieces, arranging them in a circle on the plate.

'So, let me guess how it goes with you, My Lord. Let me try to determine, and you must stop me if I speak out of turn, what must have changed for you.'

She ate one of the pieces and smiled.

'What do I know? Well that is easy: you wanted a French alliance but Edward's foolhardy marriage must have ruined that plan.'

Another morsel.

'I wonder: you pretend to have such control of your young King but this liaison he has made, well that makes your position look less sure, your influence less secure perhaps. And, if that is true, then I would guess that Louis looks at you with less regard. I am right, I think?'

Another piece; another smile.

He did not answer but any play of amusement had completely disappeared leaving his mouth thin and his face unpleasantly drawn. She had him, she knew it, so she continued, letting her tone warm to her theme.

'So I am right. Louis will not take any notice of you, then were else would you turn? Burgundy, I would guess, as I once did in your place. But that cannot sit well: unless I have it wrong, you hate Charles of Burgundy; everyone knows it and you have declared it often enough. How could you ally with a man who was such a friend of Somerset? Surely Somerset was the man King Edward chose to pardon against all your advice and the man behind your brother's sudden rise to power?'

She ate the final crumb.

'Well, I can see from your expression, My Lord, that I have the pieces correct so far but I am missing something and I do not know what it can be. Jean, help me here...'

Her brother saw her game at once and assumed a look of thoughtful concentration that belied the answer that came so smoothly to his lips.

'It must, I think, be the question of marriage that still occupies My Lord Warwick. Obviously he cannot promise the King's hand any more but he has other offers to make and I would venture to guess that it is Edward's sister who has now become the prize.'

'That is it! Why we talked about the rumours spreading from Burgundy just the other night: King Edward plans to marry his sister Margaret to Charles and form an alliance against France.'

She deliberately clapped her hands as though delighted at her own cleverness and continued as though she was playing a guessing game at a party.

'Well that would not do for you would it my dear Warwick? No, that would not do at all. So what can it be? I know! You have not come to make friends with Charles of Burgundy or to act as broker for the marriage, no: you have come to undermine it. That must be it: you have come to Louis and promised him...promised him what? Who could Margaret marry if not Charles? Let me think, perhaps Louis' brother-in-law, the Duke of Savoy? That would be a neat fix: the brother to replace the sister your Edward made a fool of? Or perhaps one of Louis' daughters could marry one of Edward's brothers? There are two to choose from, unless, of course, you want George and Richard for your own girls...'

His face was dark as thunder now which only served to entertain her more.

'I am right on every count; I can see it in your frown! I have caught you, how infuriating! But, my poor Lord Warwick, your plans have no more substance than air, do they? King Edward does not know you are here and Louis will have none of your scheming. He has guessed, hasn't he, that Edward has finished with you and that your word carries nothing?'

She paused, watching him carefully now for any pretence of friendship on his part was long gone and she wondered if his simmering fury could be contained. Yet, still he did not speak.

'So now you come to me. That is an interesting turn-about. Tell me, why do you think that I would want anything to do with your schemes? Be really honest, now My Lord, no more games. What use am I to you? What have you done to force such a change of plan? Perhaps you have killed my husband.'

There was no laughter in her voice now and both men heard the change from amusement to contempt.

'Perhaps you have killed Henry and now have a marriage in mind for me. Perhaps you will have Queen Elizabeth removed and me put in her place, a puppet Queen to control your once puppet King.'

She laughed that mirthless laugh that her household loathed to hear.

'No, that cannot be it: your influence does not stretch that far with Edward and besides no one could make me do such a thing even if it didn't stretch the bounds of credibility. But you say you will re-store the House of Lancaster so how would you do it? Perhaps it is the other way round. Perhaps you would have King Edward killed and my son marry the widow. But that is even harder to believe: you must want her gone and would surely kill them both if you are set on that course. So what am I left with? Would you remove one Edward and crown the other or is it, perhaps, your own claim you would pursue now. Is that it Warwick, do you come to kill me and my son and clear the path to real power? You like to make kings, My Lord, whose turn is it now?'

He is brave; I had not seen that before. I thought the defiance all born out of arrogance but I think there is bravery in it.

Warwick's face was as white as the lilies that filled the courtyard but he did not flinch. Reaching for the wine he took a deep drink, the break in his composure visible only in his pallor. When he did speak, his tone was measured and his voice controlled.

'You put the pieces together with skill, My Lady but you are wrong on as much as you are right. I have lost favour, I admit it. I loathe this Queen Edward has risen up and her grubbing hordes of relatives who worm their way into every position and pour corruption into every office they touch. And Edward is not the man I schooled to wear the Crown. He dotes on that woman so much he has grown soft; he would spend all his days in her bed and cares nothing for the problems that beset every corner of his country. I swear he is bewitched by her arts or her mother's potions and there will be a reckoning I cannot save him from. But I have not killed your husband, Madame and I do not weave marriages for you or for your son, no matter how diverting your fancies might be.'

'I did not truly think you did.'

His plain-speaking had removed much of her anger.

'But I am right about Louis? He knows your hold over the King is slipping?'

There was not a sound in the courtyard; the heavy summer air had stilled, the birds had silenced. Jean sat back into the shadows and Warwick and Margaret were left as though alone.

'Yes, about that you are right. Louis does not trust me and I have no intention of becoming another thread in his plotting.'

His voice had dropped so low, she had to lean forward to hear him.

This is where his charm lies: in his honesty. This is how he wooed Edward and Richard of York, with his honesty and his naked ambition. I need to take more care around him than I knew.

She felt herself being drawn into an intimacy that disturbed as much as it intrigued. The air thickened: the perfume of the lilies stole around them with a heady, deadening scent and then Jean coughed, deliberately perhaps, and the spell of the moment was broken.

Margaret blinked and saw herself as if from outside the scene and did not like the weakening woman in front of her. With a deliberately dismissive gesture, she rose to her feet and stepped away.

'This is all very interesting gossip for a sunny afternoon but it does not answer my question: why should I ally myself, my House, with you?'

The charm broken, Warwick leaned back in his seat, made himself as formal as her, and regarded her levelly.

'Because you want the throne and I can deliver it. I have armies and I have money. Your husband is alive and we will give him back the crown but it will not be truly his. He will be reinstated only to ready the throne for your son: it will be you and I, Madame, who will rule whichever of them wears the crown. Ally yourself with me and we will both get what we want.'

He hands me back what I thought I had lost. Dear God, I can almost touch it, that promise of power. But it is still too soon, he is still too strong.

She shook her head.

'How simple you make it sound and yet I think you will ask for more. Next you will come looking for my son to marry your daughter. Surely that must be part of your plan: to make a king and be father to a queen; that would be very nicely done.'

He laughed and showed her the truth in her words, clearly assuming that such a marriage would please her.

You are still too proud; it is always your undoing.

She moved a hand to her throat, deliberately directing his glance to the heavy emeralds set into her thickly enamelled necklace. He must not think her penniless or desperate even if this was the last good piece she had left.

'It strikes me, My Lord, that you have not yet learned the lessons losing control over Edward should have taught you. Henry is one thing and would be easy to influence, that I grant you. But what happens when my son no longer wants to do your bidding; who will you replace him with then?'

Warwick smiled; a smile that was too confident, too sure.

'But it will not be only my bidding that he carries out; it will be yours, his beloved mother's. We will make a pact between us, Margaret, it will be a shared rule to serve both our ends; I promise you.'

It was the so familiar use of her name that turned her hand against him.

He is a snake. He will strike at me the minute I refuse to accept his will and I will not bend to him. This Warwick is still too dangerous for me to manage, too dangerous for my son.

But she would not send him away with nothing: Louis was not the only one who could spin plots and set snares. Her smile at the last was gracious.

'You are a bold man, My Lord Warwick and you have given me much to think about. There can be no answer now and I do not imagine you would claim one: it is too great a matter for haste. But don't leave us just yet: you have been my guest today, let that continue. Even if our hospitality is far more modest than King Louis' court can offer, we will make you most welcome. Dine with us tonight: you will meet my son and we will talk of everything and anything but the crown and battles and power. You will tell me how delightful your daughters are and entertain me with gossip from the English Court and I will tell you all manner of stories about how unpleasant Duke Charles was as a boy. We will learn to know each other a little more and, when you return to England, we will begin a correspondence that, I hope, will bring friendship and understanding between us. I trust you will not deny me such a little request.'

He knew when he was matched.

The evening was as entertaining as she promised him it would be although she made very sure that Edward was the focus of attention and avoided any moments when that earlier intimacy which had weaved itself unbidden about them might be recalled. Warwick stayed the night and asked for an audience again the following day but she begged a headache and sent him on his way, unheard perhaps but with enough of a hope of a future alliance to keep his interest alive until she could better shape the engagement.

And so began a correspondence that would lead to an alliance; that would lead, in truth, to the crushing of my hopes not the flowering of them. For that I cannot blame Warwick; I can blame no one but myself.

France:
1468-1470

The last years of my exile presented themselves as though they were the opening of a new chapter. They were not. They were nothing more than the dying days of our hope, the last rallying that comes before the final breath and fools the watchers with its sudden energy.

It seemed to Margaret that more letters flew across the Channel in 1468 than seabirds filled the skies. Letters not only to Warwick, although their correspondence had begun as he had promised and was often a source of much entertainment, but back and forth with all the men who now declared themselves still loyal to Lancaster from London to the North and across to Wales. Her pen was never still.

There was no more sign of Warwick although she knew he came to Calais more than once. His letters described how he spent more and more time at his Middleham estates, far away from the English Court which he detested and described in malicious terms as a nest of grasping Woodvilles. They also told her something of the Queen: of how she had become so haughty that she demanded silence from all around her when she ate as though she was too mighty for mere mortals; of how greedy and cruel she had grown.

His letters were amusing frequently and shocking sometimes but there was a bitterness that hung heavy on them and it was clear he had lost all faith in Edward. More and more they talked about the younger brother, Clarence, and how fine a man he was; it was increasingly obvious that his attention was shifting and new plans for securing the power he clearly craved were beginning to take shape. Margaret did not question him, in truth all she did was continue to encourage his friendship and flatter his pretensions; there was still too much danger in too close an alliance there.

Those letters went undetected but too many others did not and their recipients and their authors paid a high price for their words. Margaret knew the danger and protected herself with Warwick, yet she never discouraged or concealed letters from any other who would write and was rarely circumspect in her own choice of words. She had been at Louis' side often enough to know that codes and ciphers were widely used by many with secrets to hide but she had never mastered them or cared to try and so the letters, for too many, became death warrants.

Some men paid hard for their loyalty and many more were put in danger and the stories of torture and execution that reached Margaret's household always unleashed a black fury. The details of the rack and the burning irons and the noose were ugly and made her weep but did not make her stop. So many men were fined she began to think her name had become merely an excuse for another tax to be levied to fill the Woodville purse; Warwick even dared make the accusation to Edward himself when too many of his own household were charged and made to pay but she counselled caution there and, for once, he saw the threats surrounding him and was silenced.

King Edward's fury swept the Kingdom. John Poynings, Richard Alford, Richard Stairs: three men Margaret had never heard of and yet all were executed for supposedly using Margaret of York's wedding as a cover to meet and plot with her at Koeur la Petite. Sir Thomas Tresham, Thomas Hungerford, Henry Courtenay: all hung, drawn and quartered after a mockery of a trial in November 1468 for plotting to return Lancaster to the throne and yet none of it was true. It seemed as though King Edward, feeling his throne suddenly less secure, was set upon a reign of terror that would rid himself of any mention of Lancaster and more and more voices began to call to Warwick for counsel and for help. And as Warwick's name began to grow again, so did Edward's anger until it became clear to everyone, Margaret included, that her name was only ever cited to hide a vengeance that was never about her at all. She was not the target of Edward's fury: Warwick was.

***

Time hung too heavy. She could fill it well enough with conversation, with her books, with her beloved horses but it still hung too heavy. News still came but less of it now and she felt the weight of isolation pressing on her more and more. For her son it was becoming a torment.

'When was the last time you had word from Warwick?'

It was an abrupt interruption but her brother had never been one to waste time on courtesies. He clearly had news but his lips were too tightly drawn to suggest anything pleasurable had reached him.

'Not for quite some weeks now; not since May in fact.'

Margaret folded away the needlework that held no interest and motioned him to sit.

'I assume he is sulking somewhere, mulling on some Woodville slight that he will recount as a witty story when he has his temper back. That is his usual pattern.' She saw Jean's frown deepen, 'your face suggests you might know different. What has happened to make you look so serious?'

He sighed and pulled a letter from his sleeve, pushing it across the table.

'He has been far too busy to waste time sulking. Read it, sister, it seems you understood My Lord Warwick's plans for his daughters rather well.'

The letter was marked as having come from Calais and dated the 12th of July 1469; it had reached them swift enough but, already, the news it contained was out of date and begged more questions than it answered about Warwick's silence. She read it once quickly and then again.

So I did not mistake the scale of his ambition or how quickly he would move on from any dalliance with me.

She passed the letter back.

'He has married his daughter to Clarence. To be honest, I didn't think he would do it although I teased him about his ambitions. You say I guessed his plans but I wasn't serious when I accused him of plotting such a thing. Isabel and George are cousins so a match would not be a straightforward affair and, besides, I thought the King had forbidden it.'

Her brother plucked an orange from the bowl in front of him and rolled it around his fingers.

'He did, two years ago when the idea was first suggested; he was clear that Warwick's ambitions were riding too high. But it seems that our Earl no longer cares about the King's displeasure.'

Jean began peeling the orange, rolling its scented skin into thin strips as he continued. 'You didn't know that Warwick has been in Calais for the past two months?'

'No.'

It was her turn now to frown. 'I don't receive so many letters from England as I did; people fear Edward now, they don't want to risk sending word to me. Do you know more than is contained here, did your messenger bring more news than this?'

Jean nodded and ran a hand through hair she noticed was starting to thin.

'There was more that could not be entrusted to paper. It looks like Warwick has played Edward for a fool.'

The room was becoming stifling in the summer heat, the scent of the discarded fruit too cloying. She moved to the casement and pushed it as wide as it would go but there was little breeze to be had. Jean's hesitancy was beginning to irritate her as much as the heat and she had to breathe deeply to stop the harsher tone he would hate and did not deserve.

'If the letter is not the full story, then tell me what you mean?'

Jean stayed where he was, plucking another fruit from the bowl to pull apart.

'I mean what I say, Warwick seems to have tricked Edward into thinking he was no real threat, despite the King's suspicions. You know how much Warwick has been kept from Court and it has become increasingly clear that all the trials, all the fines have been intended to curb Warwick's ambitions as much as they have been warnings against any dealings with you. You see that don't you?'

Margaret nodded: even had she not suspected it, Duke Charles had made it clear that she was of no interest to Edward, that he barely considered her anymore. Charles, in fact, had been much amused by the thought of inviting Margaret to his wedding and having his new wife try to guess who she was. It had not been a pleasant exchange.

She waited for Jean to continue, staring out of the window to try and hide her impatience as though the empty fields were more fascinating than any words of his. She doubted he was fooled for a moment. 'Well, against all advice, Warwick persuaded Edward to let him have the Captaincy of Calais again. It makes little sense to me. Perhaps Edward was distracted by some local disturbance or by Duke Charles's visit; I don't know. Perhaps he was simply glad to have Warwick out of the country. Whatever the truth of it, he agreed to Warwick's request and handed him the control of Calais and its army and the seas. What it seems that Edward didn't know was that the Earl had been secretly bargaining with the Pope: he got his dispensation and the pair are married, cousins or not.'

'So Warwick is father-in-law to a royal prince.'

She leant on the sill, knowing that she was missing something but still unsure what it could be.

'But that matters little if he is still out of Edward's favour and surely such a blatant refusal of his authority will only anger the King more? What possible use could such a marriage be to Warwick?'

And then, as she spoke, she realised the import of what Warwick had done and the sill suddenly seemed to shift beneath her hands. 'Dear God, he means to challenge Edward for the throne but not with my son or my husband but with Clarence! He would make George a king! I have the truth of it, Jean, tell me I have the truth of it.'

Her brother closed his eyes as though he could not bear to see the effect of his words.

'You have it and he has already done it. They had the marriage and then sailed straight away for England with an army to back them. He is going to take the Crown from Edward if he can and, yes, it will go on his son-in-law's head; you are nothing to him anymore. He has forgotten you and your son and, if he wins, the House of Lancaster will be gone.'

**

They waited and waited for news and, when it came, it seemed that Jean's chilling prophecy had come true.

Warwick had landed in Kent and wasted no time in raising an army there to swell the ranks he already had. He had also wasted no time in circulating rumours about King Edward: with a daring that even Margaret did not think him capable of, he openly proclaimed Edward to be a bastard, the son of some common soldier Cecilly Neville had taken to her bed in France like a common whore. And if Edward therefore had no claim, then who should have the throne but Clarence, the unsullied younger brother?

That was the only piece of news from England that brought a smile to my lips that summer: the thought of that pinched woman's discomfort at the songs being sung about her and the whispering she would have to face was some recompense for the disdain she had always shown to me.

Whether there was any truth in Warwick's words could not be answered and mattered little once the rumour took hold and married itself to the dissatisfaction with the King springing up everywhere: men flocked to Warwick's standard, they did not flock to Edward's.

And so, eight years after the horrors of Towton, there was another battle fought and more blood soaked the English countryside. News came slowly and in patches but it all told the same tale: Warwick's army at Edgecote was relentless in its attack and its pursuit. First Margaret had news of his victory, then of the beheadings of Edward's champions, the Earl of Pembroke and the Earl of Devon. Then news came of the capture of Edward himself and his imprisonment at Middleham Castle. And, finally, the news came that meant nothing to anyone save her: Richard Woodville, Lord Rivers, the father of her son was among the dead, executed at Kenilworth along with his son John.

Jacquetta was a widow and I, what was I? I didn't know how to grieve for him. I could not grieve for him, not in public certainly and barely in private for I did not dare let my women see any trace of tears. And now that I can weep for him, when there is no one to notice or to care, the tears will not come. His passing is too long ago and matters too little when stacked against the death of our child.

Late July and early August: the days were hot, dry and exhausting.

She thirsted for news and hated it when it came for it told only of Warwick's triumph and what could his triumph be if not her disaster? He had two kings imprisoned and a son-in-law desperate for a crown: every day she expected news that Henry was dead in the Tower; that Edward had met with some accident in Middleham; that Clarence was crowned King and Warwick's little daughter had pushed Elizabeth Woodville from the throne. And she waited and waited and it never came: Warwick might know how to make a king; he did not know how to break one.

***

'You will let me go. Tomorrow, I will ride out of here and you will not stop me. Do you know why?'

'Because you are the King.'

'Because I am the King.'

Edward's shout of laughter was loud enough to bring an army running, if there had been an army to come.

'Because I am the King and you are nothing.'

He smiled at Warwick, a smile of such genuine pleasure it was more frightening than anger would have been.

'You are nothing, do you understand?'

He had no arrogance left in him, no fight left. Edward was right: he was nothing. Warwick's army had gone; Edward had charmed the servants so beautifully no one would raise a finger against him; if he chose to leave, the castle walls would be as much use as thistle-down.

'What will you do?'

Edward shrugged. 'With you? I will kill you. Not now, I need to get back to London and show myself.'

The smile broadened.

'I need to see my beautiful wife and get a son on her. But I will kill you.'

He leant across the table and cupped Warwick's defeated face in his hand.

'I really don't care what you do. Go to France if you like, try your luck with the Anjou bitch if you want, but bear in mind that every day now is a borrowed one. For you and your family and for my brother whose stupid head you have pulled into this nonsense.'

Edward stood up and stretched to his full height.

'Let's put some sport into it. Go and get an army and let's make a proper contest of it. Just remember that you will pay for this.'

He turned and left and made good his promise, riding away the next day as though from a pleasant visit, only his threats remaining to poison the air and Warwick's every remaining day.

***

'I have waited more than two years to see you again but these are hardly the circumstances our last meeting led me to expect.'

And you are not the man I expected to see.

The bluster was still there and the arrogance of manner but it was less assured, more a façade than a certainty. Warwick's eyes darted about the room and his fingers knotted with nerves; there were new lines cutting grooves in the corner of his mouth and he looked tired, deeply tired. Margaret had been amused, entertained and irritated in turn by his letters and they had formed a kind of friendship, no matter that neither really trusted the other. She recognised something of herself in him and knew him as both a potential ally and a dangerous threat. And yet, when she came to the Great Hall at Angers, summoned by Louis to meet and bargain with this most unpredictable man, it was not he who first commanded her attention, it was his daughters.

'What have you reduced your family to with all your ambition?'

He did not answer; she did not expect him to.

'Isobel, Anne, come forward and let me greet you properly.'

The family grouped before her, the women bent deep to curtsey, were broken. Although they had been ashore for over a month, they still bore the marks of the terrible voyage they had endured. As the girls stepped forward, Margaret could see that Isabel was grey; no other colour could describe her. Against the bright golds and reds of the tapestries, she appeared faded: her face was all hollows and shadow and her gown hung limply from bones that had all the substance of a bird. Margaret knew that, when Isabel had sailed from England, she had been with child and near her time but the baby, born on a ship that was refused entry wherever it turned, had been lost. She had stopped Osanna and Katherine's gossip but the little she had heard of a terrible labour in a storm that threatened to capsize them all had chilled her.

Something of the mother has died with the child; she shrinks from any attempt by her husband to touch or speak to her, there is a malaise that runs too deep.

It was too much: she was angry with the father not the daughter and would not be witness to Isabel's suffering.

'Countess of Warwick, your daughter is ill and has no place here. Take her back to your chambers and let her rest, please; she has been through enough.'

As they left, Margaret turned her attention to the younger girl, Anne; she, in contrast, had a vividness about her. She was no great beauty, although pretty enough with her dark blonde hair and large brown eyes set wide in a face that had a delicacy to it, but there was a pride in the bearing that bore a look of her father. Her head was high, she watched those around her carefully and, when Edward stared at her more frankly than Margaret had seen him do to any girl, there was no maidenly blush but rather a level gaze and a slight smile that caused the boy to fluster first and look away.

'My Lord Warwick, let us sit.'

Margaret waited for the small party to settle itself and smiled at him; it was not returned.

'We have heard much about your flight to France but very little of the reasons behind it. From the news that reaches us, it seemed everything had fallen in your favour, if not perhaps in the way you promised me it would, and yet here you are in exile.'

She waited to see if he would volunteer an explanation, an apology, an excuse but he merely gazed back, his stare as level as hers, his expression blank.

He is beaten; he simply cannot accept it yet.

'You are strangely quiet today, My Lord, and I have so many questions. Will you answer a few?'

Still silence. She shrugged as though his rudeness was of little interest.

'Then let me list a few. Why did the garrison at Calais fire on you when you must have assumed you would be safely escorted in? Why would you let your daughter sail when she was so near her time?'

She could see she was needling him now so she continued, the smile never once leaving her mouth or reaching her eyes.

'Why did you betray every promise you made me? That is an interesting question. Here is a better one: why did you try to put George on the throne?'

The only answer I really care to hear; the only reason I have come.

Louis' summons to Angers, an invitation into his presence that she had long-since stopped seeking, had intrigued her. She knew the French King had no interest in her, that he had even less in Warwick and Clarence and their thwarted ambitions to cease the English throne; Louis' only aim was to stop England's warmongering against him. He saw a chance to meddle and to disrupt and so Margaret became his favourite cousin once again; she knew it and was happy to play the role. For dignity's sake, she had made a great show of refusing Louis' olive branch and spurned his staged reconciliation with Warwick, striding out of the Hall almost as soon as she was called to enter it. It was for dignity's sake alone and they both knew it. Once the public stage was cleared and the daughter and the Countess sent away, then it was a different story. She would not meet with Clarence: he was a fool and she would have no part of any scheme that put him centre-stage. With the child gone, she imagined Warwick felt the same. But to see Warwick so reduced: for that she was happy to grant any audience that was requested and play any part in Louis' plotting.

When I saw Warwick casting nervously about the Hall as if he did not know who was to be trusted, when I knew that he had let a prize so tightly caught fall from his grasp then I knew I had what I had been waiting for since that summer afternoon when we had danced around each other and measured our ambition.

It was exactly as she had wanted it: the Warwick who came before her now was an exile. He was as dependant as her on the help of others to make his dreams a reality; he was as much at the mercy of other people's whims and fancies as she had been for nine long years.

Warwick and I were, finally, in ambition, hope and defeat, equals.

'Why Clarence? Why did you seek to put him on the throne? Why not me?'

Her son's question, echoing her own, was so directly put it might have been possible to claim it came from naivety had it not been for the hard edge in Edward's voice that was as obvious to Warwick as it was to Margaret. Edward's bluntness, nevertheless, surprised her and so she watched closely as Warwick regarded him across the table as though newly appraising the boy, a faint smile washing across a face made leaner by the trials of recent weeks. This attack from Edward seemed to finally penetrate the defences he had put up.

'Well that is certainly an honest question and therefore deserves an honest answer. Why weren't you our champion? Well, we did discuss it your mother and I but there was one simple flaw: I did not trust your mother and she did not trust me.'

He looked across at Margaret as though for validation but she merely shrugged and left the response to Edward who continued to watch Warwick with an equally level stare.

He is not easily dismissed or intimidated this man my son is becoming.

It was now Edward's turn to smile but more confidently than the older man, dropping an affectionate hand on his mother's arm as he replied.

'I cannot blame her for that and I can understand your misgivings; I can also understand, if I put my mind to it, that Clarence might seem a malleable choice for your schemes although I continue to doubt your judgement there. But what I cannot understand, my dear Lord Warwick, is how you came to fail. You had the King under your control, or so we were led to believe, a prisoner essentially in your estates and yet you are here in exile with nothing to show for yourself and the King is, well, wherever the King is he is not a prisoner and he is still the King.'

Edward removed his hand from Margaret's arm and steepled his fingers as though faced with a thorny dilemma.

'No, this is where I need your help, My Lord. I have thought and thought about what happened and I am still confused. I think, perhaps, my question was not the right one: I shouldn't have asked about who you chose but why you failed? Now, will your answer still be as honest to that?'

The shadows in the room were lengthening as the evening closed in but there was no mistaking Warwick's displeasure: his face had tightened and his fists begun to clench as Edward spoke. The silence stretched like a drawn bow between the two men, for Edward could now surely no longer be called a boy, and then Warwick sighed, his tensed shoulders dropped and he rubbed his temples with his long fingers, suddenly revealing the exhaustion he had kept hidden all day. It was a far more genuine smile he bestowed on Edward now and on Margaret.

'You have taught him very well, Madame, he is clearly afraid of nothing and no one and with good cause. Unlike Clarence who only shows no fear of anything because he lacks the wit to realise what he does.'

He nodded his head at Edward who continued to watch him impassively.

'Perhaps I should have ignored my misgivings and chosen you; I cannot have made a worse fist of things. Your directness deserves the same from me although, I confess, I barely know myself what went wrong unless I am more in thrall to a golden head and a crown than even I had realised.'

'I agree: my mother and her advisors, for she chose them with a care I am grateful for, have taught me well.'

Edward had control of the conversation now and Margaret was happy to let him lead it, to let Warwick see that he was no puppet to be manipulated when future plans came to be discussed as surely they must.

'She has always asked the men around her to keep from riddles and to speak plainly and it has always impressed me how they have done just that so now I would ask the same courtesy of you. Tell us what happened in the simplest terms and leave us to draw our conclusions as to the why and tell us it all, without omission, so that we can design the next stage of this campaign in terms that all of us can trust.'

309

He is my equal now in this struggle to regain what has been stolen from us; I have never seen it before. He knows his own mind and his own heart and Warwick will never fool him. He is a man not a child and a king in the making and Warwick can see it plain.

Margaret nodded her agreement.

'My son speaks my wishes as much as his own. We know what happened at Edgecote, My Lord, but we know little of what happened after that. The battle is as good a place as any to start but it is the detail of what came after that concerns us most.'

She kept her smile and her tone warm deliberately: there was a sudden sense of togetherness in the room and she wanted to pull him further in to it; Warwick vulnerable was something new and likely not to last, she did not want to waste it.

Warwick sighed. 'Whatever you have heard, it was no great battle and there is little to tell. It was a battle won far easier than I expected, that is the story of Edgecote. And it was not won by me, if you want the real truth of it.'

Edward frowned at him, 'who was responsible if not you? All the reports we had claimed it as your victory.'

'It was my victory, yes, but the getting of it was done by Robin of Redesdale.'

Warwick shrugged at their blank faces.

'You may not know the name now but you will hear it again, count on it. Master Robin is a great one for talking and mostly about himself.'

He spread his hands in a gesture of apology.

'Forgive me, I am doing what you asked me not to do and talking in riddles. Robin of Redesdale commanded the winning army on the day but his title is an alias: he is my cousin Sir John Conyers of

Hornby, who you have met, Madame, I think when you held court at Coventry.'

He continued as Margaret nodded, 'he prefers a less public life than some of my family although his loyalty to me is unquestionable; he assumed the name so that he could distribute tracts attacking the Woodvilles and calling the people to my cause without arousing the King's suspicion. And also, and perhaps closer to the truth if you know him, because he is a fool of a romantic and felt it lent him the air of an outlaw. Well, no matter: he is as good a soldier as he is a writer and it was his troops who won the day, I merely came and took the glory.'

'And the King?'

The servants had been dismissed for privacy's sake, no man in Louis' pay could be trusted, so Edward poured wine into silver goblets as he asked the question, raising his cup as though in a toast.

'We had that right at least, you took the King?'

Warwick's smile broadened and he leant across the table as though he would clasp Edward's hand; that moment of triumph at least was still fresh for him.

'I did, I caught him at Knebworth, took him without a fight and gave him to my brother George for safe-keeping at Middleham. He was astonished at what I dared, and at what I planned to do.'

'At what you planned to do? You had him safe. And then, well what? He escaped? You let him go?'

There was a dangerous note in her son's voice Margaret had never heard there before: he was goading the older man, gently enough it was true, but still he was pushing him, taunting him. It was like watching a cub suddenly flex his muscles and begin to prowl around the pack leader; she knew Warwick sensed it and also knew he did not know how to play this sudden challenge. She settled back into her chair and sipped her wine, fascinated to see where Edward was leading.

On the other side of the table it was as though a candle had been snuffed out. Warwick looked down for a moment and drew back into his chair, his twisting fingers the only sign that he had any energy left in him.

'I threw it all away. Is that what you want to hear?' Edward made no reply, simply waited.

'I threw it all away when everything lay at my feet for the taking.'

Margaret could hear the anger now but it was not directed at Edward or at herself; Warwick was looking not at them but inward and hating what he saw.

'I had broken the Woodvilles; I had the head of the family executed before me in case they doubted how much I hated them. I had the wife accused as a witch to show that I would not be stopped. I had the King in my own castle and I held him there for six months without a challenge...'

'Who was accused as a witch?'

She could not help herself; she could not let him continue although she was conscious of Edward's irritation at the interruption and aware that Anne was watching her intently from her quiet perch. She did not dare ask about Rivers, she doubted her voice would have held steady enough, but she could not let mention of Jacquetta, for that is surely who he meant, slip by with no explanation.

Warwick looked up in surprise, as though he had forgotten he had an audience at all.

'Jacquetta Woodville of course. Why do you ask? You called her witch often enough when I was here; I wanted the family broken and could not touch the Queen so I attacked the mother. It was you who gave me the idea.'

Margaret looked at him in astonishment and had to bite back the shocked laughter rushing to her lips.

'So Jacquetta finally faced the charges she so dreaded! But how did you do it? What grounds did you use or did she implicate herself again with her own silly words?'

She was suddenly aware of both men staring and Anne leaning forward in her shadowed chair.

'What do you mean, again?'

It was Edward who asked the question both were clearly thinking.

'Why would you ask that and how do you know she feared such an accusation? Did you have some cause to think she was a witch?'

Edward looked at his mother strangely, 'that is not a charge you have ever thrown out lightly. I remember as a child that any mention of the Maid of France or Eleanor Cobham would anger you, make you furious at where superstition could lead. So why would you deal so carelessly with such accusations about a woman who was once your friend?'

I will betray myself and Edward will never forgive me; he of all people cannot know the truth.

She spread her hands as though to brush the idea away.

'You are right, Edward, that is a weapon I have never cared for and I should not welcome it here although it is a long time since I have called her friend. But, truly, I meant nothing. Jacquetta was always one to talk of potions and charms and such nonsense; I warned her it would get her into trouble one day and now clearly it has. I simply wondered how it came about. But we do not need to dwell on it; I have little interest in her when there are more important matters to hear.'

She did not know if her pretence of disinterest fooled either of them and made play of re-filling their wine while Warwick continued so that she did not have to look up.

'You might not like the method, Madame, but it works. As I said, you gave me the idea when you teased me about how Elizabeth had made Edward fall in love with her and your hints about love charms have been repeated often enough in England to make them of use. It was a simple enough matter to have one of my men accuse her of making images, to fashion some simple thing to look like figures of the King and Queen embracing and have her charged.'

He smiled at Margaret but it was not a pleasant smile.

'And I remember now. She asked if it was you who had accused her, she said you had threatened it before. It seemed a strange thing to say but then Jacquetta is a woman full of strangeness.'

He paused for a moment as though trying to catch some memory that eluded him and then laughed. 'That was not all she said. What was it? It was strange: she said that, if we were to burn her as a witch, she would reveal a secret that would take you to the fires with her. I took no notice of her at the time but now I am starting to wonder: what, My Lady, could she mean?'

It was as if time had frozen. I could not move, my heart beat so loud I knew that they must hear it and then, as I tried to find words to counter him, the moment was over and the matter dismissed.

'I knew it was nothing but talk.'

Warwick shook his head as though shooing the subject away. 'She said so much and all of it nonsense and now she is free again and all accusations melted away.'

He made some other comment about her which made Edward laugh but Margaret did not hear him and only caught the conversation again when Edward offered her something to eat, concerned that she had grown pale.

I have to make myself focus on him when all I can see is this great chasm that suddenly threatens to claim me.

'It is nothing, my dear, as she is nothing. My Lord Warwick is right: Jacquetta is a great one for speaking and it is always nonsense. She is certainly not one who could keep or be told some great secret; that would be like entrusting a jewel-case to a thief!'

She turned back to Warwick and smiled with all the composure she could muster.

'My Lord, I broke your tale and I am sorry. I know this cannot be easy to tell so I will let you speak without further diversion. Tell us what happened with the King.'

'It was as you said. I let him go because I had no means to keep him and no plan beyond taking him.'

Warwick looked away as though the memory made a fool of him.

'What did I really have? My great victory was nothing but illusion. Clarence was an idiot without a thought in his head beyond the next cask of wine; that became apparent within days of me taking his brother. He blustered and shouted orders and acted as though he was already crowned; within days everyone hated him, my daughter included I think. Parliament would have no more put a crown on his head than on one of the dogs from the yard and would have had me ridiculed if I had tried.'

He paused, 'I hear that, after Edward won the throne, people called me the Kingmaker. That is quite a title and one, I confess, I took some pleasure in. Well they must be sorely disappointed in my efforts now. I had two kings to command. Two kings, both impris oned at my order, neither with any means to defend themselves and I had no idea what to do with either of them, that is the simple truth of it. Should I have had one killed, had both of them killed?'

He waited for a moment as though in hope of an answer but then seemed to realise how foolish his question was.

'Well that was not a decision I found so easy to take or even to enforce. You see I had no army, the men who had flocked to me simply melted away.'

Warwick smiled suddenly as though in some disbelief at his own words.

'And then, after six months of pretending that I was in charge and that he was a prisoner, Edward refused to carry on with what had become little more than nonsense. He told me that he was going to return to London. He saw that I had no strategy and no support and he simply left. Edward took his men and some of mine and rode away to London as though nothing had happened, leaving me as foolish as a cuckold.'

He looked directly at Edward 'you asked for honesty and there you have it. I was a fool and I lost. I cannot make it sound finer.'

Margaret had never seen Warwick looked defeated before but he looked it then. She said nothing, merely motioned for Edward to refill the Earl's empty cup, and left him in silence for a moment to contemplate the wine and his own admission. It would have been the simplest thing to mock his failings, she imagined he expected exactly that, but there would have been a cruelty in such a response that Warwick's plain speaking did not merit. So she took a gentler path with him and Edward, who had shown himself more and more the diplomat as Warwick's story unfolded, followed her lead.

'That was not an easy thing to admit, My Lord, and your trust in us is noted.'

She nodded to Edward, giving him permission to move the conversation where it needed to go and was gratified to see how quickly he understood what was wanted.

'My Lady Mother speaks for both of us and I also thank you for your honesty.'

He hesitated for a moment, letting Warwick acknowledge the compliment.

'But you did not leave England at once, My Lord, as I would have expected if York had sought some vengeance on you. I can only think, then, that there must have been some forgiveness from him. But you are in exile, with nothing. There is still some twist in this I do not understand.'

Warwick sighed and took a deep drink before answering.

'It is because you do not know King Edward...' the younger holder of the name moved as though to correct him but Warwick shook his head. 'You may not want to call him King or hear him named so but it is not your title yet. As I said, you do not know him. The King can charm and play any man any way he chooses and he still has some plan for me and for his brother. He has forgiven me publicly, he has forgiven Clarence publicly but he does not mean it.'

Warwick laughed, a hollow sound that did not sit well on him.

'And how much better does such generosity look than to have us beheaded: his brother and his oldest friend?'

'But surely, Edward is furious that he was imprisoned? He must have suspected at the very least that you sort to restore my father even if he never believed Clarence would be treated seriously? He must have believed you wanted to kill him or why take him prisoner? What did he think you were going to do?'

If Warwick heard the refusal to use the royal title, he did not ac knowledge it.

'I don't know what he thought because he did not ask. It did not matter to him because he never believed I would harm him and he was right. And now he has said that my quarrel was with the Wood-villes and not himself; he has determined, in public at least, that his brother and I acted out of loyalty to him and out of concern for the people he was surrounded with and so, once he returned with his usual triumph to London, he was free with his pardons. All that was demanded of me was that I stopped defaming his wife's family. I had to accept that the charges of witchcraft against Jacquetta were unfounded and I had to refute the accusations of treason I had made against Lord Rivers. Then everyone could be reconciled and no one could take sides.'

It is another Loveday but this King means none of it.

'He is no fool.'

It was Margaret's turn now to drink deeply for this was a side of Edward she did not want to hear: the soldier had become the strategist. 'He did not want a direct challenge to his position so he did not let you make one and he did not want you to win sympathy so there was no punishment. It was cleverly done. And yet, even though he pardoned you and you could have surely pushed your way back to influence with the Woodvilles quietened, you still chose to run into exile and to come to me. Why do such a thing when surely you had even less chance of succeeding than before?'

If Warwick had recognised the need for honesty earlier, he knew it could not be avoided now for this was the point on which his future, on which all their futures would turn. All of them knew it and neither Edward nor Margaret would break the silence that now slipped over the room. The Earl, as she knew he would for he was no fool either, chose the truth.

'I am finished with York.'

He looked at the son then but spoke to the mother.

'Edward has told me that he will kill me and I believe him. This reconciliation is all for show: I kill him or he kills me, there is no other ending. I want power, Madame, as do you; that does not change and...'

'And my cause serves your needs.' Margaret finished the sentence for him.

He nodded. 'I have too many rivals at the English Court, men who have been shown favour by Edward and like the taste of it. The King has even betrothed his daughter to my nephew but still refuses to countenance any matches with my children. No, I was pardoned but it was merely a stay of an execution that I will not wait for.'

Edward smiled at Warwick then; there was a gentle enough expression on his face but a mocking tone had crept back into his voice that had Margaret more alert than the Earl.

'And yet still you chose Clarence. Not once but twice. I am not mistaken? You are, after all, here and not in England. And you are here as an exile because you married your daughter to the King's brother and tried to raise a rebellion in his name. You surely aren't here because you knew your mistake from the first failure and came looking for me as your champion are you, My Lord.' The last was a statement not a question and it left Warwick nowhere to hide.

'No I am not. I knew I could not trust the King so I tried to raise the country again and I was beaten before I could even build an army. I made Clarence my son-in-law and, yes, I tried to make him King because I knew I could control him and I did not stop even when I knew I could not do it. Edward has swept my support from under me. Every man I convinced to come with me in my challenge, not that many would after I had failed so publicly before, lost his head: Sir Robert Willoughby, Richard of Welles, Thomas Dymoke; all executed before we even had an army in the field. So, when Clarence and I were summoned to appear before the King at York, I knew this time he would make good his promise and have us killed. We fled because there was nothing else to do and now here I am in France with a fool for a son-in-law and a heartsick daughter and nothing left to me but my name and my ambition. And that is what makes your cause and the House of Lancaster and you seem a side worth fighting for. There is nothing else left.'

It had been a long speech and the two men were left staring across the table at each other, Warwick's hand finally open and played for Edward to see.

It is my turn now to take the lead; Edward cannot control this. He is too young: he will see an insult where there is an opportunity and play it wrong.

'Your honesty continues to do you credit, Richard.'

Margaret rarely used Warwick's name and he looked at her with some surprise but said nothing.

'I refused your plans when you last brought them to me because there was only a pretence from you then that we were equals. Now here we are, both exiles, both craving a route back to power; I think now, My Lord, I can forgive past wrongs and see a common cause between us.'

Warwick nodded but still Edward sat impassive, watching.

'Thank you. The times favour us I think. Louis wants King Edward stopped before his attacks on France become more than just bluster. He would give us the support now, Madame, which he has too long withheld. If we raise an army now, we strike while the King least expects it, while he thinks that I am beaten.'

'And who would you put on the throne this time?'

Edward's question seemed to expect one clear answer but Margaret could sense something behind it that Warwick clearly did not hear for his words came too quick.

'Why you, My Prince. Who else?'

'My father, of course King Henry.'

It was not the response Warwick expected and it flustered him.

'But your father is ill, he cannot rule, he barely could when he last held the throne. And now, well he has been imprisoned for so long, he has retreated even more into his prayers and silences. We cannot put him up against Edward; the people would never choose him.'

Edward shrugged. 'It is not about choice. It is about restoring the Crown to its rightful wearer. If my father's condition has worsened in his captivity then surely I must look to you to put matters right, for you are the author of his misery.'

I misjudged him; he is clever enough for all of us.

There was not a trace of hesitation or deference in Edward's voice.

'No, My Lord, you will not fight for me. You will fight in my father's name, with Clarence by your side if you so wish and, then, when King Henry is restored to the throne, then he will give control of the Crown to me, not to you. He can, if he wishes and I suspect he will, retreat to a monastery for the rest of his days and I will rule, with my mother's guidance and your advice when it is required, but I will rule.'

Margaret laughed, she could not help herself: to see Warwick out-manoeuvred by her son was a delight.

'Edward is right, you cannot deny it. He will not be a made King, he will be a true King saving his sainted father from the burdens he can no longer bear and keeping the Crown where it rightly belongs. The people will see the just nature of this and will be grateful that the natural order of things is returned. And you, Warwick, will be our champion. Oh it is a great plan, My Lord, you must see it.'

'Except he does not see it because all it seems to be is a promise of power with no guarantee that his attempts at influence will ever amount to anything.'

Edward stretched out his long legs and lent back in his seat; there was a moment when he could have looked boyish again but there was a new cast to his expression that a boy would not have; a secretive smile on his face that even his mother could not read.

He has plans of his own, plans that are really not so much a mother's business.

She watched him seek out Anne in the shadows, saw the smile that passed between them but was still as surprised as Warwick at Edward's declaration although she, at least, made some attempt to hide it.

'You will have your voice in the King's ear, My Lord, I promise you because I will marry your daughter, your Anne. Not King Clarence for a son-in-law but King Edward V; how well does that sit with your plans?'

And so I will be replaced; she will have the shaping of him, not me.

He had Warwick gaping like a fish marooned on dry land with no more chance of finding words than the fish would have of breathing. There was a gasp from the corner of the room where Anne sat in such silence, everyone but Edward had forgotten her.

With a gaiety she did not truly feel, Margaret answered for him.

'I think you have taken the Earl too much by surprise, Edward, and spun his plans so high he can no longer quite imagine them! My dear Warwick, you need to take a breath and tell us how you are suited by my son's proposal; are we to be related?'

I do not want this but I will lose my son if I deny him so publicly.

And then Warwick laughed, a great hearty laugh that every servant passing through the corridor must have heard and which sent gossip spinning through the castle.

'I am suited very well, Madame, very well and by the look on my daughter's face, she is hardly displeased.'

He turned to Edward and Margaret could see the admiration on his face for the boy he thought he could manage who had now showed himself as much of a strategist as the great Kingmaker himself.

'You will have your bride and we will have an army and England will finally get the King she deserves. Yes Madame, we are to be related and let us see what the Yorkist pens make of that!'

'Every Yorkist pen will say it is an alliance forged in Hell by the Devil himself and then pray for our forgiveness.'

Margaret felt a chill encircle the room that came more from her son's words than the failing fire: she tried to push the superstitious thoughts she normally would not entertain away but for once they were too strong for her.

It is as though he dips this marriage in blood to seal a pact we should never have made. I have made him a lover of power: please God the price we have to pay to take it is not higher than any of us can bear.

***

He had been all smiles at his betrothal, now he was all caged anger again. Every step forward was too slow; every gift of money that Louis, so enchanted with Anne that he had become almost benevolent, lavished on them too little; every pledge of support the French finally made, too small. Edward would not be satisfied with anything less than an invasion and had no patience to wait for one and his frustration spilled out across the Court, infecting everyone, including his mother who no longer trusted anything around her.

'Why now? After six long years of exile, six long years of constant unheard demands for help, why do you finally think my cause is worth investing in?'

She was not normally so forthright with Louis but he had finally delivered the men and arms and the words of political support that she thought would remain a hopeless dream; rather than delighting in her success, she railed at it.

'Do you think it is for the smiles of a pretty girl or the romance of a new royal dynasty or perhaps simply for the thanks I have not yet heard?'

Luckily for Margaret, Louis was in the mood to indulge rather than to anger.

'No, you may revel in flattery but you are not fool enough to suc-cumb to it.'

He inclined his head at the acknowledgement. 'But I don't believe you have suddenly become a convert to my cause, not after all this time.'

'You are clever and you are bold. I prize that in you.'

His words astonished her but she kept her expression deliberately neutral and let him continue.

'I shall tell you the truth, Marguerite, I do it rarely enough so it may prove diverting. This Edward IV unnerves me.'

He looked to her for a response but she had none; this was more than she had expected.

'He is too vocal in his pledge to re-conquer France; he invokes the spirit of Henry V with every speech and I can no longer ignore it.

Every ambassador who travels to the English Court tells me how much the people believe that this King is the one who can lead a successful invasion and restore their fortunes on the continent. And I am beginning to believe he may.'

She chose her words carefully, not wanting to lose his sudden confidence.

'You cannot trust Burgundy or Brittany?' She knew the answer: Edward's diplomatic efforts and alliances had outflanked him.

He shrugged and smiled. 'You know I cannot. I am isolated and now I must look to you and to Warwick; it is an interesting turn of events for all of us, wouldn't you agree?'

It was: from being the irritant in his kingdom, she had now become the power to be courted and Warwick, who once could no more find an audience than she, had become the champion Louis chose to put into the field.

So fear has brought me into the centre of Louis' new web; this time I am happy to take my place there.

'And to me, you also look to me.'

It was not a question, it was a command; that much was clear from Edward's tone. He had sat quietly while Louis talked, waiting for the right moment to make his voice heard; it was increasingly his way.

'To you, yes. Eventually.' Her words were intended to placate, they had the opposite effect.

'Eventually, what do you mean?'

The shift in tone was slight but it was there; Louis noticed it and sat back in his chair, observing where the play would take them.

'Warwick will sail to England and launch the campaign. Once it is concluded, you will sail to England and claim your inheritance, just as you planned it.'

'Except that is not what I planned and you know it!' Edward was on his feet, furious. 'The strategy is mine. I will lead this campaign, not Warwick. It will be me who will rally England to my father's cause and me who will lead the army who wins back the throne.'

'No.'

She waved her hand to dismiss his arguing knowing he still had too much respect for her to do anything but subside into glowering fury.

'That will not happen. Warwick will sail and he will smooth the path for you. That is how it will be.'

'Why? Mother, why? Don't you think me capable?'

She could hear less anger and more hurt in his voice and it tore at her.

'That is not the reason, I...'

'Your mother does not trust Warwick and she is right not to.'

Louis watched as Edward turned, about to interrupt.

'Listen to her and listen to me. No one doubts your bravery but we all doubt Warwick, no matter how much we let him charm us.'

'The King is right.'

Margaret waited while Edward sat again, still glowering but ready, at least, to listen.

'I cannot trust him: he has turned his coat once and can do it again just as easily. You must remember the bond he and King Edward once had; despite all our pledges and the plans we have agreed, I cannot trust that bond is broken. Think about it, Edward. Too many things are in fortune's control and not mine. What if King Edward flatters his old friend again, promises him all the power he once had, what would Warwick do with you then?'

Edward shifted in his chair but she could see he knew the truth of her words, even if he did not want to accept them.

'I cannot put you in such danger. And think of Anne: she does not want to risk a husband before she has one. Do not assume Warwick would look to her happiness and save you; you only need look at Isabel to know he would not care for his daughter at all if there was a greater prize to be had.'

'I do not like it. People will think I am a coward.' Edward's voice was mutinous still but she could hear the acceptance creeping in.

'They will not. They will see a man who can make good decisions; you have to trust me in this.'

And he did but he was angry and our last days together were coloured by that: he tried to conceal it and was as courteous as ever but he thought that I had manipulated him and there was a distance between us. That is my tragedy: I thought that I would have time to mend the hurt once he saw that my strategy was the right one, once we had the throne safe. Dear God, it pains me so much to know that I caused a wound that never was given time to heal but how could I have foreseen what was to happen? I thought I could control the danger that he faced; what a fool I must have been. And yet, I kept him alive a little longer than might have been his fate; I kept him with me and safe a little longer; I saw him married and I saw him happy. It has to be enough, there is no more.

***

The chateau had echoed all day to the sound of raised voices as Edward took out his frustration on anyone foolish enough to cross his path. Only Anne had any power to calm him and even she had given up the struggle: pleading a headache that only fresh air could cure, she had slipped away to the gardens, leaving Margaret to try and divert Edward while they waited for news. It had not been a success and both were heartily tired of each other by the time the messenger arrived.

'They have sailed, Your Majesty, Your Royal Highness.'

Fortescue clearly had more to say but Edward's scowl did not invite confidences and it was left to Margaret to acknowledge his words. 'And has their leaving gone to plan?'

Fortescue smiled but it was clear from his stiff manner that he remained uncertain how to act in the face of Edward's palpable anger. His pupil was no longer a boy to be easily chided out of poor behaviour or a show of hostility towards his mother that none were used to seeing.

'It would seem to, yes. Duke Charles had sent a fleet to block the harbour mouth at Harfleur but a gale whipped out of the sky and blew them away before any engagement was needed.'

'And every foolish peasant at the Court now talks of portents I presume.'

It was a sneer, not a question and had poor Fortescue scuttling for the door. Margaret turned to confront her son, increasingly tired of his churlishness, but was not quick enough.

'That was unkind, Edward; he is your tutor still and deserves your respect not your discourtesy.'

It was Anne, returning pinkly pretty from her walk, who spoke and with a more immediate effect on him than the tongue-lashing Margaret was about to unleash could surely have had.

'You are right and I am sorry for it.' He reached out a hand to cup her delicate chin and a much-needed calmness settled on the room.

'I know you wanted to ride out with them, Edward, but...'

'But you were afraid that I would jump on board ship without your hand to stay me.' Edward shrugged, 'and you were right to fear it.'

He waved a hand as Margaret started to speak again.

'No more, Mother. I have heard and accepted your arguments and I have stayed as you demanded but do not expect me to keep quiet if you continue. I have done my duty by you but do not think I like it or that Warwick accepts it. You have made a fool of me.'

She could not argue: she knew there was too much truth in what he said. Warwick had been all courtesy at the leave-taking, promising that he went to England only to make it safe for Edward, to prepare his path to the Throne. It was gallantly said and gallantly received but Margaret's mistrust hung heavy in the room and soured the day. So Edward's fury remained barely constrained and his mother hardly saw him until news of the army's safe landing at Plymouth reached them.

Those days were yet another agony of waiting. She filled them well-enough with all the diplomatic wranglings entailed by the papal dispensation needed before Anne and Edward could marry; Edward accused her of delaying this as much as she delayed their sailing and there was little she could say in her defence. He had sworn to Anne he would not go to England before they were wed and she knew he would honour that pledge: there was little incentive for her then to chase ambassadors and demand audiences. If it had not been for Anne keeping the balance of civility between mother and son, they would have driven each other mad with unspoken anger and resentment.

When news came of Jean's arrival from the Burgundian Court one bitterly cold October day, they both looked to it only as a welcome diversion, not realising the importance of his visit. It was a relief to Margaret at least that Jean's opening words, with the surprise and promise they contained, turned that pretence of civility into something more approaching the closeness she had once taken so for granted.

'He is in Bruges.'

'Who is in Bruges?'

Margaret sighed at Jean's opaqueness, knowing from his smile that he carried news of importance but too much still the little sister to want to play his games.

'The English King.'

Her brother burst out laughing as she and Edward both leapt to their feet. 'Well that was quite the reaction I had hoped for; you are like a pair of stranded fish!'

'One day, Uncle, I swear, you will get a reaction from me you do not want!'

But Edward was smiling now, the boyish smile no one had seen on his face for days. 'What has happened? Tell us plainly for I am beginning to think I am not a patient man and we have been waiting too long for news, especially good news.'

He took Margaret's hand as they sat and she was grateful for it.

'I had intended to come sooner but these have been strange days and I needed to know that the rumours reaching me were true.'

Jean shook his head as Margaret began to speak.

'I will tell it all, you do not need to interrupt and I will be quicker if you don't. I have spent too much time at Duke Charles's Court in Bruges lately and its dullness was beginning to bore me. I was preparing to leave but then rumours reached us that a party had landed from England at Alkmaar in the Friesian Islands and was about to arrive in Bruges, as the guests of Gruthuyse, the Governor of Holland. All that anyone knew was that the fleet was small and the men carried no markings with them but had clearly sailed in haste because the few witnesses to see them disembark all commented on their bedraggled state. Well, I stayed and it seems they came to try and seek an audience with Charles but were hustled away to private rooms at the Governor's mansion without meeting him; it took some stealth on my part to discover the truth for which I hope you will be grateful.'

His pause then was clearly for affect but Margaret bit her lip and waited and he continued with a grin.

'It seems the mystery guest was King Edward with hardly enough men to form an escort and the reason for his reduced state is that he has fled into exile and thrown himself on Charles's mercy. The Duke has not appeared much pre-disposed to Edward's plight in public but, in private, well it seems they are great friends together.'

She could not contain herself any longer.

'But how has this come about? What has happened in England to make Edward leave? Has there been a battle? And, if he is gone, who has the throne?'

'And in which order would you like your answers?'

Her brother's drawling tone was enough to make her palm tingle with the urge to slap him as she had been provoked too often to do when they were children.

'Marguerite, I will tell you everything I know if you will only let me.'

Edward's grip on her hand tightened but she sensed it was to calm not control so she subsided and gestured for Jean to continue.

'There was no battle, sister, not even a drop of blood spilt, there was no need. It seems that Edward was betrayed or trusted too much to the loyalty of those around him. He has been so confident in John Neville since Warwick fled that he demanded Neville march against his own brother; Neville appears to have remembered that his true loyalty should lie with his family not with the promise of riches and he could not do it so he marched against Edward instead. Oh he stated some grievance that Edward had favoured the Percys over him but whether that was an excuse or whether Warwick had promised him power under a new regime, well who is to know with these English lords and their constant quarrels. Whatever the cause, Neville rode to where Edward was lodging at Doncaster and made it plain that he would arrest him; the King had to flee in the middle of the night and lost half his men to the sea and the quicksands; he is lucky to be alive himself.'

'And who has the throne?'

The question this time was Edward's.

'Your father; King Henry VI is restored to the throne.'

Margaret was on her feet again and ready to cry with delight this time but something in Jean's face stopped her.

'What is it? Surely this is the only outcome we could have wanted and far quicker than we ever expected it; what could make you look so serious...'

And then she stopped, horrified by the look on Edward's face.

'You stupid woman.' There was hatred in his voice, it was unmistakeable.

'Do you really not understand, even now? Without me there, all that Warwick has done is put a madman in place of a storybook hero. Once the people blink away the romance of what they have been duped into believing is a great victory and see the reality of their returning King, how much more golden will their lost King look?'

All my delaying, all it has done is serve the wrong Edward. How could I not see it? I have become my son's enemy and he will nev-

er trust me again.

'Edward, I...'

But he was gone, flinging himself from the room in a blind fury. She turned to Jean but he shook his head and followed his nephew. Alone in the room, she curled in on herself and cried like she would never stop.

***

And still she could not sail and would not let Edward sail and he, for all his anger and all his threats to invade England without her, could neither argue against both Anne and his mother nor get Louis to agree to his leaving alone. As the chill autumn winds settled around them, Margaret's court became a snarling pit full of tears and accusations and impotent rage. And still she could not go.

She could not blame an exile's isolation for refusing to accept the reality of Warwick's undertaking. Every day seemed to bring new rumours from England and none of them played in her favour. Elizabeth Woodville, still hiding in sanctuary at Westminster Abbey, had finally given birth to a son, the heir to strengthen her husband's cause, and had named him Edward, whether to honour his father or anger Margaret she did not know but she chose to believe the latter.

Henry's claim had been reiterated in Parliament without any voice raised in dissension and Warwick had him paraded almost daily in his crown and ermine cloak but already the rumours had begun that Henry was stranger now than ever before, that the years in the Tower had taken what few wits he had left and he did not even know he was King again. People had begun to point and whisper when he rode out and all the cheers had quickly turned to muttering and doubt.

As the tide began to slowly turn again, stories came that Clarence was under more and more pressure from his formidable mother and his sisters to leave Warwick's side and return to the family fold, his folly sure to be forgiven by a brother whose image was starting to glow again. The truth was obvious to everyone: the shadow of invasion hung over the country and King Edward in exile had begun to reclaim the allure he had lost in person. England needed more than Warwick: the people needed Margaret in front of them as Queen; they needed her son as a believable heir to counter Elizabeth's new babe; they needed proof that the House of Lancaster was as splendid and as solid as any Yorkist claim could ever be. Warwick wrote as much in increasingly impatient letters, Jean and Edward said as much in terser and terser tones and still she refused every demand that ships be made ready and the order to leave be signed.

She could not explain herself. She did not trust Warwick, that did not change, but no one would accept that any more when Warwick's actions did nothing but prove his loyalty. She could not explain herself.

Because I was paralysed by fear, a fear so strong it had its own taste and certainty, a fear that my son would die.

I, who had always refused (and been so proud in my refusal) to accept the common wisdom of omens and portents and superstition was crippled by the belief that, if I was to take my son to England, he would be dead within a month and the only way to keep him safe was to keep him from his birth right.

Her actions made no sense, she knew it: the English throne belonged to her son; her life had been centred on holding it for him; that autumn of 1470, when it had never been closer, she would not let him take it.

I could not tell the truth: whether it was because the stakes were so high or because I knew how desperate my son was to prove himself in battle or because I was a mother more than a queen in those last months, I felt too many shadows circling us and let them become ropes of fear to bind my hands and my mouth. I clung to him and he hated me for it.

And then, despite all her words of protest, they sailed. But it was not Margaret who forced the change to happen, it was no longer Margaret who forced anything to happen; it was her son.

France and England:
1471

I offered you the simple fact that it was my son who changed when what I should have said was that the son outgrew the mother. It has to happen one day but none of us look for it or see the circumstances coming that speed the sudden move away. So what was it for Edward that broke the ties? Not one thing, in truth, but three that took the last traces of the boy and built the man: a wedding, a death and a promise.

As Edward's irritation with his mother's hesitancy had grown, he had begun to turn more and more to the men about him, particularly those who did not share his reluctance to see him win his spurs in battle and chief among them was Louis. For all that Margaret was becoming the Queen of waiting, Louis was becoming the King of impatience and, in that, his desires proved far stronger than hers for they more equally matched her son's. Margaret could not claim surprise: she knew that Louis could not stand aloof indefinitely. The shifting sands of allegiances would not let him even had his own love of intrigue not forced his meddling hand to action.

In England, she had learned, it was often enough to watch just English affairs, an island can afford a little arrogance and self-belief. On the Continent, countries must keep a closer eye on what their neighbours do and say and hope that the two are almost the same. Duke Charles in Burgundy had promised that he would respect his French alliance and not involve himself in England's affairs but no one believed him and everyone expected that Edward's invasion would arm itself with Burgundy's gold, Louis and Edward most of all.

They were so close, kept together no doubt by Louis' ongoing infatuation with Anne as much as his love of plotting and distrust of Charles; Margaret was never excluded from their many meetings but neither was she always informed that they were taking place and Edward had grown very clever at politely ignoring any question she put to him. When the news came then, in early December, that Louis had broken his treaty with Burgundy before Charles could do the same with him and, when further news came that French armies had invaded Charles's territory, her son showed little surprise and accepted Louis' public pledge of support for his own ambitions against England as though he knew the words before they were spoken. The fact that these actions would inevitably push Burgundy into open allegiance with King Edward seemed of little concern to either of them; Edward was pushing for the war he believed was his to win and what could Margaret do but praise his newly emerging strategic skills in public as much as she fretted over their consequences in private.

***

'She is beautiful.'

Margaret smiled in agreement with her son: she was. Whether it was the cloth of gold Louis had found for Anne that dazzled him or the beam of joy that lit her face, it did not matter: Anne was beautiful and her son was enchanted.

'I am glad this day is here; that you are so happy.'

Edward raised an eyebrow. 'Really? I thought you hoped the dispensation would never come.'

'Not today, Edward. Not today. This is what you wanted and I am happy for you.'

Margaret was and Edward acknowledged the truth of her words with a smile more tender than she had had from him in weeks. The soldier in her son had set the date and removed the discussion: Margaret understood completely that no man waiting on the fortunes of battle will deny himself anything, especially a bride, so now they stood in Louis' own palace of Amboise with the Grand Vicar of Bayeaux to officiate and a great banquet to follow, waiting to make him a husband.

'Louis has done you a great honour.'

'He is so smitten with her: I thought he intended to marry Anne himself, I am just grateful to be the bridegroom!'

His laugh was genuine now and set the tone for the day to come.

My son has taken a bride and she has taken my place. He will have a new Queen to guide him and I must learn to step back.

She nodded and waved to the smiling crowds who were gathered on every corner as the bridal party rode through the streets of Paris, streets that were decorated as though for a coronation. She was feted on every corner once more as a queen and felt the power of the pageantry, knowing how much she craved it still. She saw the streets of Paris become the streets of London, saw Edwards's bridal procession become his coronation and wanted the triumph so much, it was a physical ache. She watched her son and saw he felt it to.

And yet it was not me who rode beside him but Anne.

'It is as it should be.'

Louis, watching her intently as they rode, had no time for sentimentality.

'You have kept him close for longer than he wanted, now he will cut the apron strings and you must let him. He will make a happy marriage, something few of us expect or know. Do not begrudge him that.'

'I don't. I know that the man who leaves the wedding chamber is not the boy who entered it and so it will be with Edward.'

Margaret shook her head at Louis who had started to laugh, not unkindly perhaps but it still stung.

'I swear I hope that Anne will be a happier bride than I was ever allowed to be and I know Edward is in thrall to his little princess. He has hardly left her side and seems to have forgotten the urgency of leaving; he has not spoken of sailings or invasions for days even though ships are now at our command whenever we might call on them.'

But Louis would not allow her that indulgence. 'Do not expect it to last, Marguerite; he will be more determined now than ever to go. He has a wife to win a crown for.'

He was right, it could not last: it was merely a lull before the confidence Anne gave him strengthened Edward's hand. This time, when he insisted that they go to England as soon as the winter storms abated, there was no question or debate invited: it was a simple statement of what would happen.

Edward would not countenance any more opposition from his mother and, even had she wanted to fight him anymore, she no longer had the heart: she wanted only to be at peace with him for she had too little family left to squander. Her brother Jean had died. Sometime between the wedding celebrations and the Christmas feasts, her brother had died alone and too far away, in Barcelona where he had gone to press their father's claims for Catalonia. To add to the pain of loss, which was hard enough itself to bear, poison was suspected as the cause. Margaret could not even weep but sat hollow-eyed and sleepless in her room, overwhelmed by guilt. Jean had left her court in silent fury at her stalling, in frustrated despair at what he saw as his sister's weakness and had gone, in his stinging parting words, to find a more honourable cause to champion. She felt Jean's death on her conscience and her hesitation as a stain on her son. Edward was ready, Louis was ready, Anne would follow her husband anywhere he asked; there was no question of waiting any more.

***

My son died. My son died. He was eighteen years old and he died an agonising death on a battlefield, his body torn apart in mud and frenzy with no one to care or lighten his last moments. That fact colours every word for it is the only thing that matters.

I saw his corpse; I wish that I had not but there was no one left who cared enough to protect me from that pain. He was butchered, there was no beauty left in him, nothing but blood and horror; it has been ten years and I see his broken face every day, every single day.

My Confessor told me once that prayer would ease my suffering, well it does not. Where once I refused to listen to omens and superstitions, now I refuse to listen to the word of God and if that consigns me to Hell, as I am told it surely will, then I do not care for I have seen Hell and it has no terrors left for me.

I know now that I live in an absence of feeling. I thought I would go mad after he died, I truly did, but I had to learn that I would not have the luxury of such a release as I had to learn that I would not die simply because I wished so often that I might. So now I wish for nothing and care for little except the misery of those who caused me this pain. It is little wonder I am so much alone.

How did his death come about? Through my delaying, there is no honest answer but that. Had I sailed before Christmas, had I trusted that Warwick would stay loyal to me, had I beaten King Edward back to England, then I think my boy might have lived. No, I know that he would have lived. My son died. My son died and his death is at my door. What mother wants a legacy like that?

***

Another door flung open; another messenger who forgot the courtesies due to a queen; another day made dark. Their return to England had been so triumphant, the cheering crowds that met their ships so loud; it all did nothing except make the shock of the news even worse.

'Warwick is dead.'

There was a cry: Margaret saw Anne fall to the floor but could do nothing. It was as if she had been turned to rock, to ice.

'How can he be dead? Was he taken ill and no one thought to tell us?'

Edward was cradling Anne, holding her as she came back to consciousness. 'Surely you could have taken more care with the news,' he helped his wife to a chair as his mother remained rooted to the spot, uncomprehending. 'She has had a hard voyage, we all have; some delicacy would have been welcomed here.'

'There is no time for delicacy.'

John Courtenay, Earl of Devon, had the grace to look ashamed at the upset he had caused but he would not back down. 'And no, it was not illness that took him; he died in battle.'

'What in God's name is going on?'

Anne was weeping bitterly now and Edward was clearly torn between trying to help her and trying to understand the meaning of what Courtenay had just said.

'You are making no sense; how can he have died when the battle is not yet fought?'

He tried to stem Anne's tears but it was beyond him.

'Anne, please, this is not helping you. Alice, take her to our chambers and give her something to help her sleep.'

Margaret was as horrified, as mystified as Edward but having his wife in so desperate a state was a distraction neither of them could afford. She turned to Courtenay as Anne was led away, 'speak freely now and quickly.'

He had the wit, at least, to do as she said but his words only deepened their confusion.

'We could not wait on your armies any longer. Warwick took the field against King Edward at Barnet just hours before you anchored and he was beaten, his armies chased from the field. He is dead.'

'He had no right!'

Edward's fury exploded with the force of a cannonball and the room cringed.

'We were delayed, yes, the storms that hit our fleet have cost us two weeks and nearly broke the spirit of our men; I know it. But we were coming! How could he have fought when he knew we were coming? He should have waited!'

'If it was only a matter of waiting two weeks, perhaps he would.'

It was Somerset who spoke and his tone was mutinous.

'But we have waited far longer than that. We have waited and waited while March slipped into April and while King Edward sailed with 36ships and 1,600soldiers into Ravenspur. We have waited while men flocked to the Yorkists and still not one of your ships had even slipped anchor.'

Somerset stared at his Queen and his Prince with unconcealed bitterness. 'You forced us to wait and you forced us to fight without you. This disaster is your doing.'

Edward will blame me: he will make the waiting my fault and he will hate me again.

'This disaster makes no sense.'

Margaret had to speak first before Edward turned on her and she had to speak with the authority and attitude of a queen.

'Think before you speak like that again or you will rue it. If Warwick chose to fight he should have won; he had the forces to do it

342

without our armies, so why did he lose?'

'Because he was betrayed; it was a battle, what else would lose it for the side with the greatest strength except betrayal?'

It was John Morton who spoke this time; all the manners and charm of his quayside welcome gone.

The fight left her and she sank into a chair, leaving Edward to ask the question she already knew the answer to.

'Who betrayed him?'

Morton shrugged. 'Who else? It was Clarence. The one we thought was no more than Warwick's foolish puppy bit his new master and scuttled home to the shelter of his family, taking his army with him and clearing King Edward's path to London.'

'I should have known; I should have been here.'

Edward's words were so heartfelt the pain cut through her but she could do nothing to comfort him.

The fault is mine. It is mine. Clarence, stupid faithless Clarence: how could I think he would accept being passed over for Warwick's new favourite? How could I think he would not strike back? It was obvious but I would not see it. I would not see anything except keeping my own boy safe.

'Much good it will do him.'

She spoke almost to herself.

'Is he so desperate for his brother's approval or his mother's love or is he simply stupid enough to believe that any words of forgiveness the King bestows on him mean anything real? I presume Edward made a great show of forgiveness and brotherly love?'

Somerset nodded but did not speak.

'Then he is a fool to trust it: Clarence has sowed the seeds of his own death and everyone knows it but him.'

'What do we care what happens to Clarence?'

Edward's shock had given away again to anger.

'What was the meaning of our welcome if this was the truth of our homecoming? Why were there cheering crowds on the quayside when we arrived if the battle was already lost?'

'Because they paid for them.'

Margaret looked at the men surrounding them but not one would meet her eye.

'They paid for every cheer and every bow. They paid to make me feel that I was returning from exile in triumph because, if I guessed the truth, I would have turned the ships around and not let you sail into danger.'

Edward turned to Somerset and grabbed his arm; there was a menace in her son that chilled her, that made her afraid to speak out against his roughness. 'Is she right?'

'Yes.' Somerset shook his arm free and moved away. 'Yes. We need you here if there is to be any counter-attack and your mother would have done exactly what she said.'

'Because the risk is too great!'

Margaret was on her feet but Edward whirled around before she could continue.

'Be quiet!'

The room was silent.

'Be quiet or I swear I will have you sent from the room, Queen or not. These delays are your fault and I am sick of your meddling.' He turned away from his mother back to the men who were now watching him with an awed fascination. 'Where is King Edward now?'

'He has marched back to London and entered the City with no opposition.'

Morton's voice had a new respect in it; Margaret could hear it and did not know whether to rejoice or rail at it.

'You must understand; he has wasted no time in securing his victory. Your father is imprisoned once more and Elizabeth Woodville, and her boy, are removed from sanctuary; King Edward has promised the citizens safety for their businesses under his protection and his men have spread poisonous tales everywhere about your mother. He calls her the French Queen, quite deliberately, and whips up hatred against the French armies he says are waiting in Warwick's shadow to take England back from Englishmen.'

'And every man and besotted girl is on the streets cheering for their golden King and the one in the Tower is all forgotten again.'

There was no question in Edward's words and Morton merely shrugged in acknowledgement of the truth.

'Who else is lost?' He was all the soldier now, dealing in facts, not emotions.

'John Neville and Henry Holland.' Margaret cried out at Somerset's words but Edward paid no heed.

'And our armies?'

'The slaughter was terrible; our losses are high.'

'Then we will avenge them.'

Such simple, terrible words. I have created this: I cannot bear to hear it.

'Edward, no! It is hopeless, our cause is lost!'

She clung to his arm but he shook her off with a violence that had her half-falling to the floor. And then he turned and all the impotent rage of the long weeks of waiting spilt out in a wash of fury.

'Do not speak! My God, woman, you have lost that right! How can our cause be lost when all you have ever told me is that our cause is the only one that is true? How can it be lost if my father is God's chosen King and I am God's chosen heir? All my life you have shaped me for this moment so do not tell me that our cause is lost, Madame, because I cannot accept that and be the man you made me.'

She could neither move nor speak. She had taught him too well, she could hear it in every word he threw at her.

He truly believes the English Throne is his by right and God will champion his cause; he truly believes that all armies and opposition will melt away in front of him with no more substance than snow in sunlight. My brave, misguided boy.

His course was set and she was merely a sideshow to the scene she had so carefully crafted.

Through that long night, as she watched him plan with Somerset, noting the position of every Lancastrian sympathiser, calculating the men they would bring and the speed they would do it with, debating whether the march should be on London or to an open battlefield, she could do nothing but keep her terrors to herself and admire the soldier he was so eager to be and the commander he had so clearly become. For it was not just Margaret who saw it: Somerset, Lord Wenlock, all the seasoned campaigners in the room began to defer to their prince as his grasp of tactics became so obvious and his passion became so clear. They had a king in their midst, they could sense it and so could she. So, as the pink shadows of dawn began to fill the room and they called her to leave the quiet corner she had retired to so many hours before and listen to the strategy for victory they made sound so convincing, what could she do but grant her support? Edward made it clear that he would over-rule her if she dissented; the Queen would be sacrificed to the King in waiting. He saw the battle won and would not let any wrong word from a mother he had once deferred to in everything weaken his cause, for it would be his cause and no longer theirs if she fought him on this; that much was clear in the certainty in his voice and the light in his eyes.

So she nodded her assent and praised his courage and fine planning instead of weeping and refusing; the relief in the room was tangible. At any other time she would have rejoiced for, in many ways, the plan itself was a strong one. Their intelligence was good and Lancaster still had support in sufficient amount to make them a convincing threat if they could marshall it well enough. Jasper Tudor was amassing an army in Wales which, with the other forces they could rely on, would swell their numbers to match anything the Yorkists could field. And Edward had not just considered numbers; he knew there was more to winning battles than that. He would use subterfuge and not make the blind attack the King probably expected would be unleashed in fury at Warwick's loss. He would send out small parties of troops in different directions to confuse the enemy, arrange billets for his men along the road to London and make it look as though the main aim was to march on the City while, in fact, taking the main body through Gloucester and into Wales to join with Tudor without risking too early a battle.

Once King Edward had fallen for the ruse and marched out of London to meet the threatened attack, the strengthened Lancastrian army would swoop back from Tudor's strongholds and take the City. It was a good plan and Margaret could see the sense in it; she could see the possibility of success and the daring gamble of the trick to be played and how that would appeal to a young man thirsting to become the stuff of stories. But there was a downfall in the plan: it relied on a far less shrewd soldier than the King if it was to work. King Edward was far too battle-hardened to let any enemy go so far from his sights that they could slip into Wales uncounted. She tried to make her son see there was a flaw but he rounded on her fast, her fears were made to seem like foolishness and she was forced to silence.

And in that is my only comfort: my silence allowed him to ride with my blessing, a blessing he asked for and that I publicly gave. I hope that he died in the knowledge that I believed him to be a real soldier, a warrior in the making. And, yes, there is as little comfort to be had in that knowledge as there sounds but that is my burden to bear, not his.

***

It was a familiar dance then, that game of cat and mouse they played with York again through those hot, dry weeks of April. It was unseasonably hot, the sun seemed to blaze through every daylight hour and the soldiers saw omens in it and muttered that God was smiling on the King and would kill them with thirst before they ever got to a battle. Edward heard their disquiet and laughed at it in public, saying it was still only one sun not three in the sky and that the men should be grateful not to be drowning in spring rains, but in private he grew more pinched and pale from lack of sleep.

'He is afraid and he would die before admitting it.'

Margaret looked up from the letter she had been trying to write to her father, knowing she no longer had the words to describe the fears she currently faced even if Rene had cared to know about them.

'He comes to my bed every night and...' the girl blushed, 'I can soothe him for a little while but then he is up and pacing the room and nothing quietens him.'

Margaret pushed the paper away. 'Is it the thought of dying that frightens him?'

Because that is what haunts my nights and keeps sleep away from me.

Anne shook her head. 'No, that is not it; at least that is not what he talks about. He is frightened of failing, of taking an army into battle and not being the soldier he wants to be.'

She twisted the golden band on her thin finger and kissed it gently as though it was Edward's face she saw reflected in its gleam.

'He is frightened of failing you, of failing all of us. He knows this is the only chance he has to get the Crown he has dreamed of his whole life.' She closed her eyes as though tears were too close to falling. 'It is a terrible burden to carry into his first battle.'

'He could not fail me.'

Margaret saw the tears begin to slip down Anne's pale face and knew there was no comfort she could offer or take. 'He could not fail me or you. I would rather he lost the battle and lived, I swear it.'

Anne smiled, 'and he would rather die than lose.'

Waving away any more words, she walked out of the room with such dignity in her slender frame it was Margaret's turn to weep.

***

Margaret was proved right, although she longed to be proved wrong, and Edward's ruse, so carefully thought out in the planning, did not, in practice, work.

For three weeks the Lancastrians crept through towns that did not want to see them: through Bath, Wells and Bristol while the King marched through Cirencester and Malmesbury, shadowing their path to Wales for he knew, how could he not, that Margaret would not risk a march on London without every man she could muster. Margaret's scouts sighted the Yorkists, their scouts sighted the Lancastrians and they inched along the road to Gloucester and a safe crossing through the city like pieces in a chess game played to a stalemate. The name alone should have alerted Margaret to their fate, it should have alerted her to the city's response: Gloucester held its allegiance to Richard, its Duke and its namesake and they were not a strong enough force to make it cast its lot in with Lancaster. Gloucester barred its gates and she had no choice but to wheel around and hope the ford at Tewkesbury would provide a passage before the King could find them. It was a hollow hope and they all knew it: the Lancastrian soldiers had marched for thirty hours through a heat that was like an assault on their lowered heads; they could not push further than any place that would make a camp, a crossing was beyond them. And that camp would be the battlefield for, by the time they found it, the Yorkist army was barely three miles away.

'There is no place for you.'

Edward's tone would stand no arguing even if Margaret had had the will to try. He had been in his armour half the night and had not slept; she had kept a wakeful vigil with Anne in her tent and the strain showed clear on all of them.

'Then we will ride to Tewkesbury and await you there.'

Anne's voice was steady but fear poured from her as she gazed at the husband who no longer saw mother or wife: in his mind he was already on the battlefield.

I had seen that distracted look on so many men before: it was too hard to see it on my son.

'God will ride with me, Anne; have no need to worry. I will be at Tewkesbury before you know it, with the crown.' He believed it, it shone from him.

'Then you have our blessing; we will go and make arrangements to celebrate your return to us.'

Margaret's voice was as hollow as her words; he did not hear it. She wanted to say more: she wanted to send him into battle with noble words but there was nothing. There was barely a moment to acknowledge her goodbye, barely time to kiss his wife: her son was all caught up with strategy and troop placements and had little time to spend on women so they had to take what comfort they could in a perfunctory smile and an absent wave and leave him there.

And leave my heart there too, that is the truth of it. I left my heart with my son and it died with him. And I would swear his wife did the same and it is a ghost who moves through the life they have made for her now.

'Tell me we will see him again.'

Anne's voice as they began the lonely ride to Tewkesbury Abbey was thick with tears and yet Margaret had no words for her.

'We will, Madame, we will and with the crown he promised you.'

It fell to Katherine to offer some kindness but it was not her good-intentions Anne wanted and she repeated the question.

'Will we see him again? Do you believe he will win?'

'What choice do I have but to believe it?'

Margaret could not look at the girl who shared her pain: her face would have told a different story to her words. 'I have to believe it and I will pray for it; that is all we can do.'

There was nothing more she could say: she did not trust her voice not to descend into a scream of pain and fear so strong it would tear her heart out.

I feared his death in a way he did not. I feared it so deeply and Anne knew it. Neither of us spoke again until we arrived at the Abbey and received the Abbot's stilted welcome; we were both so full of words of worry we knew that we would surely drown if we let any spill. So we did not speak of it, or of her father's death or of her sister Isabel and her brother-in-law's betrayal. In truth I do not know what we spoke of in those few shadowy hours of waiting; perhaps we read, perhaps she prayed, I do not know, I do not care to remember.

***

The heat was thick: it smothered sound, stilled the air, cut the women off from the world around them as though they were flies caught fast in honey. Outside they knew was turmoil, chaos; inside was a stillness so complete they felt time had frozen. Margaret could not bear it to continue, she dreaded its end: when the door finally opened, she could barely remember how to breathe.

'You must leave.'

The Abbot's face was a scowling mask, his curt mouth poisonous with a message he took no pains to soften. 'The Yorkist army has won and you must leave before the King arrives and has me hanged for harbouring a nest of traitors.'

It is over; it is over and I have lost him. I cannot hear this.

'My husband, please tell me: what news is there of my husband?'

Anne's face, already pale from the strain of waiting, looked almost transparent in the cold gloom of the chamber: if the Abbot had any pity in him, he did not show it.

'Did you not hear me? King Edward has won; your men have been butchered. What news would you expect of him?'

Margaret slapped him. She slapped him hard across the face and drew blood with the jagged edge of a jewelled ring.

'You are no Christian and if my son lives, if you are wrong, you will pay for your cruelty, I swear it.'

And I will not hear this news. I will act and I will ride away from here faster than any man running from a battlefield but I will not hear this news.

She grabbed Anne from the floor where she had sunk in a half-swoon Margaret had no time for and pulled her from the room towards the stables before the Abbot had the wit to take them prisoner and win favour with their betrayal.

'I cannot ride, I cannot.'

Margaret knew Anne spoke the truth but she could not stop to care.

If I stop, I will think about Edward and I cannot do it; while I have no news, he is alive; I have to hold that, I have to hold that.

'Strap her on the horse if you have to.'

Margaret pushed the fainting girl into Katherine's kinder arms and climbed into the saddle, hitting the horse far harder with the whip than she needed.

'We have to go. We can't wait on a blood-soaked army to find us, no matter what side they might be on. There is a convent a few miles down the road; the sisters will have to give us sanctuary whether they want to or not.'

And they did and were far kinder than the Abbot had been. They bundled the women into warm rooms without question and had the kitchen send up a simple meal that no one touched and rough wine that all deadened their nerves with. Margaret heard riders come and go throughout the day and knew that the nuns had given food and water to soldiers stumbling from the battlefield but she and her women remained undisturbed: she was glad of the peace even though she knew it was only an illusion, an unreal calm.

'Madame.'

The Mother Superior's voice was gentle, too gentle; its soft tones boded nothing but pain to come. 'Madame, there are soldiers here now who are looking for you. They know you are here and...' she hesitated and Margaret thought she would drown in the sudden silence, in the pity in the nun's eyes. 'Madame, I cannot pretend that you are not here: the King is with them.'

'And my son? Is my son with them? Do they bring me a prisoner or a body?'

She did not speak but shook her head; it was enough.

Anne saw the tears on the nun's soft face and the devastation on Margaret's and it was too much for her battered frame. She fainted; she looked for all the world like a corpse. She fell into a swoon so heavy everyone thought her as lost as the husband she mourned. It was left to Katharine to pick her up as though she had no more substance than thistledown and carry her away.

If she had borne what I had to, she would have died or lost her reason. Maybe that would have been the better for her; she has surely found little happiness in the life she has now.

The Mother Superior was still waiting. With great care, as though she gestured to a cornered animal, she reached out a hand to Margaret, stroked the limp fingers as though to steady her for what was still to come.

'Madame, they have asked for you to go down to the courtyard.'

Margaret shook her head.

'You must be brave. God will watch over you, he will give you the strength you need to bear whatever you must.'

She could not speak, she could only follow.

She was a nun, a sister of God. Surely she could not have known what was waiting for me or she could not have said such words; she could not have led me there. And yet she left me at the doorway and let me go out alone.

The sun was low and there was a glare from it that took Margaret's sight and then she heard him speak her name in tones too like his father, the same mocking lilt.

'Lady Margaret, at last we have caught up with you.'

He swung himself out of the saddle as easily as if he had been riding to a picnic not returning from a battle and bowed as his men burst into laughter.

'But you look tired, too pale. I hope this waiting has not been a strain for you.'

The pleasant words and cruel tone were at such odds she began to feel dizzy. With a grin he moved towards her, slipped her arm through his as though he would lead her round a pretty flower garden and leant in close.

'Where have those pretty looks gone? My father always talked about what he would do with you but I think the bloom is gone.'

His mouth was so close to her face she could feel the bristles prickling at her skin.

'Still, I'm sure some of my men would be generous enough to lift your skirts once I'm done here. It would be a nice way to thank them for your gift.'

She looked at him blankly and he stepped back a little, pulling her further into the centre of the courtyard as though they were partners in a strangely measured dance.

'I have a gift for you, my dear Lady. I am sure you like gifts.'

He clicked his fingers and two men came forward bearing what looked like an arrow chest. It was a rough plain box and for a moment, a brief blessed moment, she did not understand its significance. As they put it on the ground the King smiled again, 'your gift, Lady Margaret, chosen especially for you.'

She knew what it was. Somehow she sensed it, perhaps in the crude way the bearers threw it on the ground.

She would have run but they dragged her down, pushed her onto her knees in the dust the horses had kicked up and prised open the lid, dragging her arms to her sides so that she could not cover her eyes.

It was not weapons in that box but my son, my beautiful beloved son, broken and crushed and defiled.

She could not breathe. She could not speak. The world had shrunk to nothing.

'She does not like my present.'

Edward had come closer until he stood over her, his shadow falling across but not hiding the twisted contents of the chest.

'Margaret, I am so disappointed. You haven't thanked me, after all the care I have taken with your gift and not a single word of thanks. Perhaps you need to look at it a little more closely to really appreciate how hard I have tried to find something you would like.'

And then she felt his hand push her head down and down until the smell of blood filled her nose and mouth and her son's butchered face was all she could see.

Screams filled her head, strangled her throat. She could not open her mouth, his skin was too close. She could not break free, every twist made the hand tighten. She closed her eyes but it was as if the lids were transparent.

'Have you seen enough?'

As quickly as he had pushed her down, Edward wrenched his fingers through her hair and pulled her back.

'Will I get my thanks now?'

There was blood on her face, she could feel it. Her boy's blood drying on her face.

Edward saw it too: he reached out and, almost gently, wiped it away before knocking her to the ground with a blow so fast she had no time to break her fall. As her cheek hit the packed mud, the dam broke. Osanna and Katherine came running to the door, convinced their mistress was being butchered: the sound she made had so much pain in it, it was unearthly.

'What have you done?'

Anne, pulled out of her trance by the commotion, was in the courtyard. Her face was the colour of ash, her thin shoulders visibly trembling beneath her cloak, but her voice was steady.

'What have you done to her?'

'Close the lid.'

Richard, Duke of Gloucester, had stepped quickly in front of the chest as he saw the girl appear.

'Now. She does not need to see this.'

His brother shrugged, bored now with his game. 'Fasten the box and do something about her.'

Edward pushed at Margaret's twitching body with his foot; the screaming had faded into sobbing but the sound was no less raw. Osanna ran forward and dragged her mistress up, cradling her as though she was a baby.

'Come with me now, we will find something to help you sleep. This will pass, it will pass.'

'You have an hour and then we leave.' Edward was already pulling his riding gloves back on.

'Have some pity for God's sake.' Anne watched as Margaret was led away. 'She needs to rest.'

Edward looked at her with interest.

'Are you giving me orders?' He moved closer. 'Warwick's daughter and the wife of the boy who wanted to steal my throne and you give orders?'

He reached out and pulled open her cloak to reveal the thin night-gown underneath.

'You are a traitor, have you forgotten? Do I need to remind you who is in charge?'

'Leave her alone.'

Richard did not raise his voice but the command was clear. Edward paused, his outstretched hand resting lightly on Anne's breast. Then he smiled and turned, dropping a mock bow at his brother.

'If that is how the land lies, you are very welcome to her. Do what you like but we leave in an hour.' His interest was gone. 'Find a hole for that' he gestured to the chest.

Anne was about to speak but he shook his head.

'If you try my patience any further, I will have that box opened and you can spend the night with your husband. Be grateful for my brother's protection; push me and you will lose that.'

She was beaten; the little strength she had been able to summon drained away as she realised what Margaret had seen. Katherine caught her as she fell and carried her into the Abbey, thankful at least that neither Margaret or Anne saw the box containing their beloved Edward's remains tipped into a drainage hole without any prayer offered over it. She could only hope that neither of them would ever ask.

I never saw his grave or heard mention of any funeral or any masses for his soul. I never asked. They gave Anne to Clarence's care and took me away. They rode me into London in the royal train, not at its head as I had so long planned but at its rear, a captive to be jeered at, not a queen any more to be feted at every corner. How they must have enjoyed it, those brothers of York, united in their unholy trinity. How little, by then, I cared.

***

'Where is my husband?' She had been in the Tower a day and a night and asked the same question over and over and still no one would answer. She had asked and asked until everyone's patience was exhausted and they had finally sent for Gloucester to quieten her demands.

I hated him. I hated him then for the way he had mocked my grief; I grew to hate him more for the way he uses Anne; that night in the Tower I learnt to fear him and the strength of his ambition.

The room they held her in was little more than a cell. There were no tapestries on the walls to hide the cold damp stone, no sweet rushes on the floor. There was a poorly covered bed and one simple chair. When Richard entered, he took it, forcing Margaret to stand.

'All these questions about your husband. Have you decided to finally become a wife now that you are no longer a mother? Or a queen?'

There was malice in his voice, pure malice. He wanted her to fear him; she did but she would not give him the satisfaction of seeing it.

That was a foolish mistake: it only deepened his cruelty.

'What happened to you?'

Margaret forced herself to look at him.

'You were such a pleasant child, I remember you. Perhaps it's jealousy that twists you. It must be hard to be the youngest and never have hope of the throne.'

It was a mistake; he laughed at her and there was more threat in his amusement than she had heard in other men's curses.

'You are quite wrong.'

He settled his soldier's frame more comfortably into the chair.

'You are the only one in here without any hope of the throne. Do you honestly believe that my brother, that either of my brothers can hold it?'

He smiled; she forced herself not to shudder.

'Think about them: a womaniser and a drunk. How can the throne not come to me?' He leant forward as though sharing some wonderful confidence, 'and do you know who I will share it with?'

Margaret shook her head, not wanting to pretend intimacy with him. 'Your little daughter-in-law.'

'Anne!' She shook her head again. 'Why on earth would you want Anne? She is disgraced.'

'And so she will be grateful which is always interesting!' He burst into laughter at Margaret's horror-struck face. 'Grateful and rich; what a wonderful combination.'

'You are evil and stupid, a far commoner mix in your family.' But the insult slipped off him like an arrow glancing off stone.

'Stupid?' He grinned. 'I get called many things but rarely stupid; that is normally reserved for my dear brother Clarence. It was Warwick's favourite word for him as I remember. But please go on dear Lady, I am sure you have your reasons.'

His taunting tone twisted at her nerves; she took a deep breath to steady myself.

'You are stupid because there are more steps to the throne than you think.'

She tried to keep her voice level, conscious of the amusement in his eyes that she would not feed by a show of fury. 'It is not just your brothers, although surely that is obstacle enough, but my husband, the House of Lancaster that blocks your way. There are still plenty of people who believe my House has the only just claim to the Throne; they won't allow your family to keep poisoning it.'

He watches me like a cat watches a mouse who thinks it has escaped the flexing claws.

'The House of Lancaster, that is interesting. Tell me, Margaret, is it still a House if the heir and the Head are gone?'

For a moment she did not understand him and then the true horror of his words struck home and she sank to her knees, not in prayer but in fear of what they had dared.

'You have killed him. You have killed Henry.' It was not a question; his face showed it was a certainty. 'When?'

'You always liked the details didn't you? No matter whose death was on your hands, my father's among them, you always liked the details.'

His smile was so twisted it was all she could do to hold the nausea

361

back; his next words were poison. 'Why do you think we showed you your boy like that? For the details of course: for every blade and foot that marked him; we wanted you to remember the details.'

He was standing now, leaning over her like a foul shadow.

'So do you need to know exactly whose hand held the pillow last night, whose hand held his arms or legs or is it enough to know we were as one in the old fool's killing?'

He came closer, his breath hot on her cheek, 'your husband is as dead as your son and there is nothing you can do.'

She was on her feet again.

'I will denounce you! I will cry Henry's murder to anyone who will listen! You have killed a king, you cannot keep the throne now; it will be war again.'

And you will kill me. As soon as I cry out murder, you will kill me. I will be allowed to die.

He knew her too well.

'Don't hope that you will be next, where would be the fun in that? The best punishment we can give you is to keep you alive.' He stood up to leave, 'besides, who would listen? All your champions are dead. There is Anne perhaps but we have her now. In a little while I will marry her unless of course she is carrying your son's child; if she is, then...well you know what will happen to her.'

He opened the door and bowed.

'Don't you see how easy it would be for us to kill you? We could say you had done it yourself in the madness of grief; there is no one left to question or to wonder or to grieve. But that would be what you wanted and where is the pleasure in that? You are alone, Madame, and you are alive and you will stay that way.'

Had she had any tears left, she would have wept.

They stained their souls with murder without a care and still they would not commit the one I prayed for. Henry would have welcomed death: he had waited to meet his God all his life. They murdered a man happy to die and he was doubly lucky: they sent him to the Heaven his mind had gone to so long before and left me to live, left me to wish for death to come for the two years they kept me locked in that unholy place with no company but my grief. It is a wonder and a torment both that I did not go mad, in madness at least there would have been a release.

Chateau du Dampierre, France: 1481

I am returned to my story's start, watching the fog roll in across the marshes, feeling my mind grow weary of the memories I try so hard to shake. It has taken months to write these words, months of reliving things I had forgotten and reliving things I cannot forget and I am so tired with it. And there are ten years still untold. Ten years in a life is a long time and yet this chapter will have no more length than if I wrote about the passing of ten months for they are ten years that mean nothing, nothing at all.

'You have a visitor.' Margaret looked up from the book lying unread on her lap and shook her head.

'I cannot have visitors, you know that.'

Alice Chaucer, Suffolk's widow and Margaret's gaoler in all but name, sat down next to her on the cushioned seat.

'No one has ever said that, Your Majesty, it was never in the orders when you were sent to me. It is simply that there is barely anyone left to come.'

Margaret smiled at the old courtesy of the title. Since she had been released, without any warning, from the Tower into the custody of her one-time lady-in-waiting, Alice had shown her nothing but kindness. She had survived the horror of her husband's death and survived every attempt to attaint her with Suffolk's sins. She had become indeed the very model of a loyal Yorkist, but she was still gentle Alice Chaucer underneath and her manor of Wallingford had gradually begun to feel like a home to Margaret, a place of peace where the world might begin to have a little colour again.

'So which brave Knight has found the courage to breech your walls?'

Alice heard the bitterness and could do little to soften it. She knew that Margaret had had no visitors for the two years she had been kept in the Tower; she had been refused permission herself and had been left in no doubt that a second request would not be well-received.

'It is not a Knight, it is a Lady but you must promise to be calm.'

Alice suddenly clasped Margaret's hand, 'you must not cry out when I tell you or when you see her; the servants must not know. She puts herself in danger coming here...'

'Dear God, it is Anne, isn't it? It is Anne?' Margaret kept her voice low but her eyes shone.

Alice nodded, smiling herself at the other woman's joy, an emotion she seldom saw.

'Yes, it is Anne. I will bring her here to you, the garden is quiet and you can talk without being overheard.'

Margaret barely had a moment to collect herself before a hooded figure slipped through the rose trees curtaining the little bower that had become Margaret's private retreat.

'It really is you.'

She pushed back the hood and held Anne's face between her hands. It was no longer a girl who stared back at her but a woman with a thin pale face and new lines about her eyes; the four years that had passed since they had been torn apart had not dealt kindly with her daughter-in-law.

'I could not come before, you do understand that?'

Margaret felt the thinness of the hand she took, the bones barely covered by the papery skin and could have cried.

What has he done to you? Where is Edward's pretty bride? You are as old as me.

'Of course I do. I can hardly believe you are here now but I am so glad. And you are a mother, Alice told me. I am so happy for you.'

She saw the shadow pass across Anne's face and knew at once where the pain truly came from.

The boy is ill. The rumours must be true. She is frightened for him.

'I have a son.'

Anne smiled as she sat down but its warmth did not reach her eyes. 'A beautiful son but he is little and sickens easily and the doctors seem to have no cures for him.'

She glanced down at her thin frame, 'and there is no sign of another, no matter how much my husband wishes for it.'

'Is Gloucester kind to you?' Margaret guessed the answer before the hollow laugh gave it.

'Kind? He doesn't know the meaning of the word. Power is all that matters to him and power means more than one weak child in his cradle. Every time I fail, it twists his anger even more...'

She shook her head and Margaret did not press the matter; the secrets of that bedchamber were too plainly written on Anne's strained face.

'No more about me now. How are you, are you comfortable here with Alice?'

Margaret smiled. 'I am; she is good to me and I am glad to be away from the Tower. I thought I would end my days there, sleepwalking out my life.'

'What did you do? I know they kept visitors away from you; it must have been hard to bear.'

Margaret shrugged. 'No, I wanted that solitude, I craved it. As to what I did? I read my days away but I have little memory of what I read. I wrote letters sometimes, to my father and to King Louis but abandoned more than I wrote for I had little to say and I doubted they had much appetite to be reminded of their ties to me. I spoke little and, once my gaolers realised their taunts had no power to reach me, I was left alone. I suppose you could say it was a life in shadow but I wanted nothing else; it was a life that wanted nothing of me and I lived it in mourning; that was all I could bear to do.'

'And now?'

She smiled again. 'And now it is a little easier. It is as quiet but I can face the world a little more, see the world a little more. And Alice indulges me: she lets me imagine my son as the great King I had hoped he would be and never berates me for dreaming it.'

She gestured at the massed flowers surrounding them, heavy with scent and the gentle murmur of bees.

'Here, in this garden, I can conjure him again and find a little plea-sure in the pain.'

'I miss him.'

To Margaret's surprise Anne was weeping. 'I miss him still, every day. I look at my little boy and I wish he had been our son, that his father had been the husband I loved not the one who will push me aside soon to God knows what fate.'

For a while there was silence in the garden as the two women held each other and wept quiet tears for the man they had never been al-lowed to mourn together. It was Margaret who finally broke the spell.

'You are the last one left who knew him. The women who stayed with me for so much of my life are scattered now: Osanna is dead and Katherine writes when she is able but I have not seen her.'

'So many ghosts; I am tired of conjuring them.' Anne wiped her eyes, 'and Jacquetta gone as well. You were close to her once and her husband weren't you?'

There it was: the moment to spill secrets, to share the truth.

'They say her husband's death left her broken-hearted.' Anne continued without noticing how white Margaret had become. 'Richard said that Queen Elizabeth took to her bed for days, they were so close that her mother's death struck her like an illness: all those long days in sanctuary together, there must have been no secrets between them.'

And the moment passed.

Could she have told her? Surely not: no daughter could forgive her mother such a deception. Jacquetta could not have told Elizabeth and I cannot tell Anne: if Gloucester is as cruelly ambitious as I think he is, if he guessed she knew something about the King's family, he would destroy her. Jacquetta is gone and our secret most likely buried with her; it must stay that way until I am buried to.

'There is something I must tell you.'

Anne's voice, something more urgent in its tone, broke through Margaret's distraction.

'There is a reason I am here, more than just to see you.'

She shook her head, mistaking Margaret's still pale face for fear. 'It is nothing to alarm you, the opposite I hope. You are going home, Margaret, to France.'

'I don't understand. I have had no letters from Louis or from my father, how can I go back?'

And then she understood.

'The King has ransomed me. My letters never mattered; Edward has been negotiating all this time.' She looked at Anne who nodded.

'I always wondered why I was released and why the conditions put on how I lived here at Wallingford were so slight; Edward has been trying to turn me from an expense into a payment and he has finally managed it. I am right?'

Anne nodded again. 'I heard him discussing it with Richard. The King needs money, he has almost emptied the Treasury with the demands of his mistresses and his children and his increasingly jealous wife. It was Richard's idea: they have sold you back to France, to King Louis, for 50,000 crowns.'

'And what does Edward get in return?'

'Peace. He is marrying his daughter Elizabeth to the Dauphin to seal the bargain.'

Margaret laughed and Anne winced at the bitterness.

'So not some glorious rescue, I am not even the jewel in the transaction.'

She pulled a rose from the branch behind her and began shredding the petals. 'He loves me, he loves me not. I was the Princess bought from France with such high hopes of healing the realm with her children and her alliances and I failed. So now this King will make good on England's losses and a disgraced Queen will be traded for a new, more beautiful Princess. Another woman will be shuffled across the chessboard and the game begins again.'

She tore the last petal off the stem and looked at Anne. 'And is that all?'

'No.'

There were tears in Anne's eyes again but this time of frustration not loss.

'They will make you sign a deed which renounces every claim you ever had to the English Throne in exchange for your return to the French Court and its protection and they will never let you return.'

'And if I don't sign it?'

Anne's face was white now; her eyes black hollows empty of any emotion.

'Richard will have me killed.'

They catch me at every turn. They will not kill me but they will destroy everything around me until I cannot breathe for hating them and still they will not let it end.

'He sent you. This was no secret visit.'

'He sent me.' There was no pleading in her voice.

'He sent me but my tears were real and my words; I loved your son, remember that. I loved him and I mourned him with you. I cannot be sorry for that.'

She left as quietly as she had come leaving Margaret alone in the garden, staring into nothing as the shadows fell and the darkness wove a cloak for her weeping.

***

And so I came here, at last, to this quiet Chateau.

The protection of the French Court was a paper promise, crafted from expediency and lies: Louis welcomed me home by invading Anjou and taking the last of my birth right. The Spider King unchanged.

I live in poverty, it is that simple. No more the spoiled queen taking luxuries for granted or the guest enjoying the pleasures of an English manor house.

It was not meant to be this way: my father, guilt finally outweighing his fury at my failure, had granted me a castle and a pension that would have amply met my needs but he died and there was nothing left for me since all his inheritance had long been the property of Charles of Maine.

I have lived on charity ever since: Dampierre is only my home through the kindness of a man I hardly know, Francois Vignolles, who loved my father once and extended his loyalty to me. But, for all its seclusion and its privations, it is a home. I have freedom here and visitors still. I have news of England and of Lancaster's supporters, who still flourish even though they have lost so much. Often now I hear rumours that centre themselves about the Earl of Richmond, another Henry who fled with Jasper Tudor in the year of my son's death and another young man with a mother who has ambitions for a crown. But I am tired and have no more wish to see boys try to make themselves into men on a battlefield and so I wave the words away and refuse to play the games of speculation my visitors would wind me in. I watch the fog weave about the walls and hide us a little more from the world and I do not weep for it.

My interest in the world has shrunk to the limits of these four walls and it is time for me to admit as much. I no longer care to know how King Edward's reign will proceed or whether his sons will hold the crown any more securely than any who went before them. I doubt that they will for the crown seems to want to sit no more safely on one head than it does on another.

I wondered at the opening whether this was a pause in my story or its ending. Now I feel the fog's cold hand lie ever more heavy on my tired bones and I think the ending is come or it is very close at least. I think I knew this from the start or the strain of the telling would have been too much.

Thirty years and still no peace: our houses ripped the country apart with our unstoppable pursuit of power; enemies became friends and enemies once again and still the Crown wavers on the head of anyone fool enough to claim it.

And my son: all through these pages the light that was my son. My hope for better things. My boy and, in the end, a man and a soldier. A brave soldier whose death I caused. The pain of his loss is as raw as if it happened yesterday and I have had to learn to put it away from me. I had forgotten that the act of writing must bring him back to life.

This is the final truth and it is for me alone to face: I have had enough of my memories; I have had enough of my life.

I am finally ready for silence.